An OPEN LOOK™ at UNIX®

An OPEN LOOK™ at UNIX®

A Developer's Guide to X

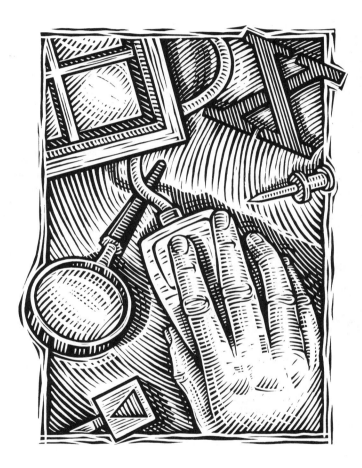

John David Miller

M&T Books
A Division of M&T Publishing, Inc.
501 Galveston Drive
Redwood City, CA 94063

Library of Congress Cataloging in Publication Data

Miller, John David, 1964–
    An OPEN LOOK at UNIX: a developer's guide to X / John David Miller
        p.   cm.
    Includes index.
    ISBN 1-55851-057-5 (book) : $29.95. — ISBN 1-55851-058-3 (book/disk) : $39.95. — ISBN 1-55851-059-1 (disk) : $20.00
    1. OPEN LOOK (Computer program) 2. X Window System (Computer system) 3. UNIX (Computer operating system) I. Title.
  QA76.76.U84M55 1990
  005.4'3--dc20   90-6153
                                                     CIP

93 92 91 90   4   3   2   1

Project Editor: Kurt Rosenthal   **Cover Design:** Lauren Smith Design
Cover Illustrator: Christine Mortensen

To René

Contents

Chapter Six: Building Applications 283

Acknowledgements

The following companies graciously loaned hardware and software for the development of this book:

AT&T
AT&T UNIX System V/386 Release 3.2.2 AT&T OPEN LOOK Graphical User Interface Release 2.0 AT&T XWIN 3.0

Graphic Software Systems
PC-Xview and PC-Xview/16 DOS X servers Xdgis UNIX DGIS X server AT1000 graphics display adapter

NEC Home Electronics
MultiSync 2A color monitor

Logitech Corp.
PC-93 Bus Mouse

Headland Technologies
VEGA VGA graphics display adapter

This book would not have been possible without the terrific staff at AT&T keeping me up-to-date with the latest-and-greatest versions of their products and answering my endless barrage of questions and comments. Thank-you, Don Alecci, John Baldasare, Tim Demarest, George Derby, Alan Hochberg, Steve Humphrey, Ruth Klein, Steve Kunkel, Marcel Meth, Val Mitchell-Stevens, Mike Ody, Greg Pasqueriello, Manish Sheth, Bill Stanger, Rich Struse, Nancy Trachtenbarg, Don Ursem, Larry Webber and all the behind-the-scenes staffers.

Thanks, also, to the Sun Microsystems staff for technical support and encouragement: Ralph Derrickson, Pam Deziel, Smita Deshpande, Tony Hoeber, Jeff Hong, Tom Jacobs, and Richard Probst.

I am especially grateful to the technical reviewers, who get the special award for patience and perseverance: Ruth Klein (AT&T), Steve Humphrey (AT&T), Cheryl Wood (Prime), and Timo Wilson (GSS). Despite all of our best efforts, there are bound to be regrettable errors and omissions. These I selfishly reserve as my own.

Scott Gibbons (GSS) and Troy Acott (GSS) did a remarkable job turning my rough pencil sketches into printable art, often under an unreasonable schedule. Thanks guys.

I really want to thank all the great folks at GSS (my "real" job), especially my manager, David Cobbley, and the entire Workstation Business Unit: Gene Daniel, Larry Hutchison, John Light, Matt Mason, David Opperman, George Peden, Richelle Riedl, Russ Sprunger, and Jim Thomassen.

I'd also like to thank Dan Fineberg, now at Intel, who helped get this project off the ground while he was Director of Marketing at GSS.

A round of applause goes to the book's producers, M&T Books, for doing such a wonderful job. My editors, Brenda McLaughlin and Ellen Ablow, were simply terrific to work for.

Lastly, I could never forget my friends and family, who provided vast amounts of moral support and encouragement. I especially thank my loving wife, René, who lost out to this project too many late nights and weekends. To her, I dedicate this book.

-- jdm

Why this Book is for You

This book is for you if:

- You are new to X programming and need a place to start.

- You have used Xlib but want the benefits of an X Toolkit.

- You have used another toolkit and now want to support the OPEN LOOK Graphical User Interface.

- You develop X servers and would like to better understand "the big picture."

- You use another window system but would like to know about X.

- You are interested in user-interface technology and want to examine OPEN LOOK applications.

An OPEN LOOK at UNIX demystifies X application programming through dozens of useful programming examples and no-nonsense explanations. Whether or not you have X programming expertise, by the time you finish this book you will be able to develop serious X applications.

How to Order a Listings Disk

All of the software listings in this book are available on disk (UNIX cpio format) with full source code.

The disk price is $25.00. California residents must add the appropriate sales tax. Order by sending a check, or credit card number and expiration date, to:

An OPEN LOOK at UNIX Disk
M&T Books
501 Galveston Drive
Redwood City, CA 94063

Or, you may order by calling our toll-free number Monday through Friday, between 8:00 A.M. and 5:00 P.M. Pacific Standard Time: 1-800-533-4372 (1-800-356-2002 in California). Ask for **Item #059-1**.

Foreword

When AT&T and Sun Microsystems announced the OPEN LOOK Graphical User Interface in April, 1988, we said it would change forever the way people think of the UNIX operating system. We hoped it would entice a whole new group of users and software vendors to discover the power and the potential of UNIX System computers.

I think we underestimated the impact of the OPEN LOOK GUI. Two years ago, pundits were debating whether users wanted GUIs or traditional command line interfaces. Today, the pundits are debating which GUI a user should buy and noting how easy it is to move from one GUI to another. UNIX software vendors (and a growing number of DOS vendors, too) are rushing one after the other to put the full power of the UNIX System at the command of even the most casual computer user through the OPEN LOOK GUI and other interfaces.

I'm convinced we're on the verge of an explosion in the availability of UNIX System GUI applications and a correlated explosion in the use of desktop UNIX Systems. In the 1990s, I believe, even the most casual and infrequent computer users will be able to deal as easily with vast networks of computers as with single desktop machines, thanks to the OPEN LOOK GUI. People will use sophisticated distributed applications without a second or third thought about where their programs or data really reside. Only system administrators will know for sure, and only system administrators will care, because, ultimately, the underlying architectures of computer operating systems, networks and applications don't matter, as long as people find it easy to use them to do real work.

AT&T's UNIX Software Operation is committed to making the OPEN LOOK GUI the interface of choice in the UNIX System market. It is available for UNIX System V Release 3.2. It is the standard "look and feel" for the UNIX System V Released 4, the most advanced, most standards-compliant version of the UNIX operating system ever designed. And, it is available on all major UNIX workstations, including those from DEC, HP, IBM, Sun, and AT&T.

When John Miller first approached us about his plans to write this book, the developers of our X Intrinsics-based OPEN LOOK toolkit were not entirely pleased. They were in the midst of finishing the second release of the toolkit and were not overly interested in taking time out to help some "book writer" with another book. However, their displeasure quickly changed. They discovered that John was not just another writer, but someone who knew graphics, and in particular the X system, as well as they. It became obvious that John would do more than just write a quick review of the toolkit, but would research and experiment with the toolkit to become as familiar with it as the developers, or, more appropriately, as its *users*.

So exhaustive was John's research of the OPEN LOOK X Intrinsics toolkit, and so complete was his review of all the tools contained within, that he proved helpful in improving the quality of the code. Now our quality control techniques are very good, and we have been applying these techniques for years in developing the UNIX System. Nonetheless, we were new at testing graphics, and missed a few of its (at the time) more subtle aspects. John's periodic "bug reports" were a welcome addition to our own testing.

We spent many weeks working with John. The work was enjoyable because of John's enthusiasm and, frankly, because he liked our work. It was clear that he looked at the OPEN LOOK GUI, at our X Intrinsics toolkit, and—liking what he saw—was determined to teach others to use this OPEN LOOK toolkit to build applications. This book is his vehicle for teaching, and we think he's done well. Thanks John.

Larry Dooling
President, UNIX Software Operation

Introduction

"I want to write X applications, but where do I start?" As Project Leader of GSS's X server development team, I was often asked this question by our X customers. The answer? You're holding it right here in your own two hands!

When, in December of 1988, I received a call from M&T Books asking for a new book proposal, I knew I had to tackle this problem. The question was not whether I would write the book, but which one of the X programming interfaces I would write about.

At the time, the X Toolkit, a powerful application programming interface combining the core Xt Intrinsics with some user-interface specific widget set, was maturing to the point where the Intrinsics would become part of the X standard. A basic widget was set available from MIT Project Athena, but was not considered complete enough for serious application development. The choice, then, was between the OPEN LOOK Graphical User Interface and OSF/Motif, both of which were much more than just a set of widgets, but neither of which would be generally available for several months.

As should be obvious, I choose OPEN LOOK. I had seen early versions of two implementations, one by AT&T and one by Sun, at the UNIX System V Release 4.0 Software Developer's Conference earlier that summer and had come away impressed. These people knew what they were doing.

One particularly important, if sometimes confusing, aspect of the OPEN LOOK Graphical User Interface is that it was developed first as a user-interface and second as actual implementations. The first step resulted in a wonderful user-interface, which I prefer even over the NeXT workstation on my desk. The second step resulted in separate implementations by Sun and AT&T, with their own respective application programming interface: Sun's XView is based on SunView and AT&T's OPEN LOOK X Toolkit is based on the now-standard Xt

Intrinsics. This is a boon to programmers, who can choose the API they like best and still present a common user-interface. Both interfaces are available in UNIX System V Release 4.0.

For this book, I chose the AT&T implementation primarily because it is based on the Xt Intrinsics, which have been adopted as part of the X standard and are the basis for other X Toolkits, including OSF/Motif. I felt that teaching this interface would give the reader better all-around X knowledge.

What's Here

Whether you have X programming expertise or not, by the time you finish this book you will be able to develop serious X applications. We start off by laying a solid foundation in the first four chapters, and then work our way through dozens of code examples in the last two:

Chapter One: The OPEN LOOK Graphical User Interface

Here we present the look-and-feel of the user interface. By the end of this chapter, you'll have a good idea of how your application will look under OPEN LOOK.

Chapter Two: The X Window System

Before we start writing code, we need to see what we're dealing with. While Chapter One looked at the user's perspective, this chapter explores the down-under features of the window system platform from the programmer's point of view. Using the OPEN LOOK X Toolkit, you may never need to know some of this information, but skimming this chapter will give you a much better perspective of the overall implementation.

Chapter Three: Object-Oriented Programming

Even though it is written entirely in C, the Xt Intrinsics programming interface manages to be surprisingly object-oriented. Since many programmers are not familiar with the terms and concepts of object-oriented programming, I thought it a good idea to devote a few pages to this topic.

Chapter Four: The Xt Intrinsics

This chapter describes the application-programming interface of the Xt Intrinsics, as opposed to the Toolkit-developer's interface to the Xt Intrinsics described in the MIT documentation. Here, we define widgets, resources, and callbacks, and the handful of subroutines used by application developers.

Chapter Five: The OPEN LOOK X Toolkit

This chapter demonstrates all 28 OPEN LOOK widgets and gadgets in various permutations and combinations. By the end of this chapter, you'll know what tools are part of the OPEN LOOK Toolkit, and understand how they work together.

Chapter Six: Developing Applications

In this final chapter, we go from writing demo programs to full-fledged X applications, using the X Resource Manager, Inter-Client Communication Conventions, and advanced features of the OPEN LOOK GUI, such as on-line help and the iconic file browser.

Appendix: The Xtutil Utility Library

The appendix contains the complete source to the utility library used throughout the book. This library greatly enhances the Xt Intrinsics, adding variable-length parameter lists, event callbacks, and simplified inter-client communications.

What You Need

You do not need prior programming experience with X or any other window system to read and understand this book. In addition, although X and OPEN LOOK are graphical in nature, you do not need to know much about graphics to use the OPEN LOOK X Toolkit. Since the emphasis of this book is on the user-interface, the examples contained herein are minimally graphical. Graphics application programmers will want to pay close attention to Chapter Two, which describes the X graphics primitives.

To get the most out of this book, all you really need is a good working knowledge of the C programming language and access to a system with the OPEN LOOK Graphical User Interface. Specifically, the code examples in this book were developed with the following software and hardware:

Software:
- AT&T UNIX System V/386 Release 3.2.2, including the C Software Development Set
- AT&T XWIN 3.0, an implementation of the X Window System, Version 11 Release 3
- AT&T OPEN LOOK Graphical User Interface, Release 2.0 Hardware
- Gateway 2000 80386 computer with 8 Mb RAM, 150 Mb hard disk
- AT&T VDC-600 800x600x4 VGA display controller
- NEC MultiSync 2A VGA color graphics monitor
- Logitech PC-93 Bus mouse

In addition, the examples were tested with the following X servers and display controllers:

X Servers:

GSS PC-Xview and PC-Xview/16 DOS X servers for EGA/VGA and DGIS display controllers

GSS Xdgis UNIX X server for DGIS display controllers

Display Controllers:

DGIS display controllers: GSS AT1000, NEC MultiSync Graphics Engine, NEC MVA-1024

Headland Technology Video-7 VEGA VGA

Chapter 1

The OPEN LOOK Graphical User Interface

The OPEN LOOK^{TM} Graphical User Interface (GUI) is a simple, consistent, and efficient paradigm for the appearance and behavior of applications in a window system. The OPEN LOOK GUI specification was jointly developed by AT&T and Sun Microsystems, based on pioneering work done by Xerox at the Palo Alto Research Center (PARC) in the 1970s. The nearly two-inch thick specification focuses solely on elements of the user interface, leaving implementors free to specify implementation details such as the window system platform and programming interface.

Together, AT&T and Sun have developed several OPEN LOOK programming interfaces, including:

- **XView**—a SunView-like toolkit for porting SunView applications to the X Window System and OPEN LOOK.
- **tNt**—an OPEN LOOK toolkit for the NeWS Development Environment.
- **OLIT**—the OPEN LOOK Intrinsic Toolkit, also known as The AT&T OPEN LOOK GUI X Toolkit, Xt+, and Xol. This toolkit is actually a *widget set*, based on the standard MIT Xt Intrinsics and is the ideal choice for new X application development, especially for developers who must support their applications with additional X interfaces such as Motif.

Although the concepts and structure may apply to other implementations, the source code examples presented here are designed for the AT&T OPEN LOOK Graphical User Interface (including the AT&T OPEN LOOK Intrinsic Toolkit), Release 2.0 and above.

1.1 Basic Philosophy

The motto of the OPEN LOOK GUI is, "Simple, consistent, and efficient." Simple, so it is easy to learn; consistent, so it is easy to remember; and efficient so it is easy to use, day after day. This theme is carried throughout the design of the various user-interface elements.

The Xerox influence that shaped the Apple Macintosh is obvious in many of the OPEN LOOK GUI controls. The OPEN LOOK GUI versions are refined for use in multitasking environments over a wide range of screen resolutions. For example, the Macintosh menu bar is fine for small, low-resolution screens, but having to move the mouse up to the top of the screen to display menus can be very frustrating for users with large screens. The OPEN LOOK GUI rectifies this by letting each application define control areas for drop-down menu buttons and the like, with the control areas located within the application's window, rather than at the top of the screen. Applications may also define menus that pop up at the current pointer location.

Other elements also demonstrate the sophistication and completeness of the user-interface. One such example is the location of the arrows on scrollbars. Rather than being at the extremes of the scroll cable, the arrows lie on either side of the position indicator, so that scrolling up and down involves only a slight repositioning of the mouse. Further, the pointer moves with the position indicator, so if you click on a scrollbar arrow, you don't have to move the mouse at all to click it again.

1.2 Environment

The AT&T OPEN LOOK Graphical User Interface is a complete application environment with several components. For the user, these components include:

Software:

- Three main OPEN LOOK "desktop" applications: the OPEN LOOK Window Manager, OPEN LOOK Workspace Manager, and OPEN LOOK File Manager

- XWIN, AT&T's implementation of the X Window System, including X display servers and client applications such as xterm, bitmap, and xwd

Documentation:

- *The OPEN LOOK User's Guide*

The programming environment includes these additional components:

Software:

- The OPEN LOOK widget set (libXol)
- The MIT Xt Intrinsics (libXt)
- The low-level C programming interface to X, Xlib (libX11)

Documentation:

- *The OPEN LOOK Programmer's Guide*
- *The OPEN LOOK Programmer's Reference*
- *The OPEN LOOK Specification*
- *The OPEN LOOK Style Guide*
- *The OPEN LOOK Level 1 Trademark Guide*
- *The XWIN Programmer's Guide*

As you work your way through this book, you may wish to have all of these components on-hand for reference. Be forewarned, however, that some of the documentation, particularly *The XWIN Programmer's Guide*, is not specific to OPEN LOOK application development. Use *An OPEN LOOK at UNIX* as a guide, and the other documentation as supplemental information.

1.2.1 The Workspace Manager

The OPEN LOOK Workspace Manager maintains the entire screen, or workspace, similar to the Finder in the Macintosh Desktop. The Workspace Manager's responsibilities include starting new applications, maintaining systemwide properties, and system shutdown.

You initiate Workspace Manager functions through the Workspace menu by pressing the mouse MENU button (typically button 3 on a three-button mouse) while the pointer is over the screen background.

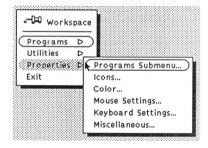

Figure 1.1 The workspace menu with the properties submenu

1.2.2 The Window Manager

Like other X Window System window managers, the OPEN LOOK Window Manager:

- controls size and placement of windows and icons,
- can close applications down to icons and open them back up,
- assigns keyboard ownership, called *input focus,* and
- terminates clients at the request of the user.

Window manager actions are activated from one of the two window menus, depending on the window type—either the Base Window menu, shown in Figure 1.2, or the Pop-up Window menu, shown in Figure 1.3. These window types are explained later in this chapter.

Figure 1.2 Window menu for a Base Window

Figure 1.3 Window menu for a Pop-up Window

1.2.3 The File Manager

The OPEN LOOK File Manager is an iconic file browser that provides direct-manipulation of files. Filename patterns are bound to icons and actions through a user-configurable file. Double-clicking on a file's icon initiates the action appropriate to that file type, such as editing a text file or executing a binary file.

Several File Manager windows may be open at one time, allowing you to move and copy files from one directory to another by simply dragging them into another File Manager window.

Figure 1.4 shows a typical File Manager window, with the path pane showing the path of the current directory, and the directory pane showing its contents.

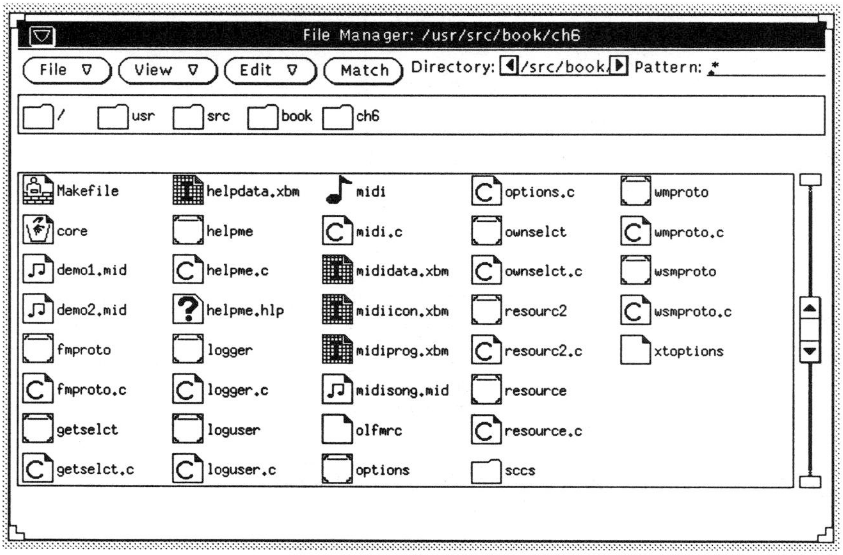

Figure 1.4 A typical File Manager window

1.3 Keyboard and Mouse Definitions

If all workstations had identical keyboard and mouse configurations, developers could hardcode applications to use specific keyboard keys or mouse buttons, assured that those keys or buttons would be available. Such is not the case, however, and applications and user interfaces that depend on special keyboard keys or a certain number of mouse buttons don't work on workstations that don't have them. Furthermore, even if keys and buttons could be hardcoded, it is not good user-interface practice to do so; what is convenient and intuitive for the developer is often awkward and clumsy for the user.

The OPEN LOOK GUI solves these problems by providing a translation layer between logical functions, such as CUT, PASTE, HELP, SELECT, and MENU, and physical actions, such as mouse <button_1>, <Ctrl>v, <Shift><middle_button>, and function key <F1>. Application programmers code and document their programs using the logical names, and users map logical names to convenient physical representations.

For example, manipulation of the standard user-interface objects centers on SELECT and MENU, and to a lesser extent, ADJUST. By default, these actions map to the left, right, and middle buttons, respectively, of a three-button mouse. As a user, if you don't like these settings or don't have a three-button mouse, you can change them using the Workspace Manager and the Mouse Settings property window.

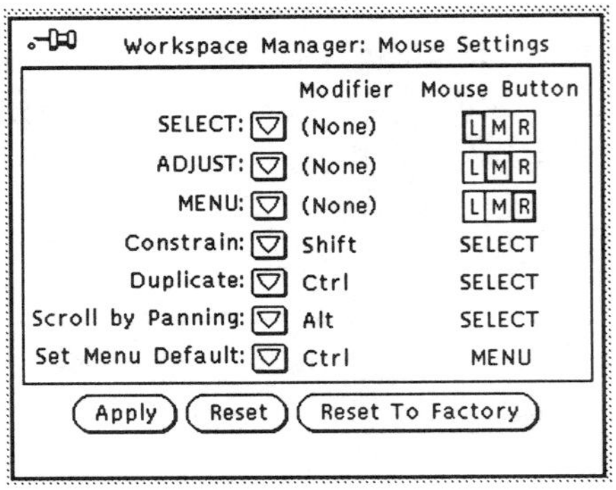

Figure 1.5 Mapping logical to physical mouse buttons

The same is true for the keyboard. On keyboards without a key labeled "Help," the default HELP key is function key 1 (often labeled "F1"). If you wish to use a different key, change the mapping using the Workspace Manager, and the Keyboard Setting property window.

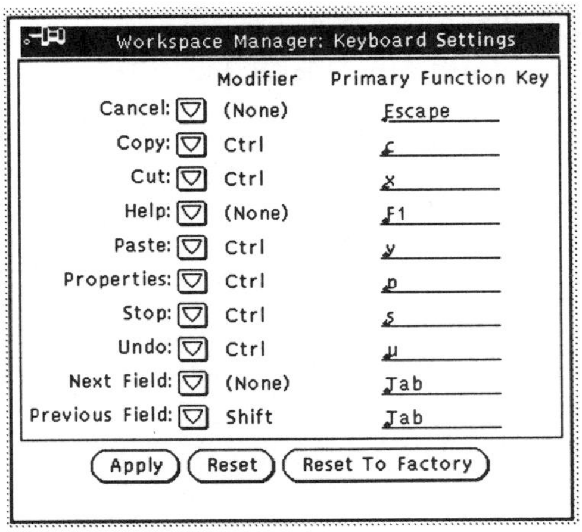

Figure 1.6 Mapping logical to physical keyboard keys

1.4 User-Interface Elements

1.4.1 Base Windows

All applications have one or more base windows, which are the application's main work areas on the workspace. Base windows have a header (otherwise known as a title bar) that displays the application title or status message, a control area for any permanently displayed application controls such as menu buttons and text fields, and one or more panes for the rest of the application's user input and output. Base windows may also have resize corners, a footer for application messages, and vertical and/or horizontal scrollbars for panning within a pane.

Figure 1.7 illustrates a base window with resize corners, a control area with four buttons (File, Print, Capture Image, and Properties), and a pane with horizontal and vertical scrollbars. Note that applications may locate control areas anywhere in the base window, not just at the top.

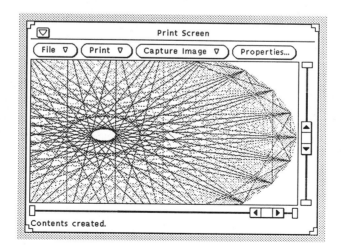

Figure 1.7 An OPEN LOOK base window

Figure 1.8 shows a control area located on the right side of the base window.

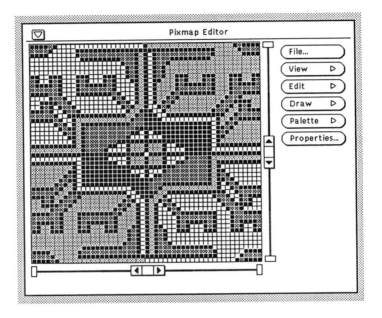

Figure 1.8 Control areas can be anywhere in the base window.

In the OPEN LOOK GUI, the term *window* is defined from the user's perspective, rather than the Xlib programmer's perspective. To a user, a window (such as a base window) is an inseparable collection of visual user-interface elements bounded by a rectangle, including the pane, header, control area, and so on.

The X Window System defines windows at a much lower level—as any rectangular area on the screen. Thus, each of the above user-interface elements is typically in its own X window. This is not as confusing as it may seem; in both cases, a window is the smallest manipulatable region of the screen. That a base window is actually comprised of many subwindows is an irrelevant implementation detail to the end-user.

Programming with the OPEN LOOK Intrinsic Toolkit is more at the level of the OPEN LOOK GUI than at the low level of the Xlib. Using the Toolkit, programmers create and manipulate complete user-interface objects called widgets. For example, an application creates a base window widget and controls its elements (such as the window title) as attributes of the newly created object.

1.4.2 Pop-up Windows

The OPEN LOOK GUI and OPEN LOOK X Toolkit provide several types of pop-up windows[1] to augment the functionality of base windows. Rather than drastically change the contents or layout of the base window, applications use pop-up windows to get command input, change settings, display help, and handle errors.

Pop-up windows are "owned" by the originating base window and are iconified when the base window is iconified. However, pop-up windows can be placed and moved anywhere on the screen.

1.4.2.1 Command Windows

Command windows get input for user-controlled actions such as search-and-replace, and save-as commands. Figure 1.9 shows a simple command window from the OPEN LOOK File Manager.

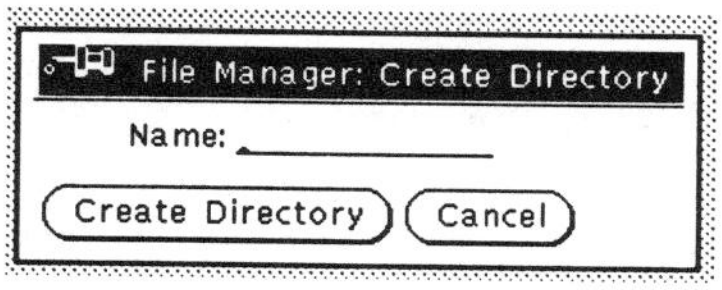

Figure 1.9 A simple OPEN LOOK command window

---

[1]Analogous to dialog boxes and alerts in other GUI's.

Notice the pushpin in the upper-left corner of the window header. The pushpin is in the unpinned position, so the pop-up window will be dismissed when you click either the Create Directory or Cancel button.[2] However, if you were to pin the window by clicking on the pushpin, the window would remain popped up, ready for another iteration. This is extremely useful for pop-up windows that users need often.

1.4.2.2 Property Windows

Property windows allow you to conveniently change the application's attributes or settings. A graphics editor may have a property window for each tool in the application to choose line width, fill style, and font characteristics.

Property windows are similar to command windows; the difference is that property window action buttons are defined by the OPEN LOOK GUI. All property windows must have Apply and Reset buttons; they may also have Set Defaults and Reset To Factory buttons as well.

Figure 1.10 illustrates a font property window for a hypothetical word processor. Like command windows, property windows also have a pushpin. In Figure 1.10 the pushpin is in the pinned state, so the window will remain on the screen after an action button is clicked.

---

[2]You could also use the window manager to dismiss the window by clicking Dismiss from the window menu. As an even shorter shortcut, pop-up windows can be dismissed by double-clicking on the pushpin, effectively pinning and unpinning the window. Windows are immediately dismissed when they are unpinned.

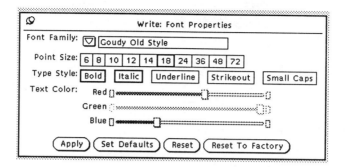

Figure 1.10 A typical OPEN LOOK property window

The OPEN LOOK File Manager has two pop-up property windows, one for customizing the application, and one for changing the attributes of files on the disk. This second property window is interesting, since it is essentially an implicit command window—the user can affect several UNIX commands by changing the contents of the window and clicking the Apply button.

This one window takes the place of this entire list of UNIX commands:

- `ls -l .Xdefaults`
- `chown jdm .Xdefaults`
- `chgrp eng .Xdefaults`
- `touch -a 1218203389 .Xdefaults`
- `touch -m 1218203389 .Xdefaults`
- `chmod u=rw,go=r .Xdefaults`

The highlighted window header in Figure 1.11 shows that the window has the keyboard focus, which means that input from the keyboard will go to this window. Specifically, it will go to the text field with the insert point, marked by a caret on the text baseline.

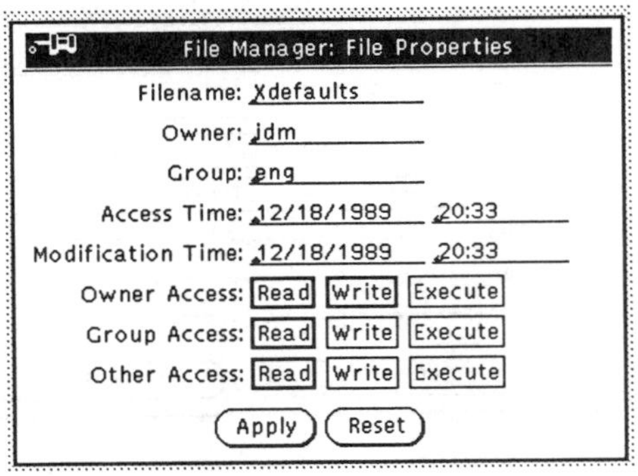

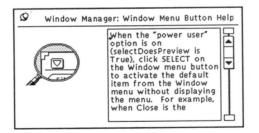

Figure 1.11 The OPEN LOOK File Manager's file properties window

1.4.2.3 Help Windows

Applications provide context-sensitive on-line help using help windows. Help windows have two panes: a magnifying glass displaying the area that was under the pointer when the HELP key was pressed, and a scrollable window containing help text for that element.

Figure 1.12 Help window for the Window menu button

The OPEN LOOK GUI requires applications to provide help for all user-interface and application elements. Using the above example, moving the pointer to the window header and pressing the HELP key would change the contents of the help window as shown:

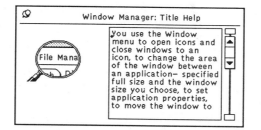

Figure 1.13 Help window for the title bar

There may be any number of help windows on the screen at any time, with the restriction of one help window per application.

A note about windows: in the previous examples, the titles in the headers of the help windows indicated that the help was provided by the window manager. Why does the window manager display help for elements of the File Manager's title bar?

In the X Window System, the window manager frames each top-level application window with window decorations, in this case the title bar (including the Window menu button or pushpin and the title area) and window border (including the resize corners). Since these areas are controlled by the window manager, the window manager is responsible for providing the help text.[3] Pressing the HELP key inside the area bounded by the window border and header triggers help for the application.

---

[3]It also means that these elements of the OPEN LOOK GUI are not provided when running a non-OPEN LOOK window manager.

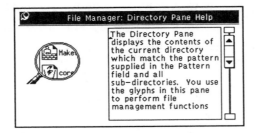

Figure 1.14 Application-supplied help text

1.4.2.4 Notices

When an application needs to ask the user how to proceed after a serious error or to confirm an operation that cannot be undone, it pops up
a notice.

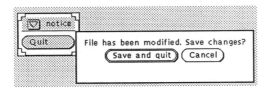

Figure 1.15 A typical notice

Notices do not have window headers or resize corners. While the notice is displayed, the application's base window is grayed-out and
keyboard and mouse input to the application is blocked, thus forcing
the user to choose one of the action buttons in the notice. This behavior is called *application modal* because it temporarily switches the
mode of control from user-driven to application-driven. Application-
modal behavior pertains only to the application that popped up the
notice; other applications continue to operate normally.

1.4.3 Controls

The OPEN LOOK GUI defines a simple and consistent set of controls for use in control areas and panes. Standard controls include buttons, settings, sliders and scrollbars, and text fields.

1.4.3.1 Buttons

Buttons are used extensively in OPEN LOOK applications, either to represent a single choice or a menu of choices. Figure 1.16 illustrates the three types of buttons.

Single Buttons perform an action or make a choice. In Figure 1.16 the Properties button is a single button. The ellipses (...) in the label indicate that clicking this button displays a pop-up window, in this case a property window.

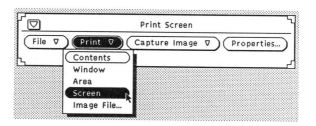

Figure 1.16 An example showing all OPEN LOOK button types

Menu Buttons display a menu. Pressing MENU with the pointer over a menu button displays the menu associated with that button.

The menu buttons in Figure 1.16 are File, Print, and Capture Image. MENU has been pressed over the Print menu button and dragged over the Screen item.

The Contents item in the Print menu is outlined to show that it is the default. Default menu items are significant if the user has enabled the "power-user" menu accelerator option from the Miscellaneous properties window of the Workspace Manager. If this option is enabled, pressing SELECT over a menu button displays the default item in that button's menu. Releasing SELECT while the pointer is still over the menu button activates the default item. Figure 1.17 shows the Print menu button with SELECT pressed.

Abbreviated Menu Buttons have the same semantics as regular menu buttons except that they have no built-in label. Window menu buttons are abbreviated menu buttons.

Within applications, abbreviated menu buttons are often paired with a "current selection" window. This window displays the last item selected from the menu and is also used for SELECT previewing, similar to regular menu buttons.

Figure 1.18 shows the abbreviated button and current selection window from Figure 1.10

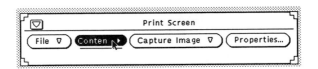

Figure 1.17 Highlighting the default menu item with SELECT

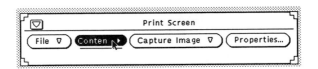

Figure 1.18   An abbreviated menu button with current selection window

1.4.3.2 Settings

Settings choose one-of-many or many-of-many items from a group. Setting controls that choose one-of-many are exclusives, while many-of-many controls are either nonexclusives or checkboxes.

The following illustrations demonstrate the different types of settings using the same data set.

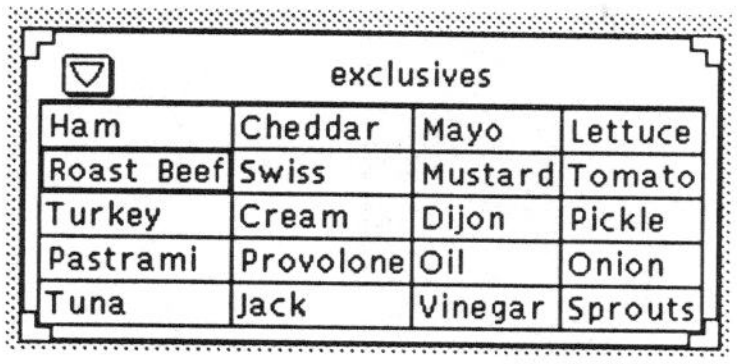

Figure 1.19 Exclusive settings

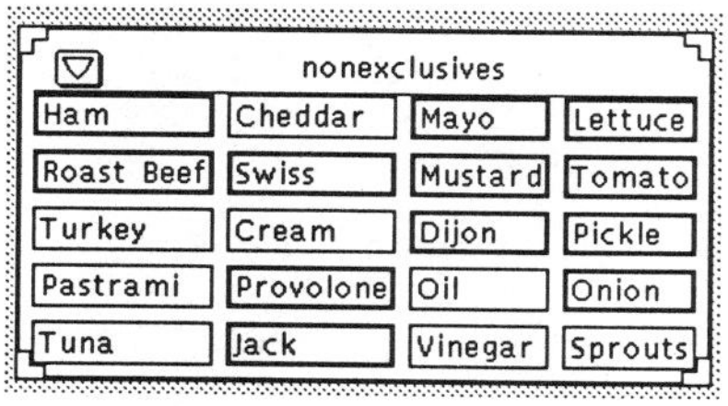

Figure 1.20 Nonexclusive settings

Figure 1.21 Checkbox settings

1.4.3.3 Sliders

Slider controls set numeric values within a range. Figure 1.22 shows several horizontal and vertical sliders, one for each channel of a simple audio mixer.

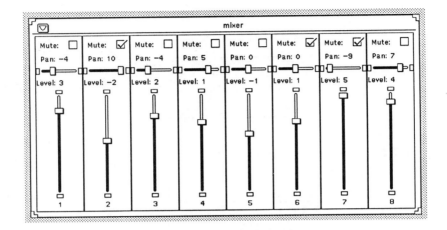

Figure 1.22 Horizontal and vertical sliders

1.4.3.4 Scrollbars

Scrollbars are visually similar to sliders but are designed to support panning within a pane. Like sliders, scrollbars can be oriented both vertically and horizontally.

Figure 1.23 Horizontal and vertical scrollbars

1.4.3.5 Text

For single-line string input, the Toolkit provides horizontally scrollable text fields.

Figure 1.24 The text field control

More sophisticated text requirements are satisfied with the text widget, which provides multi-line input and editing and horizontal and vertical scrollbars.

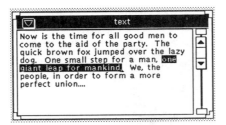

Figure 1.25 Multi-line text control

For labels and other read-only messages, the Toolkit also provides a static text widget.

1.4.4 Menus

OPEN LOOK menus can contain any combination of buttons, exclusives or nonexclusives. Figure 1.26 shows a multi-column menu of exclusive settings to set the font family.

```
 ┌─────────────────────────────────────────────────────┐
 │ ┌─┤┤┤           Write: Font Properties                │
 │ Font Family: ▼│Goudy Old Style                   │    │
 │ Point Size: ┌─┤┤┤                                      │
 │ Type Style: ┌──────────┬──────────────┬──────────┐ps  │
 │             │Avant Garde│Bookman       │Courier   │    │
 │ Text Color: │Garamound  │Goudy Old Style│Helvetica │    │
 │             │Lubalin Graph│Lucida       │Optima    │    │
 │             │Times Roman │Univers       │Zapf Chancery│  │
 │             └──────────┴──────────────┴──────────┘    │
 │    ( Apply )  ( Set Defaults )  ( Reset )  ( Reset To Factory )│
 └─────────────────────────────────────────────────────┘
```

Figure 1.26 Multi-column menu with exclusive items

We've seen how menus are associated with menu buttons and abbreviated menu buttons, and how pop-up menus display at the current pointer position. Several elements of the OPEN LOOK GUI provide pop-up menus, including scrollbars and the window header.

Applications can also define pop-up menus to pop up for a window, as shown in Figure 1.27. When the user presses or clicks MENU, the pop-up menu for that window appears, with the pointer next to the default item.

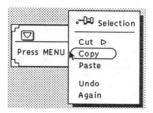

Figure 1.27 A pop-up menu

OPEN LOOK menus can be cascaded, as shown in Figure 1.28, since menu buttons can be used as items in a menu.

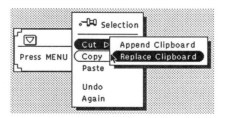

Figure 1.28 Cascading menus

1.4.5 Scrolling Lists

Often applications need to present a long list of choices, possibly allowing more than one of the items to be chosen. Scrolling lists are designed for this purpose.

Figure 1.29 shows a scrolling list containing the names of all 50 states. Two items on the list, Oregon and South Carolina, have been selected using the ADJUST button.

Figure 1.29 A scrolling list with two items selected

Applications can use an OPEN LOOK scrolling list as a visual list editor, allowing the user to interactively add, delete, and edit items in the list.

Chapter 2

The X Window System

The last chapter presented a high-level overview of the OPEN LOOK GUI, temporarily avoiding implementation details while concentrating on the user interface. This chapter looks at the other side, presenting a programmer's overview of the X Window System. Special consideration is given to how the window system architecture affects the implementation of the AT&T OPEN LOOK GUI, but most of the discussion is centered around the core X Protocol and the C language interface to the protocol, Xlib.

Low-level detail is avoided for the sake of brevity and clarity, but even so, this chapter contains much more information on X than you may ever need to write OPEN LOOK applications. Skim through it for an overview and return back to it and the *XWIN Programmer's Manual* as you need more information.

For the purposes of this discussions, X has been divided into the following logical sections:

Process Model—connections between applications and the window system.

Programming Model—language and library options available to X application developers.

System Model—defines X as an application environment.

Graphics Model—implements the X graphics machinery.

Input Model—how applications get input from the mouse and keyboard.

2.1 Process Model

The X Window System is somewhat unique among commercial window systems in that it is built around a network protocol, rather than a set of subroutine calls. The simple reason for this is: by using the network to connect applications to the display hardware, distributed graphics are designed into the system. That is, the machine displaying the graphics need not be the machine that is executing the application.

Other window systems, such as Microsoft Windows, Presentation Manager, and SunView, are physically or logically part of the operating system. They use a process model similar to that shown in Figure 2.1. Since these window systems do not use a network protocol, the application must run on the same machine as the graphics hardware.

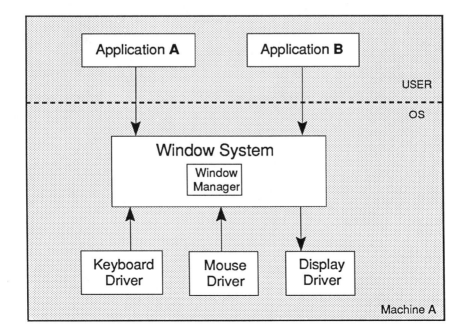

Figure 2.1 Typical window system process model

The X Window System uses the process model shown in Figure 2.2. The graphics screen(s), keyboard, and mouse are controlled by the server, running on Machine A. If Machine A is running a multi-tasking operating system such as UNIX, it can also execute X applications, known as clients. In this picture, Client A could be connected to Server A, or some other server on the network. Machine B has no graphics display or mouse, but can execute clients, such as Client B. Machine B is also running Window Manager A. In the X process model, the window manager is peer-level with clients. Like clients, the window manager can on reside on any machine with network access to the server.

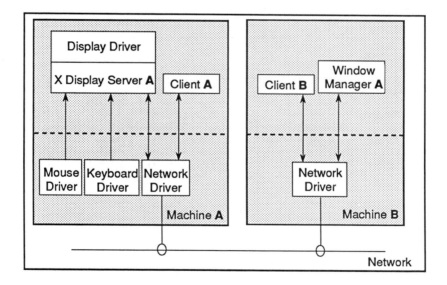

Figure 2.2 X Window System process model

This process model enables the X Window System to run on a wide range of hardware environments. In a workstation environment, it is typical to run the display server, window manager, and most clients on the same machine. In other environments, it is not uncommon to run all applications on multi-user computers, using personal computers or graphics terminals as display servers.

2.1.1 The X Protocol

The X Protocol forms the core of the X Window System. It is the formal definition of the data stream between clients and the server.

The bulk of the X Protocol is asynchronous. Data is buffered in both directions and is processed by the receiving end "at some point in the future." This is quite different from subroutine-call based window systems, in which calls do not return until the operation has completed.[1]

The X Protocol is comprised of four basic types of data packets: requests, replies, events, and errors. Figure 2.3 shows the sender, receiver, and synchronization mode of these packet types.

	Sender	Receiver	Synchronization
Request	Client	Server	Async/Sync
Reply	Server	Client	Sync
Event	Client or Server	Client	Async
Error	Server	Client	Async

Figure 2.3 X Protocol data packet types

2.1.1.1 Requests

Clients solicit action from the server by sending requests. Requests are buffered and executed asynchronously by the server.

---

[1]To aid debugging, X applications can force their server connection to be synchronous.

Some common requests include:

Request	Description
CreateWindow	Creates a new window
OpenFont	Loads a font, if not already loaded
CopyArea	Copies an area to another area
InstallColormap	Forces a colormap to be loaded in hardware

2.1.1.2 Replies

Some requests are actually comprised of two parts: the request itself, which is sent by the client, and the reply, which is sent by the server. Most requests are not sent a reply. Requests that require a reply are sometimes referred to as round-trip requests, since they require a data transfer in both directions to complete the request.

Round-trip requests force the communication between the client and server to become temporarily synchronous. When a client issues a request that requires a reply, the output buffer is flushed (with the contents sent to the server), and the client waits for the reply data to arrive from the server.

Common requests that require a reply:

Request	Description
GetWindowAttributes	Returns information about a given window
QueryTextExtents	Returns logical extent of a string
GetImage	Returns the pixel values for a given area
AllocColorCells	Returns the RGB values actually used

2.1.1.3 Events

Events are datagram-like packets sent to clients by the server[2] as an asynchronous notification that something has happened in or to a window. Apart from replies, events are the only way the server talks to a clients.

There are 33 different event types. For the most part, clients receive only the event types they explicitly request. A handful of events (MappingNotify, ClientMessage, SelectionClear, SelectionNotify, and SelectionRequest) are sent to clients without being explicitly requested. Events can be logically divided into three general categories: Input events, windowing events, and client events.

Input Events

```
ButtonPress
ButtonRelease
EnterNotify
FocusIn
FocusOut
KeymapNotify
KeyPress
KeyRelease
LeaveNotify
MappingNotify
MotionNotify
```

Input events result from keyboard and mouse activity. They are covered later in this chapter in the Input Model section.

---

[2]Clients may also send events to other clients. Client-sent events are called synthetic events.

Windowing Events:

```
CirculateNotify
CirculateRequest
ColormapNotify
ConfigureNotify
ConfigureRequest
CreateNotify
DestroyNotify
Expose
GraphicsExposure
GravityNotify
MapNotify
MapRequest
NoExposure
ReparentNotify
ResizeRequest
UnmapNotify
VisibilityNotify
```

Windowing events result from creating, destroying, moving, resizing, iconifying, or otherwise modifying windows or their appendages (e.g., colormaps). Most of these events are never used by clients, but by window managers and toolkits. The most notable exception is the Expose event, which must be handled by clients that draw to the screen.

Client Events:

```
ClientMessage
PropertyNotify
SelectionClear
SelectionNotify
SelectionRequest
```

Client events facilitate communication between clients. The PropertyNotify event is especially important and is explained later in this chapter in the Properties section.

OPEN LOOK X Toolkit applications rarely deal with these low-level X events. The Toolkit either handles the event completely or translates it into a user-interface action, such as "the slider moved," "the checkbox got checked," or "a string was typed," and calls any callback subroutines the application has registered for that action.

Unlike some window systems, X does not guarantee to preserve the contents of a window obscured by another window or otherwise not visible on the screen. Rather, when a portion of the window becomes visible, the application receives an Expose event containing the geometry of the newly exposed region. It is the application's responsibility to redraw the region's contents as soon as possible.

Toolkit objects (widgets) know how to redraw themselves on the screen, so exposures are usually transparent to OPEN LOOK X Toolkit applications. However, applications that draw to the screen themselves using Xlib must be able to repaint those areas in response to an Expose event.

2.1.1.4 Errors

Errors are a special type of event, and are handled separately through error handlers. By default, nonfatal errors print a message, while fatal errors print a message and terminate the application. Applications may define their own error handlers and replace these defaults.

Like normal events, error events are buffered. Thus, a client may not realize that an error has occurred until well after it has happened.

Here are some examples of errors:

Error	Description
`Alloc`	The server couldn't allocate the resource.
`Request`	The request opcode is not valid.
`Value`	Some numeric value falls outside the valid range.
`Match`	Some argument is not correct.

2.2 Programming Model

Although the X Window System protocol does not stipulate a particular language or programming interface, the vast majority of toolkits and applications use the C programming interface, Xlib, which as been adopted by the MIT X Consortium as part of the X standard.

Applications are typically not written directly to Xlib however, but are instead developed with the toolkits, which relieve much of the complexity of the window system.

Figure 2.4 illustrates X applications written to the various programming interfaces.[3] Client A uses Xlib, exclusively. Some of the first applications ported to X used this approach, since the toolkits were not yet available. Client B uses the AT&T OPEN LOOK X Toolkit, libXol (based on the MIT Xt Intrinsics), while Client C uses another OPEN LOOK programming interface, the Sun XView Toolkit.

Client D uses the XVT virtual toolkit. The idea behind virtual toolkits is that different window systems (X, NeWS, Presentation Manager, Microsoft Windows, Macintosh, et al) actually have a lot of similarities. The virtual toolkit extrapolates these similarities into

---

[3]The relative size of the boxes is not intended to show code proportions.

a single, common programming interface. Application source code is then portable across any platform that supports an implementation of the virtual toolkit.

Finally, Client E represents applications that do not use Xlib at all. This application happens to be written in Common Lisp; it uses CLX as the Lisp interface to the X Protocol.

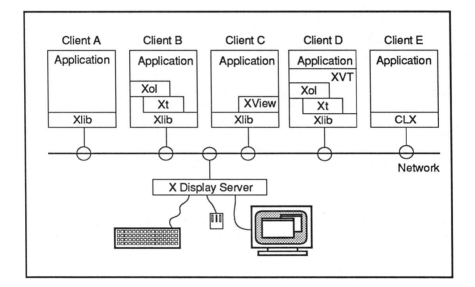

Figure 2.4 X programming interfaces

2.3 System Model

X windows are organized in a hierarchical tree. An X server can support more than one screen (physical or logical display surface), and each screen has its own tree. At the top of the tree is the root window.

Figure 2.5 shows a screen and window tree for a client with a single top-level window.

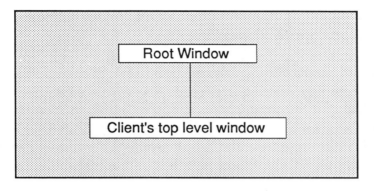

Figure 2.5a Window tree of a simple client

Figure 2.5b Screen image of a simple client

Top-level windows have special significance in X. For example, window managers only manage clients' top-level windows. As the topmost node in a client's window subtree, they act as a logical interface to other clients.

The window hierarchy also plays an important part in event reporting. Starting with the source window where the event occurred, the X server searches up the window tree until it finds the first window interested in the event or the first window that has set the do-not-propagate window attribute. A window with the do-not-propagate attribute stops all events from being passed further up the window tree.

2.3.1 Coordinate Space

Every window has its own coordinate space. All operations inside a window are performed in this space. Coordinates are in pixels, with the origin (0,0) in the upper-left corner. The x-axis increases horizontally to the right; the y-axis increases vertically down. The origin point is inside any border that the window may have. The width and height specify the window dimensions in pixels.

A window's location on the screen is relative to its parent. The window's origin coordinates specify the offset from its parent window's origin. Thus, a window positioned at (3, 4) would have its origin 3 pixels to the right and 4 pixels down from the origin of its parent (see Figure 2.6). This parent-relative addressing strategy allows window trees to be moved by merely updating the top node of the tree.

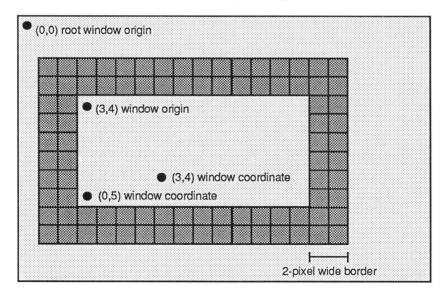

Figure 2.6 Parent-relative window coordinates

2.3.2 Mapping

One important aspect of windows is that they are only viewable on the screen when they, and all of their ancestors, are *mapped*. Creating a window allocates its data structures and adds it to the window tree, but does not make it visible. Mapping a window makes it eligible for display on the screen.

Menus exploit this mapping feature by creating their window tree once and mapping all but the top-most window in this tree. Whenever the menu is to be displayed, it is made viewable (eligible for display) by merely mapping this window.

2.3.3 Visibility

Mapping a window makes it logically viewable, but only the portion of the window that is not obscured by other windows is actually visible. In X, the portions of a window, or regions, that are not visible are not guaranteed to be drawn or preserved. As mentioned above, applications receive Expose events when window regions become visible, and they are expected to redraw these regions as soon as they can.

Some servers provide optional *backing-store* and/or *save-unders* that preserve nonvisible areas. Backing-store preserves the contents of a window when it is obscured by another window. Save-unders save the area directly under a menu or other temporary window. However, the server may terminate these services at any time, due to memory constraints. Thus, applications must always be able to redraw their windows.

As an example of how this works in practice, Figure 2.7 shows a client drawing a circle in Window A. Window A is partially obscured by Window B. The pixels behind Window B are clipped when the circle is drawn. If either Window A or Window B is moved, the region that was under Window B becomes exposed. The client is notified by an Expose event describing the region and must take steps to redraw its contents.

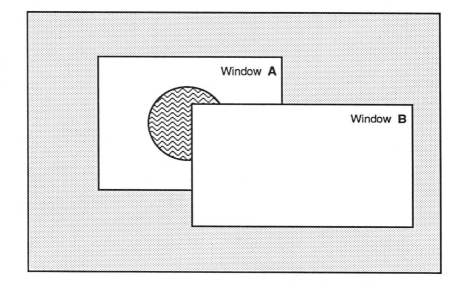

Figure 2.7 Window A is partially obscured by Window B.

2.3.4 Window Managers

The flexibility of the X process model gives users the freedom to choose their own window manager. While this flexibility has been an asset to the development of new window managers and graphical user interfaces, it has also created problems for applications that expect to operate in a particular environment.

The AT&T OPEN LOOK Window Manager is an important component of the OPEN LOOK Graphical User Interface. However, if you adhere to the client/window manager conventions discussed later in this chapter and in Chapter Six, your applications will operate with any window manager that also conforms to these conventions.[4]

2.3.4.1 Reparenting

Window managers typically add decorations to an application's top-level windows, such as a title bar and resize corners. They do this in two steps. First, the window manager creates a window large enough to hold the client's window plus the decorations. Then, the window manager *reparents* the client's top-level window to make it a child of this new window.

Figure 2.8 shows the screen and window tree for the client shown in Figure 2.5 after the OPEN LOOK Window Manager has reparented its top-level window. Note that if the window manager is running when a client maps its top-level window, the window manager intercepts the operation and automatically reparents the window before it is actually mapped.

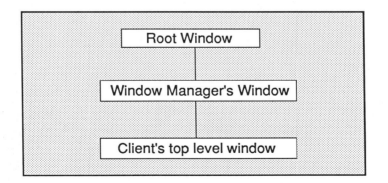

Figure 2.8a Window tree of a reparented xclock window

---

[4]Of course, features provided by the OPEN LOOK Window Manager, such as pushpins and Help windows, will not be available.

Figure 2.8b Screen image of a reparented xclock window

2.3.4.2 Pop-ups

Although normal windows are subservient to the window manager, window manager intervention is not appropriate for all windows. In particular, pop-up menus, notice boxes, and other temporary windows do not need title bars or other standard window decorations. They need to be displayed quickly and not be constrained to the particular layout policy enforced by the window manager.

The *override-redirect* window attribute overrides the window manager and prevents it from reparenting or otherwise interfering with a window. Windows with override redirect enabled are called *pop-up* windows in the Xlib documentation. What the OPEN LOOK GUI classifies as pop-up windows (e.g., property windows, command windows) are actually secondary top-level windows, called *transient* windows in other X documentation.

The exception to this are OPEN LOOK pop-up menus, which use over-ride-redirect while they are not pinned (see Figure 2.9). Pinning a pop-up menu turns off override-redirect, transforming the menu into a transient window by allowing the window manager to manage it (Figure 2.10).

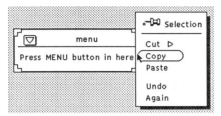

Figure 2.9 OPEN LOOK pop-up menus use override-redirect.

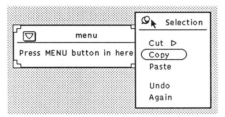

Figure 2.10 Pinning an OPEN LOOK pop-up menu transforms it into a transient window.

2.3.5 Properties

Properties are an extensible, client-to-client, data-exchange mechanism. Properties allow clients to communicate arbitrary information by associating named and typed data with windows.

Properties are very similar to global variables in the C programming language. Each property is a variable of a particular property type and can be assigned values of that type. Like C variables, applications can define new properties and property types. However, properties are associated with individual windows, and thus have tighter scoping than C global variables.

The server keeps each window's properties in a linked-list of property structures, as part of its per-window information. The server doesn't do anything with properties, except store and retrieve them at the request of clients. As a convenience, the server byte-swaps the data for clients on different architectures, but it does no other interpretation or type-casting. This is adequate, since, for any given property, at least one of the following statements is probably true:

- The property record contains enough information for the client to interpret the data.

- The convention that prompted one client to read the property is the same convention that prompted another client to put it there.

Property records contain the following components:[5]

```
typedef struct _PropertyRec {
    PropertyRec  *next;           /* next property in list */
    ATOM         propertyName;    /* name ID of property */
    ATOM         type;            /* ignored by the server */
    short        format;          /* data format {8,16,32} */
    long         size;            /* #bytes of data */
    pointer      data;            /* private to client */
} PropertyRec, *PropertyPtr;
```

The propertyName and type fields are atoms: integer IDs generated by the server to represent property name strings and property type strings.

---

[5]The fields listed here are from the MIT sample servers, on which almost all servers are based. The data may be represented differently on other servers, but the information will be the same, out of necessity to support the X Protocol.

Clients obtain atoms by registering, or *interning*,[6] a string with the server. If the string has already been registered, its atom is returned. Otherwise, the server registers the string and a new atom is generated and returned. To clients, atoms are a convenient integer representation of a symbolic name; but to the server, atoms are just an index into a table of strings. Once interned, atoms remain interned for the lifetime of the server and cannot be deleted.

The format field in the property record specifies how the data is accessed by the client: 8, 16, or 32 bits at a time. For example, ASCII string properties typically have format 8, while numbers or other data could have any format large enough to hold the largest desired value. If the format is 16 or 32, the server byte-swaps the data for clients on machines with an architecture different from the server's.

Properties are used exclusively for inter-client communication, not for client-server communication. Furthermore, all interpretation of property contents is by convention. The X Protocol provides mechanisms for creating properties and getting/setting property values, and it even defines several standard properties and property types, but it does not specify the semantics of any window properties or property values. Chapter 6 will discuss the Inter-Client Communication Conventions Manual, which addresses the need for standard property interpretation and behavior to promote interoperability between clients and window managers.

---

[6]That some of the original X designers were fond of the Lisp programming language is evident in their choice of terminology (e.g., Atom, interning, properties, property lists).

The following table summarizes the property functionality provided by the X Protocol and Xlib:

Protocol Request	Xlib Function	Description
InternAtom	XInternAtom	Registers a symbolic string with the server and return its atom identifier.
GetAtomName	XGetAtomName	Returns the symbolic string identified by an atom.
ChangeProperty	XChangeProperty	Creates or modifies a property. Properties can be appended, prepended, or replaced.
GetProperty	XGetWindowProperty	Gets the value, type, and format of a property.
ListProperties	XListProperties	Gets the property list of a window.
DeleteProperty	XDeleteProperty	Deletes a property from a window.

2.4 Graphics Model

This section highlights the X graphics model, covering:

- general characteristics
- drawing primitives
- color

2.4.1 General Characteristics

2.4.1.1 Coordinate Space

X uses a raster image model to render drawing primitives. This image model presents the application with a device-level view of the drawing space: coordinates map one-for-one to physical pixels.

Some graphics systems (CGI, GKS, PostScript™, et al) provide a coordinate-space transformation layer. Applications specify device-independent coordinates in user-space that the graphics system translates into device-space. In X, there is no difference between device-space and user-space. While this gives applications precise control for pixel operations, it also burdens the application with the responsibility for adjusting to different resolutions.

2.4.1.2 Drawables

Pixmaps and windows are collectively known as drawables. Drawables function as the destination (and sometimes source) for graphical operations.

2.4.1.2.1 Pixmaps

A pixmap is a rectangular array of off-screen pixels. Like windows, pixmaps are defined in their own coordinate space, with an origin of (0, 0) in the upper-left corner and extents specified as width and height in pixels. Pixmaps are said to be *off-screen* since they always occupy memory outside the visible frame buffer.

Unlike windows, pixmaps cannot be mapped to the screen, and, as such, drawing into a pixmap is never directly visible. Conversely, pixmaps are never obscured by other pixmaps or windows. Pixmaps are a per-screen resource. A server may support multiple physical or logical display screens, but pixmaps can only be used on the screen where they were created.

Pixmaps can be created any depth (bits-per-pixel) supported by the server for that screen. Servers are required to support at least one depth: one bit per pixel. By convention, pixmaps of depth 1 (one bit per pixel) are referred to as *bitmaps*.

2.4.1.2.2 Windows

Simplistically, a window is a rectangular area on the screen. In the trivial case, a window can be thought of as an on-screen pixmap. In practice, windows must share screen resources, such as pixels and colormaps, with other windows.

Not all windows act as on-screen pixmaps. X supports two classes of windows: InputOutput, the "normal" drawable window type, and InputOnly, transparent windows used exclusively for special input processing, such as mouse clicks on user-interface objects.

2.4.1.3 Clipping

Drawing into a window is clipped to the intersection of four separate clipping parameters:

- the window's own extents
- the extents of the parent window
- the extents of child windows (optional per window)
- a client-specified clipping region, specified either as a bitmask or a clipping rectangle list

Pixmaps do not have parent or child windows, so are only clipped to their own extents and the client-specified clip region.

2.4.1.4 Logical Drawing Functions

Drawing operations combine source and destination pixels using one of 16 possible logic functions shown in Figure 2.11.

Name	Index	Action
GXclear	0	0
GXand	1	source & dest
GXandReverse	2	source & (~dest)
GXcopy	3	source
GXandInverted	4	(~src) & dest
GXnoop	5	dest
GXxor	6	source ^ dest
GXor	7	source I dest
GXnor	8	(~source) & (~dest)
GXequiv	9	(~source) ^ dest
GXinvert	10	~dest
GXorReverse	11	source I (~dest)
GXcopyInverted	12	~source
GXorInverted	13	(~source) I dest
GXnand	14	(~source) I (~dest)
GXset	15	1

Figure 2.11 Logical drawing functions

2.4.1.5 Plane Masking

The plane mask affects which planes in the destination drawable are modified by the drawing operation. By default, the mask is set to all 1s (0xFFFFFFFF), such that drawing modifies all planes.

Both the plane mask and logical drawing function are used to compute the final destination pixel value:

((source function dest) & plane_mask) | (dest & (~plane_mask))

2.4.1.6 Graphics Contexts

Graphics Contexts (GCs) hold a particular state of the X graphics machinery, specifying foreground color, background color, function, plane mask, clipping, and other attributes necessary for drawing operations. When applications request the server to draw a line, text, or other graphics primitive, they specify a GC for the server to use for that request.

Applications can create as many GCs as they need. It is usually easier and more efficient to create several GCs than to create only one and continually change it. For example, a CAD package might create a GC for each line color or type it needs. A drawing package might create a GC for each function or tool it provides. However, GCs are server resources and they occupy memory on the server. Like any other resource, GCs should be used where necessary but not wasted.

2.4.2 Drawing Primitives

The X Protocol defines several basic primitives, including lines, filled areas, bitmap operations, text, and image transfers.

The protocol also provides for growth. New functionality can be added to X through extensions. As of this writing, several extensions are under development and may eventually be adopted as part of the protocol standard. These include:

- **PEX**—the PHIGS Extension to X. PHIGS (Programmer's Hierarchical Interactive Graphics Standard) is a GKS-like 3-D package being standardized by the American National Standards Institute (ANSI).

- **VEX**—the Video Extension to X. Servers supporting VEX can display real-time video in a window and control video play-back- and recording-equipment.

- **XIE**—the X Imaging Extension. XIE defines image-processing operations, such as image analysis, filtering, and half-toning.

- **Others**—Bezier curves, outline fonts, and Display PostScript^{TM}.

This section discusses the drawing primitives that X currently supports. At the end of this section, Figure 2.26 illustrates a schematic view of the X graphics machinery.

2.4.2.1 Line Primitives

Line primitives select pixels through a path drawn on a grid. Here, a line is defined as a point followed by a list of points. The algorithm for the particular line primitive determines the move direction to get to the next point. Since the line is being drawn on an xy-grid, the move direction, or step, is calculated as x-step and y-step components.

For example, with a horizontal line, the y-step is always zero and the x-step is always either 1 or -1, depending on the drawing direction. Diagonal lines calculate x-step and y-step independently to draw a close grid-approximation of a straight line. Arcs and circles are also drawn this way, using algorithms to approximate curves.[7]

The X Protocol currently defines the following line primitives. As mentioned above, the protocol is extensible, so this list will grow:

Protocol Request	Xlib Function	Description
PolyPoint	XDrawPoint XDrawPoints	Draws unconnected points.
PolyLine	XDrawLine XDrawLines	Draws lines between each pair of points.
PolySegment	XDrawSegments	Draw unconnected line segments.
PolyRectangle	XDrawRectangle XDrawRectangles	Draws rectangle outlines. Rectangles are specified as an upper-left coordinate and width and height, in pixels.
PolyArc	XDrawArc XDrawArcs	Draws circular or elliptical arcs. Arcs are specified by a rectangle, a starting angle, and an ending angle.

---

[7]For more information on graphics algorithms, refer to the references listed in the bibliography.

2.4.2.2 Line Attributes

X lines are drawn with GC attributes similar to those defined by the PostScript page-description language:

- **join style**—specifies how to draw the intersection of two line segments. Join style is either JoinMitre, JoinRound, or JoinBevel (see Figure 2.12).

- **cap style**—specifies how to draw the non-intersecting ends of line segments. Cap style choices are CapNotLast, CapButt, CapProjecting, and CapRound (see Figure 2.13).

- **dashes and dash offset**—specify an arbitrary on-off dash sequence for line drawing (see Figure 2.14).

- **line style**—specifies how to use the dash list for line drawing. Line style can be one of three types: LineSolid, LineOnOffDash, or LineDoubleDash (see Figure 2.15).

- **line width**—specifies the line width. The protocol specifies a particular line drawing algorithm to ensure visual consistency. A line width of zero relaxes this specification and allows the server to use its native line drawer for increased speed.

The line attributes determine only which pixels are drawn, not how they are drawn. That is a function of the fill style, described later in this section.

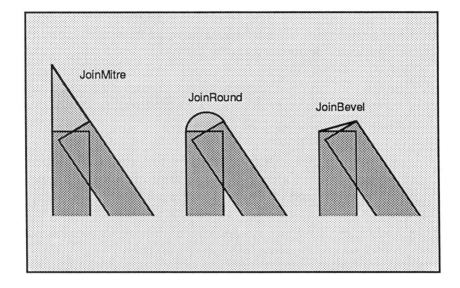

Figure 2.12 Join styles attach two line segments.

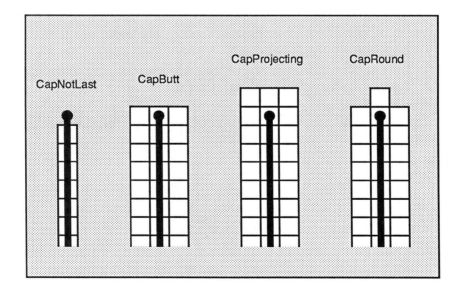

Figure 2.13 Cap styles shape line end patterns.

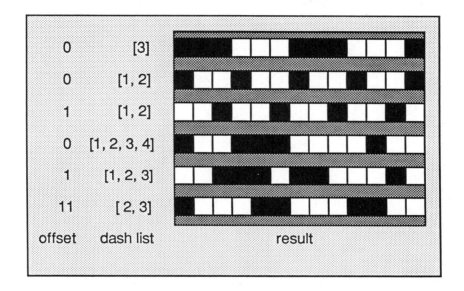

Figure 2.14 Dash list with offset.

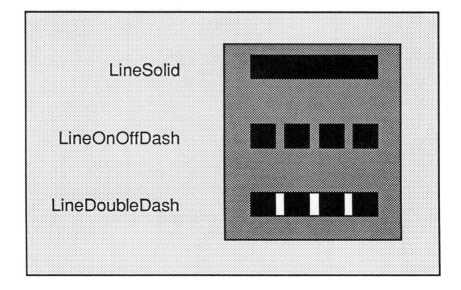

Figure 2.15 Line styles determine dash pattern color expansion.

2.4.2.3 Fill Primitives

In addition to the line drawing primitives, X provides fill primitives for rectangles, arcs, and arbitrary polygons:

Protocol Request	Xlib Function	Description
PolyFillRectangle	XFillRectangle XFillRectangles	Fills rectangular areas. Rectangles are specified as an upper-left coordinate, a width, and a height.
PolyFillArc	XFillArc XFillArcs	Fills arcs. Arcs are specified by a rectangle, a start angle, and an end angle.
FillPoly	XFillPolygon	Fills arbitrary area, specified by a path.

Arcs are closed either with a straight line joining the angles (chord) or with straight lines to the center (pie-slice), according to the GC arc_mode. Figure 2.16 shows an arc filled with arc_mode set to ArcPieSlice and again with arc_mode set to ArcChord.

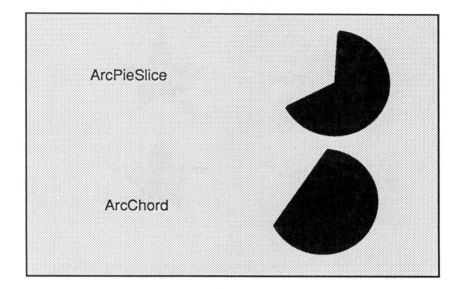

Figure 2.16 Filled arcs with different arc modes.

Polygons can be self-intersecting. The fill_rule determines the result. The EvenOddRule does not draw areas if they overlap an odd number of times. The WindingRule draws all areas the path encloses. Figure 2.17 illustrates the effect of the fill_rule on complex polygons.

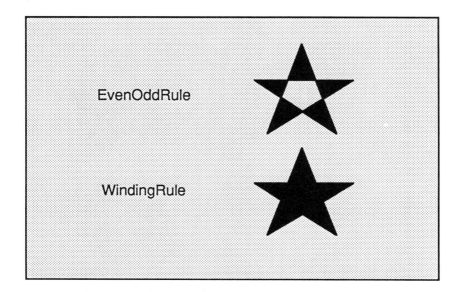

Figure 2.17 Filled polygons with different fill rules.

2.4.2.4 Fonts

X uses nonscalable raster (bitmap) fonts, with each font stored in a file on the display server's machine. Font files are distributed as plain ASCII text in the Binary Distribution Format (BDF). Server implementations provide a way to compile these files into Server Natural Format (SNF) to fit their bit and byte architecture. Each font file contains bitmap and size information for each glyph, as well as optional font properties.

Font properties are name/value pairs that provide additional information about the font, such as minimum interword spacing, italic angle, or the offset in pixels of where subscripts should begin. Currently, the X Protocol does not require fonts to have any properties, although the proposed X Logical Font Description (XLFD) conventions mandate a standard set of properties, including FONT_ASCENT, FONT_DESCENT, and DEFAULT_CHAR. Perhaps more importantly, the XLFD conventions describe a standard font-name syntax, making it much easier for applications to determine information about the available fonts.[8]

The following table lists the Xlib and protocol functions to load fonts and obtain font information. Note that the OPEN LOOK X Toolkit automatically selects and loads a default font to match the server's screen resolution.

Protocol Request	Xlib Function	Description
OpenFont	XLoadFont	Loads the named font.
QueryFont	XQueryFont	Obtains information about a loaded font, including metrics and properties.
OpenFont, QueryFont	XLoadQueryFont	Performs an XLoadFont and XQueryFont in a single operation.
CloseFont	XUnloadFont	Frees a font loaded with XLoadFont.

---

[8]For more information, refer to the "X Logical Font Description Conventions V1.3" in the *XWIN Programmer's Guide.*

Protocol Request	Xlib Function	Description
CloseFont	XFreeFont	Frees a font and info structure from XLoadQueryFont.
ListFonts	XListFonts	Returns pattern-matched list of available fonts.
ListFontsWithInfo	XListFontsWithInfo	Like XListFonts, but returns XQueryFont-type info for each matched font.

2.4.2.5 Text Primitives

The X text primitives support 8- and 16-bit character sets. Eight-bit character sets have up to 256 characters, or glyphs, and 16-bit character sets have up to 65,536 glyphs. The 16-bit character sets are needed to support Japanese Kanji and other fonts having a very large number of characters.

Applications can draw text with or without a character cell. Both methods draw glyphs the same way, but character cell text first draws a filled rectangle to the destination to clear out a background area for the glyph.

Figure 2.18 illustrates the difference between text with a character cell and text without.

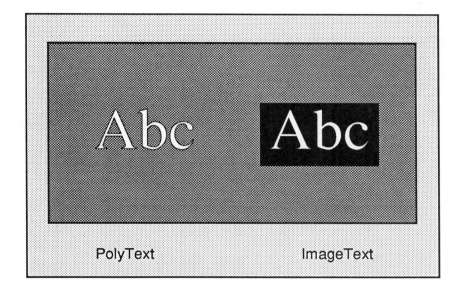

Figure 2.18 Text without and with character cells

Protocol Request	Xlib Function	Description
PolyText8	XDrawString XDrawText	Draws text using 8-bit characters.
PolyText16	XDrawString16 XDrawText16	Draws text using 16-bit characters.
ImageText8	XDrawImageString	Draws text using 8-bit characters and a character cell.
ImageText16	XDrawImageString16	Draws text using 16-bit characters and a character cell.

2.4.3 Fill Style

The fill style attribute defines how source bits (points to be drawn) translate to source pixel values, which are externally applied to the destination through the GC function and plane_mask:

- **FillSolid**—"on" source bits are color-expanded to the foreground pixel value (see Figure 2.19).

- **FillStipple**—source bits are pushed through a bitmap stencil, or stipple pattern, with the resulting "on" source bits color-expanded to the foreground pixel value. "Off" source bits are ignored, leaving the destination unchanged (see Figure 2.20).

- **FillOpaqueStipple**—same as FillStipple, except that "off" source bits (see Figure 2.21).

- **FillTile**—"on" source bits are expanded to pixel values read from a tile pattern. Unlike stipple patterns, tiles can be more than one pixel deep. In fact, the tile must be the same depth as the destination. The effect is that the tile is stenciled through the source bits onto the destination (see Figure 2.22).

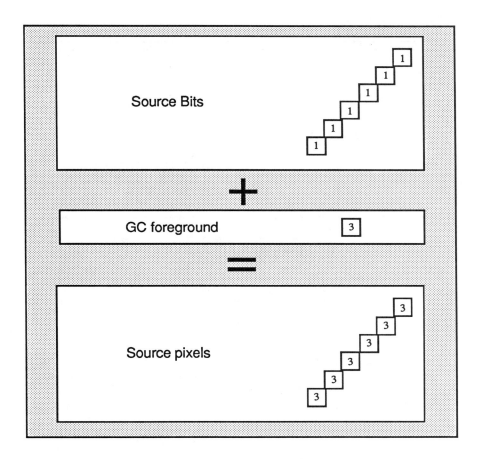

Figure 2.19 Graphics drawn with FillSolid

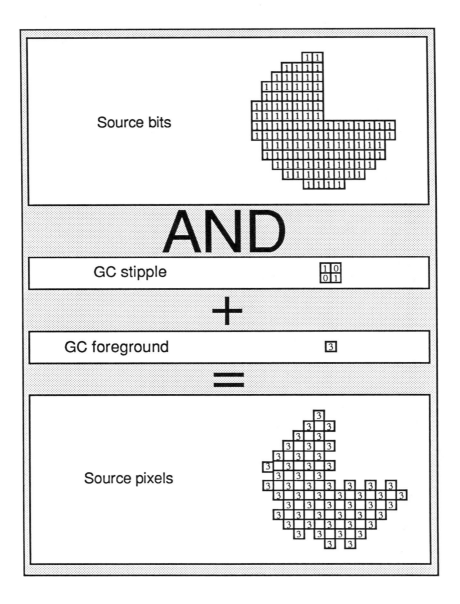

Figure 2.20 Graphics drawn with FillStipple

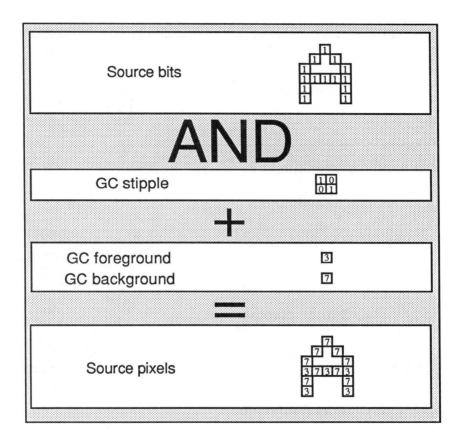

Figure 2.21 Graphics drawn with FillOpaqueStipple

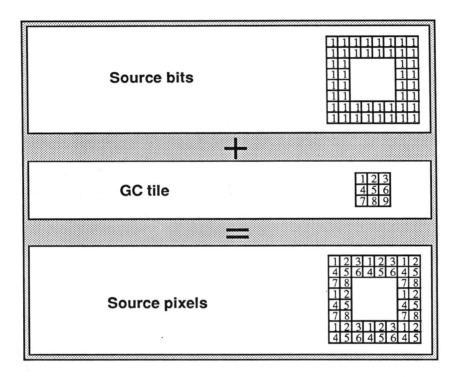

Figure 2.22 Graphics drawn with FillTile

2.4.4 Raster Operations

2.4.4.1 Pixmap Copy

Pixmap copy operations graft a rectangular array of source pixels onto a rectangular array of destination pixels.[9] The source and the destination areas may partially overlap and may even be the same. However, the source and destination rectangles are always the same size, as X does not currently provide primitives to stretch or shrink pixmaps.

Two pixmap operations are provided, one for copying pixmaps to pixmaps, the other for copying bitmaps to pixmaps:

Protocol Request	Xlib Function	Description
CopyArea	XCopyArea	Copies one rectangular array of pixels to another. Source and destination drawables must be the same depth.
CopyPlane	XCopyPlane	Color-expands a rectangular array of bits to an array of pixels on the destination.

---

[9]This operation is popularly known as a bitblt, for Bit-Block-Transfer.

Figures 2.23 and 2.24 demonstrate CopyArea and CopyPlane, respectively.

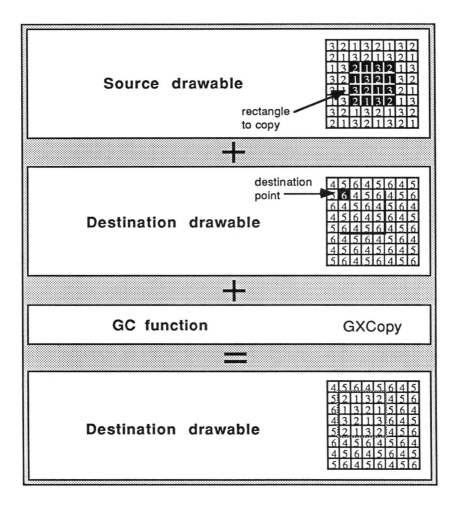

Figure 2.23 Copying a pixmap to another pixmap using CopyArea

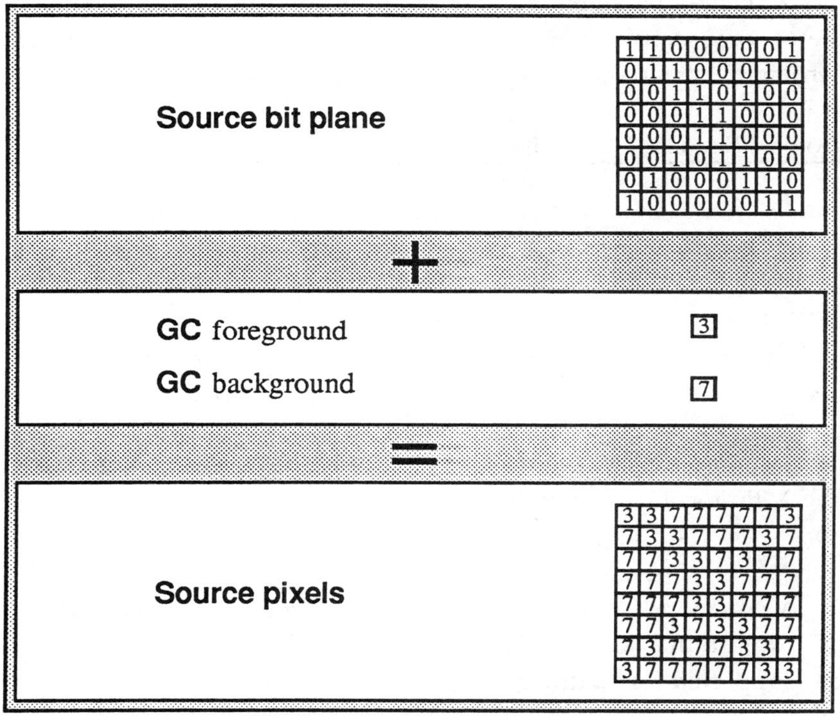

Figure 2.24 Color-expanding a bitmap to a pixmap using CopyPlane

2.4.4.2 Images

The X image operators allow clients to transfer pixel data to and from the server. Applications use image operators for image processing, hardcopy "screen dumping," and creating icons and fill patterns.

Protocol Request	Xlib Function	Description
GetImage	XGetImage	Reads a rectangular array of pixel values from a drawable.
PutImage	XPutImage	Writes a rectangular array of pixel values to a drawable.

The X Protocol gives applications three data-format options to choose from:

XYBitmap—transfers a single-plane bitmap, color expanding to foreground and background colors (XYBitmap format is not supported for GetImage).

XYPixmap—transfers an image as an array of bitmaps.

ZPixmap—transfers an image as an array of pixel values.

Xlib provides convenience routines (XCreateImage, XDestroyImage, XPutPixel, XGetPixel) that handle different image bit and byte orders. These routines allow clients to read and write images independent of the bit and byte order of the server and client machines.

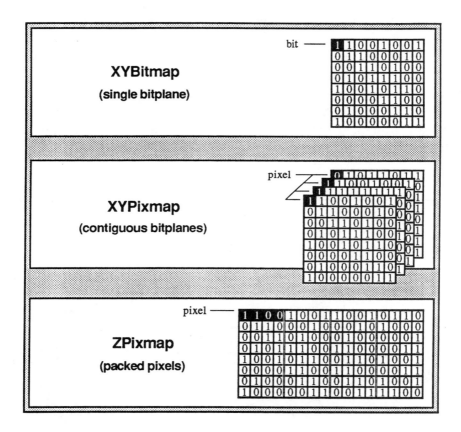

Figure 2.25   XYBitmap, XYPixmap, and ZPixmap image formats

2.4.5 Graphics Summary

Figure 2.26 pictorially summarizes the X graphics machinery.

Starting at the top are the source bits, which specify which pixels to draw. Source bits are determined either algorithmically by the drawing primitives or by bits set in character glyphs. Source pixels result from color-expansion or tile-matching of source bits. Source pixels are combined with destination pixels according to the drawing function and plane mask.

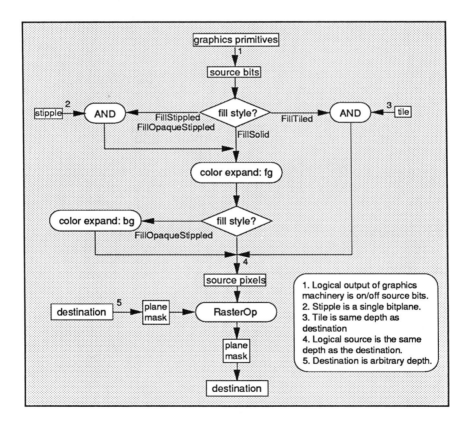

Figure 2.26 Graphics machinery logic

The following shows the graphics logic in C-like pseudo-code:

```
source_bits = DoGraphicsPrimitive(request);

switch (fill_style) {
case FillStipple:
    source_bits = BitMask(source_bits, stipple_pattern);
    source_pixels = ColorExpandFg(source_bits, fg);
    break;
case FillOpaqueStipple:
    source_bits = BitMask(source_bits, stipple_pattern);
    source_pixels = ColorExpandFgBg(source_bits, fg, bg);
    break;
case FillSolid:
    source_pixels = ColorExpandFg(source_bits, fg);
    break;
case FillTile:
    source_pixels = PixMask(tile_pattern, source_bits);
    break;
}

dest_pixels =
    ((source_pixels FUNCTION dest_pixels) AND plane_mask)
    OR (dest_pixels AND (NOT plane_mask))
```

Figure 2.27 Graphics machinery logic pseudo-code

2.5 Color Model

X accommodates a wide range of display hardware capabilities, from monochrome to 32 bits of color resolution per pixel. Servers make color resources available through the following constructs:

Visuals—Visual structures define the color model(s) available on a given display.

Colormaps—Arrays of colorcells. To translate a pixel value into an RGB value, the pixel value is used as an offset into the colormap, accessing a single colorcell.

Colorcells—Discrete entries in a colormap table. Each colorcell holds an RGB color value for one pixel value.

2.5.1 Visuals

Servers tell clients about their color capabilities through visual structures. A visual structure defines a color model, including the colormap type (visual class) and the number of bits per pixel. A server may support several color models simultaneously, and each model is described with a visual structure in the list of visuals associated with each screen.

Six visual classes specify how pixel values map into RGB values:

PseudoColor—pixel values index into a changeable colormap to produce RGB values. This is by far the most common visual class, given today's hardware.

StaticColor—predefined by the server and cannot be changed by applications.

GrayScale—pixel values index into a changeable colormap to produce shades of gray.

StaticGray—colors are predefined by the server and cannot be changed by applications. All entries have identical values for red, green, and blue, defining shades of gray.

DirectColor—pixel values consist of red, green, and blue components, which index into separate, changeable, red, green, and blue colormaps.

TrueColor—pixel values consist of red, green, and blue components, which index into separate red, green, and blue colormaps. The values in the colormaps are predefined by the server and cannot be changed. Typically, the colormaps entries span linearly from off to maximum intensity for that electron gun.

2.5.2 Colormaps

X colormaps are a virtual server resource. Each window can have its own unique colormap, although the vast majority of color display hardware available today only supports one installed colormap at a time.

The obvious problem here is that when more colormaps are used than the hardware can support, the colors are correct only for the window whose colormap is currently installed. Other windows will have "false color."[10] The window manager has full responsibility for ensuring that the "right" colormap is currently installed. Usually, this is the colormap for the window directly under the mouse pointer, or alternatively, the window with the keyword focus.

When the server is initialized, a default colormap is created for each screen. Clients are encouraged to use this colormap whenever possible.

2.5.3 Colorcells

Colorcells are the entries of a colormap, defining an RGB value for a given pixel value. In X, colorcells are a resource within the colormap resource. That is, the colorcells of a colormap can be allocated and freed by clients as needed.

There are two ways to allocate colorcells, shareable with other clients or private to an application. When a colormap is created, the server initializes its colorcells to some server-dependent default values. These colorcells are unallocated, even though they have been initialized to some value. At any point in time, a colormap will

---

[10]This effect is known as "going technicolor."

probably contain some mixture of shareable, private, and *uninitialized* colorcells (see Figure 2.28).

	R	G	B	Allocation
0	0000	0000	0000	Shared
1	FFFF	FFFF	FFFF	Shared
2	FFFF	0000	0000	Shared
3	F000	8000	8000	Shared
4	4000	4000	8000	Private
5	8000	8000	8000	Private
6	FFFF	0000	FFFF	Shared
7	FFFF	FFFF	0000	Unallocated

Figure 2.28 Shareable, private, and unallocated colorcells in a typical colormap.

2.5.3.1 Shareable Colorcells

Shareable colorcells are allocated read-only, meaning that their values cannot be changed after they are allocated. Clients that allocate shareable colorcells can conserve resources yet be assured that the color will not be changed by other clients.

The server allocates two shareable colorcells out of the default colormap, one for a dark color (typically black) and one for a light color (typically white). These two colors are adequate for use by a monochrome application or as defaults for foreground/background colors. In fact, the server uses these colors when creating the cursor and root window stipple pattern. It is very important to note that these colors are not guaranteed to be pixel values 0 and 1. Programs written with this assumption (often developed on monochrome systems) may yield unexpected colors on other X servers. Clients should use the Xlib macros BlackPixel and WhitePixel to obtain these color values from the server.

2.5.3.2 Private Colorcells

Clients may allocate nonshareable, read/write colorcells for colors that may need to be changed over the course of the application.[11] For example, a factory-control program may need to change the color of some graphics from green to red to indicate a warning condition. Using writeable colorcells, the value in the colorcell can be changed from green to red and all graphics drawn with that pixel value will change from green to red without having to be redrawn.

X does not explicitly support sharing private colorcells between applications. That is, if a client allocates a read/write colorcell and sets the value to red, subsequent requests by other clients for the color red will not use the colorcell allocated by the first client. Therefore, private colorcells should be used sparingly and only when necessary.

---

[11]On hardware that has an immutable colormap, only read-only colors can be allocated, since the hardware palette cannot be changed.

2.5.3.3 Named Colors

As an alternative to specifying RGB values for colors, applications may allocate shared colorcells by color name. Servers define common colors in a database with a name string and RGB values:

RGB value	Color Name
112 219 147	aquamarine
50 204 153	medium aquamarine
50 204 153	MediumAquamarine
0 0 0	black
0 0 255	blue
95 159 159	cadet blue
95 159 159	CadetBlue
66 66 111	cornflower blue
66 66 111	CornflowerBlue
107 35 142	dark slate blue
107 35 142	DarkSlateBlue
191 216 216	light blue
191 216 216	LightBlue
143 143 188	light steel blue
143 143 188	LightSteelBlue

Figure 2.29 Named colors

This allows users to easily specify a recognizable color and encourages the reuse of colors. It is much easier to specify "LightSteelBlue" than to remember and specify the exact RGB values each time the client is run.

2.5.4 Color Summary

Colormaps and colorcells are limited server resources. Most display hardware today can support only one colormap, and this colormap typically has no more than 256 colorcells. To coexist peacefully in the cooperative X environment, clients must use color resources intelligently. X encourages the best use of color resources by providing:

- shareable (read-only) color cells, so clients using the same colors can use the same color cell.

- private (read/write) color cells, for clients that need to change colors during the course of the application.

- "named" colors, so users can specify the name of a color as options to clients. Typically, this results in fewer cells being used by applications that do not need exact color representations.

- a default colormap, which should be used by all windows that do not have special color requirements.

- virtual colormaps, for clients with exacting color requirements that cannot be satisfied with the cells remaining in the default colormap.

The X Protocol provides the following color-related functions:

Protocol Request	Xlib Function	Description
AllocColor	XAllocColor	Allocates a shareable colorcell with the closest hardware-supported color.
AllocColorCells	XAllocColorCells	Allocates nonshared colorcells.
AllocColorPlanes	XAllocColorPlanes	Allocates nonshared color planes.
AllocNamedColor	XAllocNamedColor	Allocates a shareable colorcell using the RGB values out of the color-name database.
CopyColormapAndFree	XCopyColormapAndFree	Allocates a new colormap and initializes it with another colormap.
CreateColormap	XCreateColormap	Allocates a new colormap.
FreeColormap	XFreeColormap	Frees a colormap allocated by XCreateColormap.

Protocol Request	Xlib Function	Description
InstallColormap	XInstallColormap	Forcibly installs a colormap into the display hardware. Clients should never do this, as installing colormaps is the window manager's job.
UninstallColormap	XUninstallColormap	Removes the colormap from the display hardware and loads the default, if it is not already installed. Clients should never do this, as installing (and uninstalling) colormaps is the window manager's job.
N/A	XGetStandardColormap	Gets the property defining the standard colormap.
N/A	XSetStandardColormap	Defines or changes a colormap property. Clients should leave this up to the window manager.

Protocol Request	Xlib Function	Description
ListInstalledColormaps		
	XListInstalledColormaps	Returns a list of the currently installed colormaps.
N/A	XSetWindowColormap	Sets the colormap attribute for a window.

2.6 Input Model

Every X server has a keyboard and pointing device, such as a mouse, tablet, trackball, or light pen. Windows receive keyboard and pointer input by electing to receive the following input events:

Event	Description
KeyPress KeyRelease	A keyboard key was pressed or released. Every key generates KeyPress and KeyRelease, including modifier keys such as Shift and Control.
ButtonPress ButtonRelease	A pointer key was pressed or released. The server sends the matching ButtonRelease event to the application that received the ButtonPress event. (See Keyboard and Pointer Grabbing, later in this section.)
KeymapNotify	This event tells an application what keys were pressed at the time it was sent a FocusIn or EnterNotify.
MotionNotify	The pointer has moved. (See Pointer Motion, later in this section.)

Event	Description
EnterNotify LeaveNotify	The pointer has entered or has left a window.
FocusIn FocusOut	The keyboard focus has been attached to or detached from a window. (See Keyboard Focus, later in this section.)
MappingNotify	The keyboard mapping or pointer button mapping has been changed. (See Keyboard Mapping, later in this section.)

2.6.1 Pointer Motion

If you need pointer input in a window, you can either (a) ask for all motion events in that window or (b) ask for a single motion event to be sent when the pointer moves in that window.[12]

Plan A is appropriate if you need to know every intermediate pointer position. The granularity of the pointer motion is not guaranteed, but the server will always generate at least one motion event for every move of the pointer.

Plan B lets the server send just one motion event when the pointer moves. The application then polls to get the current pointer location. This approach generates far fewer motion events and is adequate when pointer history is not important.

---

[12]The single event is a hint that the pointer has moved.

2.6.2 Pointer Shapes

Each window can define its own cursor for special visual feedback. Cursors are defined by:

- a mask bitmap of the cursor shape
- foreground and background color
- a source bitmap, color-expanded using the above foreground and background color
- an XY hotspot to report the pointer position

Cursors can be any size and shape, although some servers limit the size to 16x16 pixels.

2.6.3 Keyboard Focus

At any given time, only one window may receive KeyPress and KeyRelease events. This window has the keyboard focus. Some window managers (such as uwm) assign keyboard focus to the window directly under the pointer. OPEN LOOK window managers let the user explicitly assign keyboard focus by clicking the SELECT mouse button in that window.

When a window is assigned the keyboard focus, it receives a FocusIn event. Likewise, when the focus is taken away, it receives a FocusOut event.

2.6.4 Keyboard and Pointer Grabbing

When necessary, clients may grab all keyboard or pointer input, or grab a particular key or button sequence. As the name implies, grabbing prevents anyone else from having it.

Grabbing the pointer and keyboard is generally left up to the Toolkit and window manager, since it has serious systemwide implications. The exception to this is the implicit, automatic grab that results from a ButtonPress event. Simply stated (and there are extenuating circumstances, of course), a ButtonPress automatically grabs the pointer until a ButtonRelease happens. In this way, button releases are always sent to the same window, where the pressed button is allowing clients to depend on button releases to terminate actions initiated by button pressing, such as dragging an object.

2.6.5 Keyboard Mapping

Keyboard mapping translates the raw key numbers of the keyboard hardware into ASCII string representations.

The server sends KeyPress and KeyRelease events to the window with the keyboard focus. These events contain the keycode of the key that caused the event and state information of the modifier keys.[13] A keycode is a number in the range of [8,255] inclusive, representing a physical or logical key on the keyboard. The server defines the mapping of raw keys to keycodes, and this mapping cannot be changed using the X Protocol.

The server provides a table containing a list of keysyms for each keycode. Each keysym list represents the set of symbols for that key, with individual keysyms indexed by the combination of the keycode and modifier keys.

The final keymapping step translates the four-byte logical keysym into an ASCII text string.

Clients may modify the global keycode-to-keysym table to remap the keyboard for all clients, or alternatively, clients may locally rebind keysyms to text strings.

---

[13]There are eight possible modifiers: Control, Shift, Shift Lock, and five definable keys.

Note that this entire mechanism may change radically in the future to better support multilingual keyboards.

2.7 Chapter Summary

This chapter presented a lot of information in a short space. Indeed, entire volumes have been devoted to this subject. The material presented here was selected as being globally useful in developing X Window System applications.

Here is a summary of some of the key points:

- The X Window System is built around a network protocol to facilitate distributed graphics. This protocol is comprised of four basic types of data packets: requests, replies, events, and errors.

- A window must be mapped, and all of its ancestors must also be mapped for it to be viewable.

- Clients must be able repaint their windows at any time, since the server does not guarantee to preserve the contents obscured by other windows.

- Clients can communicate with other clients and the window manager using properties associated with their top-level windows.

- The *Inter-Client Communication Conventions Manual* (ICCCM) defines conventions for using the standard properties. Clients and window managers conforming to the ICCCM should achieve a high-degree of interoperability.

- Pop-up windows with the override-redirect attribute bypass the window manager and become children of the root window.

- All X coordinates are in pixel space and are relative to the drawable's origin. The origin of pixmaps is always (0,0).

- Graphics Contexts (GCs) contain the drawing attributes for a given drawing operation.

- Windows are clipped to the extent of their parent window. Drawing in a window can also be clipped by the extents of the window's children and a client-specified clip region. Drawing in a pixmap is clipped only by the client-specified region and the extent of the pixmap.

- Line, Fill, Text, and Pixmap operations are provided by the core protocol, and the protocol can be extended to provide additional functionality, such as 3-D, video, and image processing.

- X accommodates a wide range of color hardware. Color capabilities are conveyed to clients through a list of supported visuals associated with each screen.

- Each window can allocate its own colormap, although most display hardware can only accommodate one colormap at a time.

- Colorcells can be allocated as private or as shareable among clients. In addition, shareable cells can be allocated by specifying a color name, such as "red."

- Pointer button release events are always sent to the window that received the button press event.

- Keyboard input is directed to the window with the keyboard focus, which is assigned by the window manager.

- The translation of keyboard keys to ASCII is programmable per application or per server.

Chapter 3

Object-Oriented Programming

To simplify developing X applications, the X Toolkit employs elements of object-oriented programming (OOP) methodology. This is somewhat of a feat, since the toolkit is written in and for the C language, which does not directly support objects.

Object-oriented programming is certainly one of the software industry's latest buzzwords, but what does it actually mean? Simply stated, OOP is the application of two interrelated programming techniques,

- Classing, and
- Encapsulation.

The chapter illustrates these ideas with simple real-world examples. With a working knowledge of these concepts, you will be much better prepared to understand and use of the OPEN LOOK Intrinsic Toolkit.

3.1 Classing

Classing organizes objects in a hierarchical tree. Each node of the tree represents an object type, or class. A parent of a class is its superclass, and its children are its subclasses.

Probably the most familiar classing system is the one biologists use to class organisms. While programmers use the word "class" to name categories, biologists group organisms into the divisions kingdom, phylum, class, order, family, genus, and species. In the animal kingdom alone (and there are four other kingdoms), scientists have used classing to organize and categorize more than a million species.

An object is an individual occurrence, or instance, of a class. Consider Lassie as an instance of the class Collie. From Figure 3.1 we can see that Collies share the traits of other dogs (barking, tail wagging), carnivores (meat eating), mammals (warm blooded), vertebrates (skull, well-developed brain), and chordates (central spinal column). From the top of the tree down, the attributes of each class add to those in their superclass. These traits, handed down from each class, are inherited by subclasses.

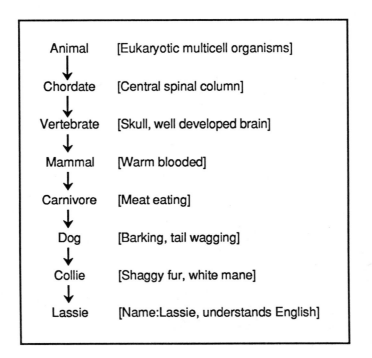

Figure 3.1 Inheriting attributes through classing

Note, however, that objects and classes can override characteristics of their superclasses. For example, barking is a trait shared by most dogs, but Basenji dogs do not bark. Thus, class Basenji would override the barking behavior specified in class Dog.

3.2 Encapsulation

Classes are to objects as types are to variables. The difference in terminology can be attributed to the distinction between variables and objects. The word "types" is really short for "datatypes," which define the format of variables. Common C language types include integers, characters, floating-point numbers, and structures. Objects, on the other hand, are the marriage of data and procedures into a self-contained capsule.

The data in an object is private to that object. Users of an object cannot directly access the object's data. Rather, they must interface with the object through object-supplied services, called methods.[1] Typically, objects define methods for such general-purpose operations as create, destroy, get_values, set_values, and init,[2] as well as class-specific functions such as draw, rotate, next, sqrt, and size.

Instance methods and instance variables are methods and variables private to each instance of an object. Class methods and class variables are methods and variables that are shared across all instances of that class. For example, Lassie has long, shaggy fur, the same as other collies. But Lassie is also an individual and therefore has individual traits, as well. Her name, age, home, and owners are unique to her. Considering Lassie as an instance of class Collie, her instance variables hold her individual attributes, and traits common to all collies are held in class variables.

The same principle applies to the class and instance methods. Lassie wags her tail much the same as any collie (or any dog, for that matter), but only Lassie can understand the English language and save

---

[1] Methods in C++ are called member functions.
[2] Instantiation is the allocation and initialization of an object. Initialization functions are sometimes referred to as constructors, and cleanup functions are called destructors.

people from burning buildings. Obviously, Lassie has a few more instance methods than most collies!

The goal behind this data hiding, or encapsulation, is to make it unnecessary for the consumer (code that uses the object) to know the implementation details of the supplier (the object). This simplifies application code and increases its flexibility.

For example, consider the sort operation. Its job is to take an arbitrary number of "things" and organize them in some progressive order. For different "things," this order may be alphabetical, numerical, chronological, or any other ordering that makes sense for those "things." The sort developer can choose to hardwire the comparison between two elements, as in:

```
if (ptr1->size < ptr2->size)
```

or allow someone who knows more about the elements to decide:

```
if (CompareSize(ptr1, ptr2) == LESS_THAN)
```

A fully encapsulated example asks the object itself to make the comparison, as in this C++ code:

```
if (ptr1->isLessThan(ptr2))
```

Using this approach, a graphics application could handle expose events by executing the following code on each graphics object in its display list, regardless of type:

```
graphicsObject->redraw(exposedRegion);
```

Since we're not using C++ (or any other object-oriented language) we'll have to invent a different syntax, say, something like:

```
CallObject(
        graphicsObject,          /* target object */
        REDRAW, exposedRegion,   /* message and data */
        0                        /* terminate message list */
);
```

This pseudo-code sends the message REDRAW and message data exposedRegion, to the object graphicsObject, just as the previous C++ code does. The difference, of course, is that the latter example requires superficial code (CallObject and implicitly routines such as CreateObject and DestroyObject) to support objects. In the OPEN LOOK Intrinsic Toolkit, this object-support code is the infrastructure known as the MIT Xt Intrinsics. The other part of the OPEN LOOK Intrinsic Toolkit, the AT&T-developed widgets, are the objects themselves.

Widget objects provide internal methods for low-level actions, such as drawing and resizing. In addition, each widget defines a set of external method hooks by which applications register callback procedures to be invoked as part of that method. For example, an application may register a callback with a slider widget that adjusts the speaker volume whenever the user moves the slider's thumb.

3.3 Program Architecture

To see how programming with Xlib and X Toolkit differs from more traditional techniques, let's look at three sample implementations of the venerable "Hello, World" program.

First, a nonwindowed *stdio* version. As you can see from Figure 3.2, the control flow is trivial. No other program can obscure its output. No user can provide random input. If the application required input, it would prompt for it. In short, the application is in complete control.

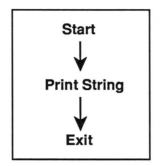

Figure 3.2 Control flow of Hello World, written to UNIX stdio

```
/*
 * Simple "Hello, World" program, using stdio
 * @(#) sccs/s.hw_stdio.c 1.2 last delta 10/31/89 21:50:33
 */
#include <stdio.h>

main()
{
    (void) printf("Hello, World\n");
    exit(0);
}
```

In a windowed graphics environment such as X, applications must handle random, spontaneous, nontrivial interactions with the user and window system: areas of the application's window(s) may be obscured or exposed, or the application may shrink down to an icon. What's worse, these interactions can occur at any point in time. User-initiated events are up to the unpredictable whim of the user. Remember that the user drives the application, rather than the other way around.

Using only Xlib, even simple programs that correctly handle these interactions require a large amount of complex code. Compare the control flow of the Xlib version of "Hello, World" in Figure 3.3 to the trivial example.

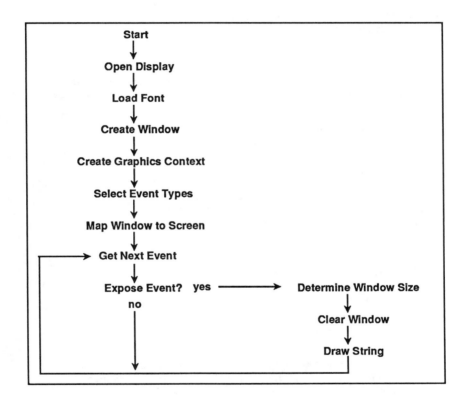

Figure 3.3 Control flow of Hello World, Xlib-only version

```
/*
 * Xlib-only version of Hello World
 * @(#) sccs/s.hw_xlib.c 1.2 last delta 10/31/89 21:50:35
 */
#include <stdio.h>
#include <X11/Xlib.h>
#include <X11/Xutil.h>

#define STRING      "Hello, world"
#define BORDER      1
#define FONT        "fixed"

/*
 * This structure forms the WM_HINTS property of the window,
 * letting the window manager know how to handle this window.
 * See Section 9.1 of the Xlib manual.
 */
XWMHints    xwmh = {
    (InputHint|StateHint),   /* flags */
    False,                   /* input */
    NormalState,             /* initial_state */
    0,                       /* icon pixmap */
    0,                       /* icon window */
    0, 0,                    /* icon location */
    0,                       /* icon mask */
    0,                       /* Window group */
};

main(argc,argv)
    int argc;
    char *argv[];
{
    Display    *dpy;         /* X server connection */
    Window     win;          /* Window ID */
    GC         gc;           /* GC to draw with */
    XFontStruct *fontstruct; /* Font descriptor */
    unsigned long fth, pad;  /* Font size parameters */
    unsigned long fg, bg, bd; /* Pixel values */
    unsigned long bw;        /* Border width */
    XGCValues   gcv;         /* Struct for creating GC */
    XEvent      event;       /* Event received */
    XSizeHints  xsh;         /* window manager size hints */
    char        *geomSpec;   /* Window geometry string */
    XSetWindowAttributes xswa; /* Set Window Attribute struct */

    /*
     * Open the display using the $DISPLAY environment
     * variable to locate the X server.
     */
    if ((dpy = XOpenDisplay(NULL)) == NULL) {
        fprintf(
```

```
    stderr,
    "%s: can't open %s\n",
    argv[0],
    XDisplayName(NULL)
);
    exit(1);
}

/*
 * Load a font to use.
 */
if ((fontstruct = XLoadQueryFont(dpy, FONT)) == NULL) {
    fprintf(
        stderr,
        "%s: display %s doesn't know font %s\n",
        argv[0],
        DisplayString(dpy),
        FONT
    );
    exit(1);
}
fth =
    fontstruct->max_bounds.ascent +
        fontstruct->max_bounds.descent;

/*
 * Select colors for the border, the window background,
 * and the foreground.
 */
bd = BlackPixel(dpy, DefaultScreen(dpy));
bg = WhitePixel(dpy, DefaultScreen(dpy));
fg = BlackPixel(dpy, DefaultScreen(dpy));

/*
 * Set the border width of the window,
 * and the gap between the text and the edge
 * of the window, "pad".
 */
pad = BORDER;
bw = 1;

/*
 * Deal with providing the window with an initial
 * position & size. Fill out the XSizeHints struct
 * to inform the window manager.
 */
xsh.flags = (PPosition | PSize);
xsh.height = fth + pad * 2;
xsh.width =
    XTextWidth(fontstruct, STRING, strlen(STRING)) + pad * 2;
xsh.x =
```

```
        (DisplayWidth(dpy, DefaultScreen(dpy)) - xsh.width) / 2;
    xsh.y =
        (DisplayHeight(dpy,DefaultScreen(dpy)) - xsh.height) / 2;

    /*
     * Create the Window with the information
     * in the XSizeHints, the border width, and the
     * border & background pixels.
     */
    win =
        XCreateSimpleWindow( /* easiest way to create a window */
            dpy,                    /* handle to server */
            DefaultRootWindow(dpy), /* parent window */
            xsh.x,                  /* window origin, x */
            xsh.y,                  /* window origin, y */
            xsh.width,              /* # of pixels in x */
            xsh.height,             /* # of pixels in y */
            bw,                     /* border width */
            bd,                     /* border color */
            bg                      /* background color */
        );


    /*
     * Perform the most basic communication with
     * the Window Manager, including information about
     * the name of this program, what we want the icon
     * to look like, the requested size of the window, etc.
     */
    XSetStandardProperties( /* set WManager properties */
        dpy,                /* handle to display server */
        win,                /* set properties of this window */
        argv[0],            /* null-terminated window name */
        argv[0],            /* null-terminated icon name */
        None,               /* optional icon pixmap */
        argv,               /* application's argument list */
        argc,               /* number of arguments */
        &xsh                /* ptr to size hints for window */
    );
    XSetWMHints(dpy, win, &xwmh);   /* set WManager hints */

    /*
     * Ensure that the window's colormap field points
     * to the default colormap, so that the window
     * manager knows the correct colormap to use for
     * the window.  Also, set the window's Bit Gravity to
     * automatically center the text if the window is expanded.
     * This is a short-cut to reduce Expose events.
     */
    xswa.colormap = DefaultColormap(dpy, DefaultScreen(dpy));
    xswa.bit_gravity = CenterGravity;
```

```
XChangeWindowAttributes(
    dpy,
    win,
    (CWColormap | CWBitGravity),
    &xswa
);

/*
 * Create the Graphics Context for writing the text.
 */
gcv.font = fontstruct->fid;
gcv.foreground = fg;
gcv.background = bg;
gc =
    XCreateGC(
        dpy,
        win,
        (GCFont | GCForeground | GCBackground),
        &gcv
    );

/*
 * Specify the event types we're interested in.
 * Exposure: means part of the window became
 * exposed and needs painted
 */
XSelectInput(dpy, win, ExposureMask);

/*
 * Map the window to make it visible.
 */
XMapWindow(dpy, win);

/*
 * Loop forever,  examining each event.
 */
while (1) {
    XNextEvent(dpy, &event);     /* wait for next event */

    switch (event.type) {
        case Expose: {
            XWindowAttributes    xwa;
            int                  x, y;

            /*
             * Only repaint if there are no other
             * Expose events in the queue.
             */
            if (event.xexpose.count != 0)
                break;
```

```
        /*
         * Find out how big the window is now,
         * so that we can center the text in it.
         */
        if (XGetWindowAttributes(dpy, win, &xwa) == 0)
            break;

        x =
            (xwa.width -
                XTextWidth(
                    fontstruct,
                    STRING,
                    strlen(STRING)
                )
            ) / 2;

        y =
            (xwa.height +
            fontstruct->max_bounds.ascent -
            fontstruct->max_bounds.descent) / 2;

        /*
         * Fill the window with the background color,
         * and then paint the centered string.
         */
        XClearWindow(dpy, win);
        XDrawString(
            dpy,
            win,
            gc,
            x,
            y,
            STRING,
            strlen(STRING)
        );

        break;
        }
    }
  }
}
```

Enter the X Toolkit. The X Toolkit handles the complexity of the window system and hides it from applications. Rather than dealing with low-level X events, applications instantiate user-interface objects, such as windows and menus, and attach callbacks, as in the above example with the slider. The application then turns control over to the Toolkit machinery, which dispatches the events it receives from the server (including user actions and events from other applications) to the objects.

Figure 3.4 illustrates the control flow for the OPEN LOOK X Toolkit version of "Hello, World."

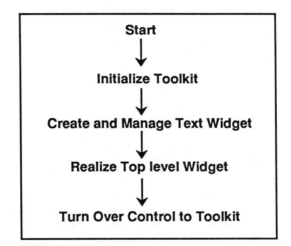

Figure 3.4   Control flow of Hello World, using the OPEN LOOK Intrinsic Toolkit

```
/*
 * AT&T OPEN LOOK Toolkit version of Hello World
 * @(#) sccs/s.hw_xol.c 1.2 last delta 10/31/89 21:50:37
 */
#include <stdio.h>
#include <X11/Xlib.h>
#include <X11/Intrinsic.h>
#include <X11/StringDefs.h>
#include <Xol/OpenLook.h>
#include <Xol/StaticText.h>

#define STRING  "Hello,  World"

Arg _tmpArgs[] = {
    {XtNstring, (XtArgVal) STRING},
};

main(argc, argv)
```

```
    int argc;
    char *argv[];
{

    Widget      w_top, w_text;

    /*
     * Initialize the OPEN LOOK Toolkit machinery.
     */
    w_top =
        OlInitialize(
            argv[0],            /* toplevel widget name */
            "HelloWorld",       /* name of resource file */
            NULL,               /* option array */
            0,                  /* number of options in array */
            &argc,              /* init destructively removes args */
            argv                /* ...from argc and argv */
        );

    /*
     * Create a Widget to display the string,  using _tmpArgs
     * to set STRING as its value.
     */
    w_text =
        XtCreateManagedWidget(
            "text",                 /* arbitrary widget name */
            staticTextWidgetClass,  /* widget class */
            w_top,                  /* widget id of parent */
            _tmpArgs,               /* create resources */
            XtNumber(_tmpArgs)      /* # of resources in array */
        );

    XtRealizeWidget(w_top);     /* make widgets "real" */

    XtMainLoop();               /* turn over control */

    /* never get here */
}
```

Using the OPEN LOOK Intrinsic Toolkit, it is possible to write complete programs using very few lines of code, making it much easier to concentrate on developing applications, rather than on handling complex, low-level window system mechanics.

Perhaps as important, X Toolkits explicitly provide a specific user-interface, or "look-and-feel." Designing and implementing a user-interface from scratch would normally make up a major portion of an application's development, but by using the OPEN LOOK Intrinsic

Toolkit, your development builds on the work of user-interface experts who have done this work for you.

Chapter 4

The X Toolkit Intrinsics

Most X toolkits, including the OPEN LOOK Intrinsic Toolkit, consist of two parts: the Xt Intrinsics and a collection of user-interface widget objects.[1] Together they present the developer with an object-oriented programming interface to the X Window System.

This chapter discusses the architecture of X Toolkits and the Xt Intrinsics programming interface. Chapter 5 details the entire OPEN LOOK widget set, with example code demonstrating each widget.

4.1 Why Use the Toolkit?

Although it is possible to write applications directly to Xlib, it is rather inefficient to do so; as we saw in the last chapter, it takes over 200 lines of code just to write "Hello, World." This is not really a fault with Xlib. After all, it is intended to be a portable interface to the X Protocol, not an application-programming interface.

The X Toolkit *is* designed as an application-programming interface, using object-oriented programming methodology to bring the application-programming task up to the user-interface level. With the Toolkit, applications deal with scrollbars, buttons, and menus, rather than an undirected collection of windows. This results in far fewer lines of code (approximately 50 for "Hello, World") and a much shorter development time.

---

[1]The phrase X Toolkit (with toolkit capitalized) refers to the combination of the Xt Intrinsics and a particular widget set, such as the OPEN LOOK widget set described in this book.

The Toolkit does not completely replace Xlib, rather, it augments it. Applications still use Xlib for nonuser-interface graphics drawing and some aspects of inter-client communication.

4.2 X Toolkit Architecture

As mentioned above, the Toolkit is built as two parts: a widget set, which implements a specific user-interface such as the OPEN LOOK GUI, and the Xt Intrinsics, the glue that holds it all together.

4.2.1 Widgets

4.2.1.1 Widget Classes

Widgets are statically classed objects, each one implementing a user-interface component such as a button, slider, scrollbar, or menu. Widget classes define the procedures (methods) and data common to all widget instances of that class.

The widget classes form a hierarchy supporting simple inheritance: subclasses can inherit the procedures and data of their parent widget class. All widget classes are subclasses of the *Core* widget class, which defines methods and data common to all widget classes.

In the OPEN LOOK widget set, the Core class has two direct subclasses, *Primitive* and *Composite*. Primitive widgets are simple and self-contained, while Composite widgets are more complex and usually consist of several simpler widgets.

Composite has two special subclasses, *Shell* and *Constraint*. Shell widgets represent top-level X windows and are the root of widget trees. Constraint widgets manage the size and position of their children according to application-defined geometry rules.

Figure 4.1 shows the class hierarchy of the OPEN LOOK widget set, with subclasses indented and listed behind their superclass.[2]

Core
    Primitive   `AbbreviatedMenuButton`
                            `FlatCheckbox`
                            `FlatExclusives`
                            `FlatNonexclusives`
                            `MenuButton`
                            `OblongButton`
                            `RectangularButton`
                            `StaticText`
                            `Stub`

    Composite   `ScrollBar`
                            `Slider`
        Shell   `BaseWindowShell`
                              `NoticeShell`
                              `MenuShell`
                              `PopupWindowShell`

        Constraint   `BulletinBoard`
                              `Caption`
                              `Checkbox`
                              `ControlArea`
                              `Exclusives`
                              `FooterPanel`
                              `Form`
                              `Nonexclusives`
                              `ScrolledWindow`
                              `ScrollingList`
                              `Text`
                              `TextField`

Figure 4.1 OPEN LOOK widget classes

---

[2]Except for important superclasses (shown in italics), internal widget classes are not depicted in this chart.

117

Composite widgets can have children; primitive widgets can't. The exception to this rule are *pop-up children*, which applications use to create windows that are outside the main widget tree's window hierarchy. Recall from Chapter 2 that windows are clipped to their parent's extents; pop-up widgets create their window as a child of the root window, allowing the window to be placed anywhere on the screen. Since parents of pop-up children do not actively manage them, even primitive widgets can have pop-up children.

In the OPEN LOOK widget set, any subclass of Shell (BaseWindowShell, NoticeShell, MenuShell, and PopupWindowShell) can be a pop-up child.

4.2.1.2 Resources

Widget instance variables are called *resources*. Applications read or write widget resource values by sending a variable-length resource list message to the widget object.

A resource list is an array of name value pairs, where the name is the string constant name of the resource. Resource name, class, and representation string constants are defined by the individual widget classes according to the following conventions:

- Resource name strings have the prefix XtN, have no underscores, and capitalize the first character of each word, except the first (for example, XtNbackgroundPixmap, XtNwidth, XtNmappedWhenManaged).

- Resource class strings have the prefix XtC, have no underscores, and capitalize the first letter of each word, including the first (for example, XtCPosition, XtCLayoutType, XtCCallback).

- Resource representation strings have the prefix XtR, have no underscores, and are spelled exactly like the representation type (for example, XtRString, XtRBoolean, XtRInteger).

The *OPEN LOOK Programmer's Reference Manual* lists the class-specific resources for each class. These are, in effect, the options available for widgets of that class.

4.2.1.3 Callbacks

When a user pushes a button, moves a slider, or checks a checkbox, that widget provides the appropriate visual feedback: the button reverses colors, the slider moves, and the checkbox toggles. Applications define additional semantics for these actions by registering *callbacks* with the widgets.

A callback is essentially a programmer-defined widget method executed in response to user input or other state changes in the widget. For example, if an application creates a button labeled Quit, it might register the UNIX *exit* function as an XtNselect callback. The widget would then call *exit* when the user clicked SELECT on the Quit button.

Widgets keep callback procedures in a list, called a *callback list*. Thus, more than one callback can be defined for the same action for any given widget. Be careful when using multiple callbacks, however, since the calling order is not guaranteed.

Callback lists are widget resources of the class XtCCallback, and are listed in the *OPEN LOOK Programmer's Reference Manual* for individual widget classes.

4.2.1.4 Instantiating Widgets

Instantiating widgets is done in three distinct steps, of which the first two are usually combined. The third is usually only applied to the top-level shell widget, since it traverses down through the widget tree.

The first step is to *create* the widget. Creating a widget allocates the data structures for a new widget of a particular widget class. From this point on, the widget is a living entity, and the application can read and write its resources, including callback lists. However, the widget is not yet visible on the display.

The second step is to *manage* the widget. This step tells the widget's parent that it has the widget as a child, at which point the parent (which must be a subclass of Composite) adds the child to its list of dependent children. The widget is still not visible on the screen.

During the management phase, the parent widget judiciously computes the geometries of its children, taking into account the size specified by the user and the preferred sizes computed by the children. Rather than going through this negotiation every time a widget is created, Composite widgets are usually managed after all of their children have been created and managed.[3]

The third and final step is to *realize* the widget tree. Realizing the tree completes the geometry calculations and creates the windows for each widget. At this point, the widgets become visible on the screen.

In special cases, the widget may want to create its windows but not have them displayed immediately. Recall from Chapter 2 the *mapped* window attribute and how it controls window visibility: For a window to be displayable, it and all of its ancestors must be mapped.[4] Using this same mechanism, the Xt Intrinsics allows

---

[3]Since this is not an issue when creating primitive widgets (they can't have children), Xt also provides a function to create and manage a widget in a single call.

[4]The window manager uses this feature to iconify an application by simply unmapping its top-level window and mapping its icon window.

applications to map or unmap widgets, which maps or unmaps all of that widget's windows. Widgets that wish to remain temporarily invisible set their XtNmappedWhenManaged resource to FALSE, which keeps their windows from being mapped during creation.

Perhaps the most significant aspect of this three-part process is that the X windows aren't created until the last phase. While this is not usually a problem, it means that applications must defer accessing widget windows (say, to use as a parameter to an Xlib call) until after the widget has been realized.

4.2.2 Intrinsics

Application programmers use only a fraction of the Xt Intrinsics; the rest are used by widget programmers to construct new widgets. The Toolkit designers did a commendable job in separating the tasks of widget writing and application development, making it as easy as possible to develop applications without knowing the details of the Toolkit machinery.

Unfortunately, the Xt Intrinsics documentation[5] makes little or no distinction between application and widget developer details. However, the documentation is useful as reference material, and you might want to have it available when going through the examples in this book.

Figure 4.2 illustrates the control flow of a typical X Toolkit application. The top box represents the mainline, where the Toolkit is initialized and the widgets are created, managed, and realized. The last thing the mainline does is turn control over to the Toolkit machinery, which eternally processes events from the X Server and

---

[5]The *AT&T Xwin 3.0 Graphical Windowing System Programmer's Guide, Volume 2*, roughly equivalent to *X Toolkit Intrinsics - C Language Interface* from MIT.

hands them off to the widgets created in the mainline, which in turn calls any application-registered callbacks for that event.

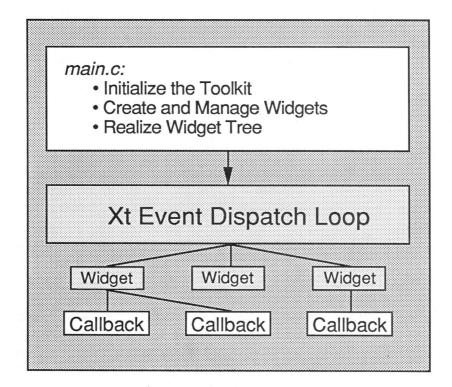

Figure 4.2 Control flow of a typical X Toolkit application

There is nothing particularly magical about this architecture, but the paradigm is very powerful: the callbacks implement the application's functionality, while the Xt Intrinsics handle the control flow according to X events. This action/reaction model becomes intuitive and natural very quickly and greatly simplifies the design of user-driven applications.

Widget callbacks are free to do whatever they need to accomplish their task, such as drawing graphics, constructing new widgets, or, in rare cases, modifying control flow by temporarily taking over the event dispatch loop.[6]

4.3 Getting Started

Certainly the best way to learn something is to use it, and the OPEN LOOK Intrinsic Toolkit is no exception. This section covers a basic handful of Xt Intrinsic functions to get us started. We'll use these and other routines in the next chapter, where we examine the entire OPEN LOOK widget set.

All of the Xt Intrinsic functions are contained in the library libXt.a, typically installed in /usr/X/lib or /usr/lib/X11. For obvious reasons, all of the examples in this book use this library.

The examples also use this book's utility library, Xtutil. The complete source for this library is listed in the appendix. Xtutil ties up many of the Toolkit's loose ends with convenience routines and additional functionality.

4.3.1 Initializing the Toolkit

The Toolkit must be initialized before you can use any of the other Xt Intrinsic functions. The OPEN LOOK Toolkit has a special routine for this purpose, OlInitialize:

```
Widget OlInitialize(
    String              shell_name,    /* obsolete, specify NULL */
    String              application_class,
    XrmOptionDescRec    *options,
    Cardinal            num_options,
    Cardinal            *argc,         /* &argc */
    String              argv[]
);
```

---

[6]Although callbacks must not use the UNIX system calls setjmp or longjmp.

The first two parameters describe the application's name and class for matching options (resources) in the .Xdefaults file. The name parameter is for compatibility with applications written to an older version of the Toolkit; the Toolkit now uses argv[0] as the application's name.

The next two parameters specify how to parse the command line for application-specific resources. This command line parsing is also the reason for passing the address of argc and argv as parameters to OlInitialize. Options that match the standard resource options or those specified in options are removed from argv by OlInitialize, and the value of argc is adjusted accordingly. For now, we'll specify all resources within the application and ignore command line and .Xdefaults options until we get to Chapter 6.

As the name implies, OlInitialize initializes the OPEN LOOK Toolkit. It is basically the same as the standard MIT XtInitialize routine, with the addition of some OPEN LOOK GUI-specific functionality. All OPEN LOOK Toolkit applications must use OlInitialize rather than XtInitialize.

OlInitialize returns a BaseWindowShell[7] widget, the top-most widget for this application. After the application has created and managed all its other widgets (descendents of this widget), this top-level widget is passed to the *realize* procedure to complete construction of the widget tree.

---

[7]The BaseWindowShell class is a subclass of Shell.

4.3.2 Creating Widgets

Applications create new widgets through XtCreateWidget:

```
Widget XtCreateWidget(
    String        name,
    WidgetClass   widget_class,
    Widget        parent,
    ArgList       args,
    Cardinal      num_args
);
```

The widget name is an arbitrary string to identify the widget for resource matching. It does not have to be unique, but for resource-matching conventions (which are detailed in Chapter 6), it should start with a lowercase letter and not contain spaces, as in "quitButton." The string can also be any identifiable widget legend, as in the case of a button labeled "Quit."

The widget_class is the type of widget to create. The appropriate value for this parameter is listed in the *OPEN LOOK Programmer's Reference Manual* on the page for that particular widget class. Note that widget classes are initialized during OlInitialize; the value listed in the manual is actually the name of the global variable containing the class object.

By convention, class names contain no spaces, capitalize the first character in each word except the first, and end in "WidgetClass." Examples are checkBoxWidgetClass, formWidgetClass, and staticTextWidgetClass.

The OPEN LOOK Toolkit also contains some optimized widgets called *gadgets*. The procedure for creating gadgets is the same as creating widgets, except that the class name ends in "GadgetClass" (for example, checkBoxGadgetClass).

The third parameter to XtCreateWidget, parent, specifies the parent widget. The parent must be a subclass of Composite. In addition, many composite widget classes, notably Shell, have restrictions on the number and/or type of children they can have. Shell widgets, for example, can only have one child. As always, consult the *OPEN LOOK Programmer's Reference Manual* for details on specific widget classes.

The last two parameters to XtCreateWidget specify a variable-length name/value argument list to override the resource defaults. The Xt Intrinsics define argument lists as

```
typedef struct {
    String      name;
    XtArgVal    value;
} Arg, *ArgList;
```

XtArgVal is large enough to hold a caddr_t,[8] char *, long, int *, or a pointer to a function. If the size of the resource is less than or equal to the size of an XtArgVal, value contains the actual resource value; otherwise, value contains a pointer to the data.

The Xt Intrinsics documentation describes two different ways to create argument lists: dynamically, at run-time:

```
Arg args[20];
int n;

n = 0;
XtSetArg(args[n], XtNheight, 100);          n++;
XtSetArg(args[n], XtNwidth, 200);           n++;
XtSetArg(args[n], XtNlabel, "Quit");        n++;
XtSetArg(args[n], XtNrecomputeSize, TRUE);  n++;
....
```

---

[8] caddr_t is a generic UNIX pointer type, typically defined in /usr/include/sys/types.h to be equivalent to (char *).

or statically, at compile-time:

```
static Args args[] = {
    { XtNheight, (XtArgVal) 100 },
    { XtNwidth, (XtArgVal) 200 },
    { XtNlabel, (XtArgVal) "Quit" },
    { XtNrecomputeSize, (XtArgVal) TRUE },
};
```

Note that in the first example, n is not auto-incremented in the XtSetArg call. This is because XtSetArg is a macro that references the first argument more than once. Therefore, if you use this technique, you must not use auto-increment (or auto-decrement, for that matter) in XtSetArg invocations.

Our utility library, Xtutil, provides a third alternative:

```
extern Arg tmpArg[];       /* implicitly filled */
extern int TmpArgList();

TmpArgList(
    XtNheight,             100,
    XtNwidth,              200,
    XtNlabel,              "Quit",
    XtNrecomputeSize,      FALSE,
    0                      /* terminate the list */
);
```

TmpArgList fills the global variable tmpArg with the name/value pairs and returns the number of pairs in the list.

All of the examples in this book use TmpArgList rather than the other methods listed above, resulting in calls to XtCreateWidget that look like this:

```
Widget              w_button, w_parent;
extern Arg          tmpArg[];
extern int          TmpArgList();
...
w_button =
    XtCreateWidget(
            "quitButton",               /* widget name */
            oblongButtonWidgetClass,    /* widget class */
            w_parent,                   /* parent widget */
            tmpArg,                     /* argument list */
            TmpArgList(                  /* ret: arg count */
                XtNheight,          100,
                XtNwidth,           200,
                XtNlabel,           "Quit",
                XtNrecomputeSize,   FALSE,
                0                   /* terminate list */
            )
    );
```

Another convention used here is naming widget variables with a w_ prefix.

4.3.3 Managing Widgets

Managing widgets is trivial. Simply call XtManageChild or XtManageChildren to add widgets to their parent's list of geometry-managed children:

```
void XtManageChild(
    Widget          widget
);

void XtManageChildren(
    WidgetList      widgets,
    Cardinal        count
);
```

As a convenience, the XtCreateManagedWidget function creates and manages the widget with a single call. The syntax is identical to XtCreateWidget. As a general rule, it is good practice to create composite widgets with XtCreateWidget, then create and manage any children, and finally manage the composite widget with XtManageChild.

4.3.4 Realizing Widgets

Finally, after creating and managing all of the application's widgets, call XtRealize with the top-level Shell widget returned from OlInitialize:[9]

```
void XtRealizeWidget(
    Widget w_toplevel
);
```

4.3.5 Modifying Resources

Valid resources and the defaults for each class are listed in the *OPEN LOOK Programmer's Reference Manual* page for that widget class. Listed with each resource is the access permission, given as some combination of the letters *I*, *S*, and *G*. *I* means that the resource value can be set during creation; *S* indicates that the resource can be set after creation; and *G* says that the application can inquire the current value.

To write widget resource values, use XtSetValues:

```
void XtSetValues(
    Widget        widget,
    ArgList       args,
    Cardinal      num_args
);
```

---

[9]Strictly speaking, you may pass any widget to XtRealize and realize the tree from that widget down.

Alternately, Xtutil provides a convenience function, SetValue, to write a single resource value:

```
void SetValue(
    Widget          widget,
    String          resource_name,
    XtArgVal        resource_value
);
```

To read widget resources, use XtGetValues:

```
void XtGetValues(
    Widget          widget,
    ArgList         args,
    Cardinal        num_args
);
```

The value field of each args item contains the address to write the resource value specified by the corresponding name field.

Xutil provides a convenience function, GetValue, to read and return a single resource value:

```
XtArgVal GetValue(
    Widget          widget,
    String          resource_name
);
```

4.3.6 Adding Callbacks

To add a callback procedure to a widget's callback list, use XtAddCallback:

```
void XtAddCallback(
    Widget              widget,
    String              callback_name,
    XtCallbackProc      callback_proc,
    caddr_t             client_data
);
```

The callback_name is the XtN-prefixed resource name listed in the resource table for that widget class in the *OPEN LOOK Programmer's Reference Manual*. Callback lists are of the resource class XtCCallback. Examples include XtNselect, XtNmenu, XtNsliderMoved, and XtNexpose.

The third parameter, callback_proc, is the address of the application procedure to put on the callback list.

The last parameter, client_data, is passed to callback_proc when it is invoked. The Toolkit does nothing with this parameter, so applications can use client_data any way they like.

All widget callbacks have the following synopsis:

```
void CallbackProc(
    Widget        widget,
    caddr_t       client_data,
    caddr_t       call_data
);
```

The widget parameter is the widget instance that is invoking the callback. Note that a single callback can be on any number of callback lists, including lists for widgets of different classes.

The client_data parameter is whatever was specified as client_data in the call to XtAddCallback. The type and contents of client_data is left to the application, with the restriction that it must fit into sizeof(caddr_t) bytes.

Finally, call_data is widget-specific data for this callback. For example, the Slider widget has an XtNsliderMoved callback list. When the user moves the slider, the widget invokes the callbacks on this list, with call_data pointing to the current slider value.

4.3.7 Using Utility Functions

Xlib doesn't know about widgets, so when using Xlib functions, applications need to provide lower Xlib-level identifiers such as Display, Screen, and Window. The example programs use Xt and Xlib utility functions to initialize global variables with handy Xlib identifiers:

```
Widget      w_toplevel;
Window      toplevelWindow;
Window      rootWindow;
Display     *ourDisplay;
Screen      *ourScreen;

...
w_toplevel = OlInitialize(...);
...
/* create and manage widgets */
...
XtRealize(w_toplevel);

toplevelWindow = XtWindow(w_toplevel);
ourDisplay = XtDisplay(w_toplevel);
ourScreen = XtScreen(w_toplevel);
rootWindow = XDefaultRootWindow(ourDisplay);
...
```

Note that the XtDisplay, XtScreen, and XDefaultRootWindow calls are valid before the call to XtRealize, but XtWindow is not, since a widget's windows are not created until the widget is realized.

4.3.8 Starting the Application

Following the above code fragment, the only thing left to do is turn control over to the X Toolkit machinery with a call that never returns:

```
void XtMainLoop();
```

XtMainLoop loops indefinitely, calling XtNextEvent to read the X input queue and XtDispatchEvent to hand events to the widgets.

Applications may implement this loop themselves if they have special event processing requirements. All of the examples presented here use XtMainLoop, but in Chapter 6 we use two utility library functions, GetTimestamp and Notice, that take over the event loop to alter the normal control flow.

Chapter 5

The OPEN LOOK Widget Set

The AT&T OPEN LOOK widget set is a collection of user-interface objects implementing the OPEN LOOK Graphical User Interface. Together, the OPEN LOOK widgets and Xt Intrinsics form an object-oriented programming environment for the X Window System.

In this chapter, we will develop simple programs to demonstrate each and every OPEN LOOK widget. You may find it useful to have available a copy of the *OPEN LOOK Programmer's Guide* and *The OPEN LOOK Programmer's Reference Manual*.

5.1 Getting Started

5.1.1 The Mainline

Rather than repeat the initialization code in each of the examples, we'll put it in main.c and link it into each program executable:

```
/*
 * main.c - OPEN LOOK Toolkit widget demo mainline.
 * @(#) sccs/s.main.c 1.15 last delta 3/12/90 19:14:50
 */
#include <X11/Intrinsic.h>
#include <Xol/OpenLook.h>

Widget  w_toplevel;     /* top level widget in the tree */
Window  toplevelWindow; /* window of toplevel widget */
char    *ProgramName;   /* printable name of our application */
Display *ourDisplay;    /* server display we are using */
Screen  *ourScreen;     /* screen we are using */
Window  rootWindow;     /* root window of ourScreen */

void main(argc, argv)
    unsigned int argc;
    char *argv[];
{
    /*
```

```
     * Initialize the OPEN LOOK Toolkit.  The first parameter
     * to OlInitialize() is the name of this program, which
     * gets used as our icon name.  Note that the address
     * of the argc gets passed so OlInitialize() can
     * destructively parse the command line for toolkit
     * options.
     */
    w_toplevel = OlInitialize(
        NULL,                   /* app name - filled by Xt */
        "OlExample",            /* app class */
        NULL,                   /* option list */
        0,                      /* # of options */
        &argc,                  /* addr of main argc */
        argv                    /* main argv */
    );

    /*
     * CreateInitialWidgets is the application's hook
     * for building the initial widget tree.
     */
    (void) CreateInitialWidgets(w_toplevel);

    /*
     * Recursively realize all the widgets, starting
     * with top level shell.
     */
    (void) XtRealizeWidget(w_toplevel);

    /*
     * initialize misc global variables
     */
    toplevelWindow = XtWindow(w_toplevel);
    ourDisplay = XtDisplay(w_toplevel);
    ourScreen = XtScreen(w_toplevel);
    rootWindow = XDefaultRootWindow(ourDisplay);

    /*
     * Turn control over to the X Toolkit machinery.
     */
    (void) XtMainLoop();
}
```

This simple mainline performs the following tasks:

- Initializes the OPEN LOOK X Toolkit
- Lets the application define the rest of the widget tree
- Realizes all of the initial widgets by realizing the top-level widget.
- Initializes some handy global variables
- Starts the application by turning control over to the Xt machinery

The C header files included by main.c

```
#include <X11/Intrinsic.h>
#include <Xol/OpenLook.h>
```

are included in every source module using the OPEN LOOK Intrinsic Toolkit. The module must also include the header file for each widget class it references.

Most of the example source modules in this book also include xtutil.h, which defines the services of this book's utility library, Xtutil. The complete source for Xtutil (including xtutil.h) is listed in the appendix.

5.1.2 Building the Examples

The makefile for the programs in this chapter assumes that the source for Xtutil is in ../xtutil and that the directory contains a makefile that knows how to build libxtutil.a. The default makefile settings know how to build the example programs for AT&T XWIN installations. If you are not using the AT&T XWIN and OPEN LOOK packages, you may have to modify the makefile to specify the correct include and lib directories for your installation.

```
#
# Makefile for Chapter 5 of "An OPEN LOOK at UNIX"
# by John David Miller
#
# @(#) sccs/s.Makefile 1.20 last delta 4/8/90 23:53:05
#

# DEBUG = -g -lg
STRIP = -s
# OPTIM = -O

# The next few lines are for AT&T XWIN installations
CFLAGS = $(OPTIM) $(DEBUG) \
    -I../xtutil -I/usr/X/include -I/usr/include
LDFLAGS = -L/usr/X/lib $(STRIP)
LIBES = $(UTIL) \
    -lXol -lXt -lXol -lXt -lX11_s -lpt -lnls -lnsl_s -lc_s

# MIT-style X Window System installations
# might use these lines:
# CFLAGS = $(OPTIM) $(DEBUG) -I../xtutil
# LDFLAGS = $(STRIP)
# LIBES = $(UTIL) -lXol -lXt -lX11

UTIL = ../xtutil/libxtutil.a
OBJS = main.o

ALL = \
        abbrev bboard caption checkbox cmdwin \
        cntlrows cntlcols cntlwdth cntlhght exclusiv \
        flatchex flatexcl flatnonx footer form \
        menu menubutt mixer nonexclu notice oblong panel \
        propwin rectbutt scrbar scrlist scrwin slider stattext \
        text txtfield

all : $(ALL)

$(ALL) : $(OBJS) $(UTIL) $$@.o
    $(CC) $(LDFLAGS) $@.o $(OBJS) $(LIBES) -o $@

cntlrows.o : control.c
    cp control.c cntlrows.c
    $(CC) $(CFLAGS) -DUSE_FIXEDROWS -c cntlrows.c

cntlcols.o : control.c
    cp control.c cntlcols.c
    $(CC) $(CFLAGS) -DUSE_FIXEDCOLS -c cntlcols.c

cntlwdth.o : control.c
    cp control.c cntlwdth.c
    $(CC) $(CFLAGS) -DUSE_FIXEDWIDTH -c cntlwdth.c
```

```
cntlhght.o : control.c
    cp control.c cntlhght.c
    $(CC) $(CFLAGS) -DUSE_FIXEDHEIGHT -c cntlhght.c

flatchex.o : flatwidg.c
    cp flatwidg.c flatchex.c
    $(CC) $(CFLAGS) -DUSE_CHECKBOX -c flatchex.c

flatexcl.o : flatwidg.c
    cp flatwidg.c flatexcl.c
    $(CC) $(CFLAGS) -DUSE_EXCLUSIVES -c flatexcl.c

flatnonx.o : flatwidg.c
    cp flatwidg.c flatnonx.c
    $(CC) $(CFLAGS) -DUSE_NONEXCLUSIVES -c flatnonx.c

$(UTIL) :
    (cd ../xtutil; make)

clean:
    -rm -f $(ALL) *.o
    -rm -f cntlrows.? cntlcols.? cntlwdth.? cntlhght.?
    -rm -f flatchex.? flatexcl.? flatnonx.?
```

On AT&T systems, simply type

```
make
```

to build all of the programs in this directory. Building all of the programs for this chapter requires about 18 megabytes of disk space. You may also build each program separately, as in

```
make propwin
```

which executes

```
cc   -I../xtutil -I/usr/X/include -I/usr/include -c main.c
cc   -I../xtutil -I/usr/X/include -I/usr/include -c propwin.c
cc -L/usr/X/lib -s propwin.o main.o ../xtutil/libxtutil.a -lXol
-lXt -lXol -lXt -lX11_s -lpt -lnls -lnsl_s -lc_s -o propwin
```

If you need to debug a program using *sdb*, you will want to edit the makefile to comment out the STRIP definition and uncomment out the DEBUG definition.

5.2 Using the Widgets

The remainder of this chapter demonstrates each of the widgets in the OPEN LOOK widget set. Each section contains a brief description of the widget and an example program showing its use. (Each example module in this chapter hooks into main.c by defining the function, CreateInitialWidgets.)

The simplest widgets are presented first, and the more complex widgets and examples are covered later in the chapter.

5.2.1 Static Text

Static Text displays a block of read-only text in a variety layout styles. It is perhaps the simplest, but most often used, widget class.
In the following example, stattext.c, the routine CreateInitialWidgets makes a single function call to create and manage the Static Text widget, w_staticText:

```
/*
 * Demonstrate the OPEN LOOK Static Text widget
 * @(#) sccs/s.stattext.c 1.6 last delta 2/7/90 17:55:17
 */
#include <X11/Intrinsic.h>
#include <X11/StringDefs.h>
#include <Xol/OpenLook.h>
#include <Xol/StaticText.h>
```

```
#include "xtutil.h"

#define MESSAGE \
"Now is the time for all good men to come \
to the aid of the party.  The quick brown fox \
jumped over the lazy dog.  All men are created equal. \
We, the people, in order to form a more perfect union...."

Widget CreateInitialWidgets(w_parent)
    Widget  w_parent;
{
    Widget  w_staticText;
    void    PrintStatus();

    w_staticText =
        XtCreateManagedWidget(
            "staticText",           /* instance name */
            staticTextWidgetClass,  /* widget class */
            w_parent,               /* parent widget */
            tmpArg,                 /* arg list */
            TmpArgList(
                XtNstring,      MESSAGE,
                XtNwidth,       300,
                0
            )
        );

    return(w_staticText);
}
```

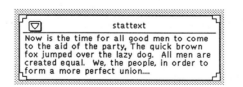

Figure 5.1 The Static Text widget class

141

Notice the addition of three header files:

```
#include <X11/StringDefs.h>
#include <Xol/StaticText.h>
#include "xtutil.h"
```

The first of these, StringDefs.h, defines common XtN-prefixed resource string constants. The StaticText.h header file defines the public interface to the Static Text widget class, including any widget-specific XtN resource names.[1] The header file xtutil.h defines the utility library interface, used here for tmpArg and TmpArgList.

When creating the widget, we set the XtNstring resource to the text we want to display and the XtNwidth resource to the initial width of the widget, in pixels. By not specifying other resources, we use the defaults (listed in the resource table for the Static Text widget class in the *OPEN LOOK Programmer's Reference Manual*). Of particular interest are the XtNwidth, XtNheight, and XtNrecomputeSize resources. The default for XtNrecomputeSize is TRUE, so when we specify either XtNwidth or XtNheight, the other dimension is automatically computed to accommodate the text in XtNstring.

Another interesting resource is XtNwrap, which is TRUE by default. Using the mouse, resize stattext to be long and narrow. Notice how the text automatically wraps to fit the new border:

---

[1] Header files ending with a capital P (for example, StaticTexP.h, OpenLookP.h) are private to the widget implementation and are not intended to be included by applications.

Figure 5.2 Automatic line wrap

Experiment with stattext.c to better understand how resources affect widget behavior. Try each of these resource assignments one at a time or in groups:

- Set XtNalignment to OL_CENTER.
- Set XtNgravity to SouthEastGravity.
- Set XtNrecomputeSize to FALSE.
- Set XtNwrap to FALSE.

5.2.2 Oblong Button

An Oblong Button lets the user activate application-specified actions. Oblong Buttons are about as common as Static Text widgets and almost as simple.

The key feature of Oblong Buttons is the XtNselect callback-list resource. When the button is pressed (that is, when the SELECT mouse button is clicked on it), the widget invokes the callbacks on this list. In the Oblong Button example, oblong.c, we define CBQuit as our XtNselect callback:

```
/*
 * Demonstrate the OPEN LOOK Oblong Button widget
 * @(#) sccs/s.oblong.c 1.1 last delta 4/5/90 20:46:15
 */
#include <X11/Intrinsic.h>
#include <X11/StringDefs.h>
#include <Xol/OpenLook.h>
#include <Xol/OblongButt.h>
#include "xtutil.h"

#define USE_GADGETS


Widget CreateInitialWidgets(w_parent)
    Widget  w_parent;
{
    Widget  w_quit;
    void    CBQuit();

    /*
     * Create the quit button
     */
    w_quit =
        XtCreateManagedWidget(
            "quit",                     /* instance name */
#ifdef USE_GADGETS
            oblongButtonGadgetClass,    /* widget class */
#else
            oblongButtonWidgetClass,    /* widget class */
#endif
            w_parent,                   /* parent widget */
            tmpArg,                     /* arglist */
            TmpArgList(
                XtNlabel,               "Quit",
                XtNrecomputeSize,       FALSE,
                0
            )
        );

    /*
     * Add callback routine
     */
    XtAddCallback(w_quit, XtNselect, CBQuit, NULL);

    return(w_quit);
```

```
}

void CBQuit(w, client_data, call_data)
    Widget  w;
    caddr_t client_data;
    caddr_t call_data;
{
    exit(0);
}
```

Figure 5.3 The Oblong Button widget class

This example uses a text string label, but the label can also be an X bitmap or pixmap image. An example later in this chapter (see section 5.2.8, "Control Area") uses Oblong Buttons with bitmap labels.

Oblong Buttons are available as widgets or gadgets. Gadgets are special versions of the OPEN LOOK user-interface objects that are slightly more efficient than the equivalent widget implementation. For all practical purposes, gadgets are identical to widgets and should be used whenever possible. Unless otherwise noted, wherever this book uses a widget, its corresponding gadget may be substituted.[2]

5.2.3 Rectangular Button

The other type of OPEN LOOK button is the Rectangular Button. Rectangular Buttons have two states, *set* and *not set*, which are toggled each time the user clicks SELECT. A different callback can be invoked for both state transitions.

---

[2]About the only notable limitation of gadgets is that they may not be the parents of pop-up children.

Rectangular Buttons expect their parent widget to be of the Exclusive Settings or Nonexclusive Settings widget class. These classes are discussed later, but for now, we can demonstrate the widget and its callbacks using Base Window Shell as the parent:

```
/*
 * Demonstrate the OPEN LOOK Rectangle Button widget
 * @(#) sccs/s.rectbutt.c 1.6 last delta 2/7/90 20:39:12
 */
#include <X11/Intrinsic.h>
#include <X11/StringDefs.h>
#include <Xol/OpenLook.h>
#include <Xol/RectButton.h>
#include "xtutil.h"


Widget CreateInitialWidgets(w_parent)
    Widget  w_parent;
{
    Widget  w_button;
    void    CBPrintStatus();

    /*
     * Create the quit button
     */
    w_button =
        XtCreateManagedWidget(
            "button",               /* instance name */
            rectButtonWidgetClass,  /* widget class */
            w_parent,               /* parent widget */
            tmpArg,                 /* arg list */
            TmpArgList(
                XtNlabel,    "Rectangular Button",
                0
            )
        );

    /*
     * Add callbacks
     */
    XtAddCallback(w_button, XtNselect, CBPrintStatus, NULL);
    XtAddCallback(w_button, XtNunselect, CBPrintStatus, NULL);

    return(w_button);
}


static void CBPrintStatus(w, client_data, call_data)
    Widget  w;
```

```
    caddr_t client_data;
    caddr_t call_data;
{
    Boolean set;

    set = GetValue(w, XtNset);
    dbg("button status: %s\n", set ? "SET" : "NOT SET");

    return;
}
```

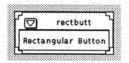

Figure 5.4 The Rectangular Button widget class

The function CBPrintStatus doubles as both the XtNselect and
XtNunselect callback. It inquires the current value of XtNset to determine the button's state and prints out a message. Alternatively, instead of passing NULL, we could have passed TRUE and FALSE to
CBPrintStatus as client_data.

5.2.4 Slider

Sliders allow users to visually set a numeric value within a range.
The application has complete control of the range and granularity.

In the example program, slider.c, note that the XtNsliderMoved callback, CBSliderMoved, gets the current value from call_data, rather
than using XtGetValues on XtNsliderValue.

```
/*
 * Demonstrate the OPEN LOOK Slider widget
 * @(#) sccs/s.slider.c 1.7 last delta 2/7/90 21:20:44
 */
#include <X11/Intrinsic.h>
#include <X11/StringDefs.h>
#include <Xol/OpenLook.h>
#include <Xol/Slider.h>
#include "xtutil.h"
```

```
Widget CreateInitialWidgets(w_parent)
    Widget  w_parent;
{
    Widget  w_slider;
    void    CBSliderMoved();

    w_slider =
        XtCreateManagedWidget(
            "slider",                   /* instance name */
            sliderWidgetClass,          /* widget class */
            w_parent,                   /* parent widget */
            tmpArg,                     /* arg list */
            TmpArgList(
                XtNorientation,     OL_VERTICAL,
                XtNheight,          200,
                XtNgranularity,     10,
                0
            )
        );

    /*
     * Add callback routines
     */
    XtAddCallback(w_slider, XtNsliderMoved, CBSliderMoved, NULL);

    return(w_slider);
}


static void CBSliderMoved(w, client_data, call_data)
    Widget  w;
    caddr_t client_data;
    caddr_t call_data;
{
    dbg("Current value = %d\n", (int) *call_data);

    return;
}
```

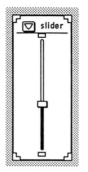

Figure 5.5 The Slider widget class

5.2.5 Scrollbar

The Scrollbar is a sophisticated Slider-like device to control text or graphics window scrolling. The Scrollbar provides only the user-interface; it does *not* perform the scrolling. The application (or widget, such as Scrolling Window, Scrolling List, or Text) is responsible for defining and implementing any such additional semantics.

From the example program, scrbar.c, we see that Scrollbar has a slightly more complicated callback than Slider. The call_data parameter is a pointer to an OlScrollbarVerify structure, rather than just the current position. Among the additional information is an OK flag, which the callback may set to FALSE, if it needs to block the scroll.

The Scrollbar's other notable feature is the menu. After creating the widget, the application inquires the value of the XtNmenuPane resource, which is a subcomponent of Scrollbar. As shown in the example, applications may add button items to the menu by specifying this widget as the parent in the call to XtCreateManagedWidget.

```
/*
 * Demonstrate the OPEN LOOK Scrollbar widget
 * @(#) sccs/s.scrbar.c 1.9 last delta 2/18/90 09:20:02
 */
#include <X11/Intrinsic.h>
#include <X11/StringDefs.h>
#include <Xol/OpenLook.h>
#include <Xol/Scrollbar.h>
#include <Xol/OblongButt.h>
#include "xtutil.h"


Widget CreateInitialWidgets(w_parent)
    Widget  w_parent;
{
    Widget  w_scrollbar, w_menu, AddOblongButton();
    void    CBScrollbarMoved();

    w_scrollbar =
        XtCreateManagedWidget(
            "scrollbar",                /* instance name */
            scrollbarWidgetClass,       /* widget class */
            w_parent,                   /* parent widget */
            tmpArg,                     /* arg list */
            TmpArgList(
                XtNorientation,         OL_VERTICAL,
                XtNheight,              200,
                XtNgranularity,         10,
                XtNsliderMin,           0,
                XtNsliderMax,           100,
                XtNsliderValue,         0,
                XtNproportionLength,    10,
                XtNtitle,               "Scrollbar Menu",
                0
            )
        );
    XtAddCallback(
        w_scrollbar,
        XtNsliderMoved,
        CBScrollbarMoved,
        NULL
    );

    /*
     * Get scrollbar menu wid and add a button item to it.
     */
    w_menu = (Widget) GetValue(w_scrollbar, XtNmenuPane);
    (void) AddOblongButton(w_menu, "additional button");

    return(w_scrollbar);
}
```

150

```
static void CBScrollbarMoved(w, client_data, call_data)
    Widget  w;
    caddr_t client_data;
    caddr_t call_data;
{
    OlScrollbarVerify   *pVerify =
                                (OlScrollbarVerify *) call_data;
    int val=0;

    if (pVerify->ok == FALSE)  {
        dbg("PrintStatus: ok is FALSE\n");
        return;      /* some other callback veto'd the action */
    }

    dbg(
        "delta = %d, new_location = %d\n",
        pVerify->delta,
        pVerify->new_location
    );

    pVerify->ok = TRUE; /* confirm the action as okay */

    return;
}


Widget AddOblongButton(w_parent, label)
    Widget  w_parent;
    String  label;
{
    Widget  w_button;
    void    PrintOblongButtonStatus();

    w_button =
        XtCreateManagedWidget(
            label,                      /* instance name */
            oblongButtonWidgetClass,    /* widget class */
            w_parent,                   /* parent widget */
            tmpArg,                     /* arg list */
            TmpArgList(
                XtNlabel,   label,
                0
            )
        );
    XtAddCallback(
        w_button,
        XtNselect,
        PrintOblongButtonStatus,
        NULL
```

```
    );

    return(w_button);
}


static void PrintOblongButtonStatus(wid, client_data, call_data)
    Widget  wid;
    caddr_t client_data;
    caddr_t call_data;
{
    String  label;

    label = (String) GetValue(wid, XtNlabel);
    dbg("%s button selected\n", label);

    return;
}
```

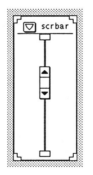

Figure 5.6 The Scrollbar widget class

5.2.6 Checkbox

The Checkbox is similar in operation to the Rectangular Button. However, unlike a Rectangular Button, Checkboxes can be used with most Composite parents, not just Exclusives and Nonexclusives.

```
/*
 * Demonstrate the OPEN LOOK Check Box widget
 * @(#) sccs/s.checkbox.c 1.6 last delta 2/8/90 16:21:03
 */
#include <X11/Intrinsic.h>
#include <X11/StringDefs.h>
#include <Xol/OpenLook.h>
#include <Xol/CheckBox.h>
#include "xtutil.h"


Widget CreateInitialWidgets(w_parent)
    Widget  w_parent;
{
    Widget  w_button;
    void    CBButtonChanged();

    /*
     * Create the quit button
     */
    w_button =
        XtCreateManagedWidget(
            "button",               /* instance name */
            checkBoxWidgetClass,    /* widget class */
            w_parent,               /* parent widget */
            tmpArg,                 /* arg list */
            TmpArgList(
                XtNlabel,   "A-OK",
                0
            )
        );

    /*
     * Add callbacks
     */
    XtAddCallback(w_button, XtNselect, CBButtonChanged, NULL);
    XtAddCallback(w_button, XtNunselect, CBButtonChanged, NULL);

    return(w_button);
}


static void CBButtonChanged(wid, client_data, call_data)
    Widget  wid;
    caddr_t client_data;
    caddr_t call_data;
{
    Boolean val=0;
    String  label=NULL;

    /*
```

```
 * get resource values from the widget
 */
label = (String) GetValue(wid, XtNlabel);
val = (Boolean) GetValue(wid, XtNset);

dbg(
    "%s button: %s\n",
    label ? label : "NULL",        /* only print if non-NULL */
    val ? "SET" : "UNSET"
);

return;
}
```

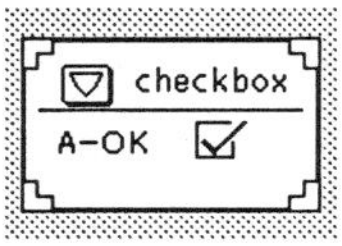

Figure 5.7 The Checkbox widget class

5.2.7 Caption

Caption attaches a string label to a child widget. The label can be positioned to the left, right, top, or bottom of the child, with various alignment options.

The example, caption.c, adds a label to a Slider widget, which is created as a child of the Caption.

```
/*
 * Demonstrate the OPEN LOOK Caption widget
 * @(#) sccs/s.caption.c 1.8 last delta 2/8/90 17:01:38
 */
#include <X11/Intrinsic.h>
#include <X11/StringDefs.h>
#include <Xol/OpenLook.h>
#include <Xol/Caption.h>
#include <Xol/Slider.h>
#include "xtutil.h"


Widget CreateInitialWidgets(w_parent)
    Widget  w_parent;
```

```
{
    Widget  w_caption, AddSlider();

    /*
     * Create the caption, but don't manage it until we
     * have attached the child.
     */
    w_caption =
        XtCreateWidget(
            "caption",              /* instance name */
            captionWidgetClass, /* widget class */
            w_parent,               /* parent widget */
            tmpArg,                 /* arg list */
            TmpArgList(
                XtNlabel,    "Volume :",
                0
            )
        );

    /*
     * For this example, we'll use the caption to label a slider.
     */
    AddSlider(w_caption);

    /*
     * Tell the caption widget's parent about it.
     */
    XtManageChild(w_caption);

    return(w_caption);
}


Widget AddSlider(w_parent)
    Widget  w_parent;
{
    Widget  w_slider;
    void    CBSliderMoved();

    w_slider =
        XtCreateManagedWidget(
            "slider",               /* instance name */
            sliderWidgetClass,  /* widget name */
            w_parent,               /* parent widget */
            tmpArg,                 /* argument list */
            TmpArgList(
                XtNorientation,     OL_HORIZONTAL,
                XtNwidth,           200,
                XtNrepeatRate,      1,
                0
            )
```

```
        );

    /*
     * Add callbacks
     */
    XtAddCallback(w_slider, XtNsliderMoved, CBSliderMoved, NULL);

    return(w_slider);
}


static void CBSliderMoved(wid, client_data, call_data)
    Widget  wid;
    caddr_t client_data;
    caddr_t call_data;
{
    dbg("slider value = %d\n", (int) *call_data);

    return;
}
```

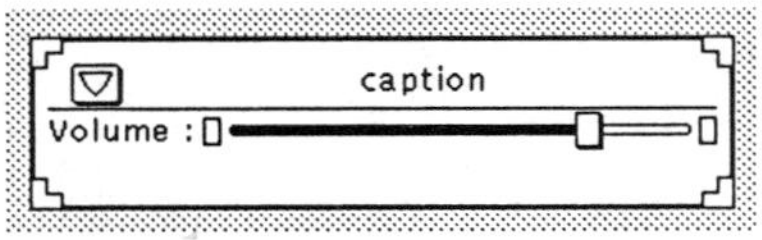

Figure 5.8 The Caption widget class

5.2.8 Control Area

Among Composite widgets, Control Area is probably the most extensively used. It is conceptually quite simple: Control Area is a general-
purpose row/column layout manager, arranging children according to
one of four options:

FIXEDROWS—Children are arranged in column-major order to form *N*
rows.

FIXEDCOLS—Children are arranged in row-major order to form *N*
columns.

FIXEDWIDTH—Children are arranged in row-major order to fit *N* pixels wide.

FIXEDHEIGHT—Children are arranged in column-major order to fit *N* pixels tall.

Using Control Area, applications can physically group widgets together without manually computing their geometries. Control Area does this work automatically and gives the application options such as:

XtNsameSize—Forces children to be the same size, either within a column or within the entire Control Area.

XtNalignCaptions—Automatically aligns the child Caption widgets' labels.

XtNhPad
XtNvPad—Adjusts the space around the Control Area.

XtNhSpace
XtNvSpace—Adjusts the space between children.

XtNlayoutType—Arranges the row/column layout style, as described above.

XtNtraversalManager—Automatically manages the keyboard focus among Text and Text Field children (see sections 5.2.13, "Text Field" and 5.2.14, "Text").

The first Control Area example program, control.c, can be built four different ways to demonstrate the four layout types.[3] This simple program creates a Control Area and a number of Static Text children.

---

[3]The makefile does this automatically.

157

The layout mode, XtNlayoutType, determines how the Control Area arranges the children within the Control Area's extents.

```
/*
 * Demonstrate OPEN LOOK ControlArea widget
 * @(#) sccs/s.control.c 1.2 last delta 2/9/90 09:30:34
 */
#include <X11/Intrinsic.h>
#include <X11/StringDefs.h>
#include <Xol/OpenLook.h>
#include <Xol/ControlAre.h>
#include <Xol/StaticText.h>
#include "xtutil.h"


Widget CreateInitialWidgets(w_parent)
    Widget  w_parent;
{
    register char   chr;
    Widget          w_control;
    char            buf[10];

    /*
     * Create the Control Area.   Try XtNlayoutType
     * with different values.
     */
    w_control =
        XtCreateWidget(
            "control",
            controlAreaWidgetClass,
            w_parent,
            tmpArg,
            TmpArgList(
#ifdef USE_FIXEDROWS
                XtNlayoutType,      OL_FIXEDROWS,
                XtNmeasure,         5,
#endif
#ifdef USE_FIXEDCOLS
                XtNlayoutType,      OL_FIXEDCOLS,
                XtNmeasure,         5,
#endif
#ifdef USE_FIXEDWIDTH
                XtNlayoutType,      OL_FIXEDWIDTH,
                XtNmeasure,         100,
#endif
#ifdef USE_FIXEDHEIGHT
                XtNlayoutType,      OL_FIXEDHEIGHT,
                XtNmeasure,         100,
#endif
                0
```

```
            )
        );

    /*
     * Create a bunch of children to demonstrate the Control Area
     */
    for (chr = 'A'; chr <= 'z'; chr++) {
        buf[0] = chr;
        buf[1] = NULL;
        XtCreateManagedWidget(
            NULL,
            staticTextWidgetClass,
            w_control,
            tmpArg,
            TmpArgList(
                XtNstring,          buf,
                XtNborderWidth,     1,
                0
            )
        );
    }

    XtManageChild(w_control);
    return(w_control);
}
```

Figure 5.9 The Control Area widget class, using FIXEDROWS layout

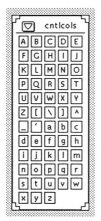

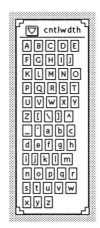

Figure 5.10 The Control Area widget class, using FIXEDCOLS layout

Figure 5.11 The Control Area widget class, using FIXEDWIDTH layout

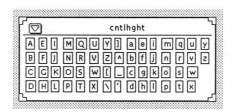

Figure 5.12 The Control Area widget class, using FIXEDHEIGHT layout

The next example, mixer.c, shows just what you can do with some of the widget classes we've looked at thus far: Static Text, Slider, Checkbox, Caption, and Control Area. The program implements the user-interface for a simple audio mixer, building each channel out of the following components:

- a Control Area to contain the widgets for each channel
- a Checkbox labeled Mute
- a Caption labeled Pan, to display the left-to-right pan amount
- a Slider to adjust the pan
- a Caption labeled Level, to display the fader level
- a Slider to adjust the level
- a Static Text channel label

In addition, CreateInitialWidgets instantiates a Control Area to lay out all of the channels as a single row.

```
/*
 * Demonstrate several OPEN LOOK widgets simultaneously
 * @(#) sccs/s.mixer.c 1.1 last delta 2/8/90 16:04:07
 */
#include <X11/Intrinsic.h>
#include <X11/StringDefs.h>
#include <Xol/OpenLook.h>
#include <Xol/Caption.h>
#include <Xol/CheckBox.h>
#include <Xol/ControlAre.h>
#include <Xol/Slider.h>
#include <Xol/StaticText.h>
#include "xtutil.h"


Widget CreateInitialWidgets(w_parent)
    Widget   w_parent;
{
    register    i;
    Widget      w_control, CreateChannel();
    char        str[10];

    w_control =
        XtCreateWidget(
            "control",
            controlAreaWidgetClass,
```

```
                w_parent,
                tmpArg,
                TmpArgList(
                    XtNlayoutType,          OL_FIXEDROWS,
                    XtNmeasure,             1,
                    XtNhSpace,              0,   /* pack tight */
                    0
                )
            );

        for (i=1; i <= 8; i++) {
            sprintf(str, "%d", i);
            CreateChannel(w_control, str);
        }

        XtManageChild(w_control);
        return(w_control);
    }


    /*
     * CreateChannel() - build a mixer channel
     */
    Widget CreateChannel(w_parent, label)
        Widget  w_parent;
        String  label;
    {
        Widget  w_control;
        void    CreatePan(), CreateFader();

        /*
         * Create the control area to hold all the controls
         * for this channel.
         */
        w_control =
            XtCreateWidget(
                "control",
                controlAreaWidgetClass,
                w_parent,
                tmpArg,
                TmpArgList(
                    XtNalignCaptions,   TRUE,
                    XtNlayoutType,      OL_FIXEDCOLS,
                    XtNmeasure,         1,
                    XtNhPad,            0,
                    XtNborderWidth,     1,
                    XtNhSpace,          0,
                    0
                )
            );
```

```
    /*
     * Add the mute toggle switch
     */
    (void) XtCreateManagedWidget(
        "mute",
        checkBoxWidgetClass,
        w_control,
        tmpArg,
        TmpArgList(
            XtNlabel,    "Mute:",
            0
        )
    );

    CreatePan(w_control);            /* Add pan control group */
    CreateFader(w_control);          /* Add fader control group */

    /*
     * label the channel as requested by our parent
     */
    XtCreateManagedWidget(
        "label",
        staticTextWidgetClass,
        w_control,
        tmpArg,
        TmpArgList(
            XtNstring,  label,
            0
        )
    );

    XtManageChild(w_control);
    return(w_control);
}


/*
 * CreatePan() - build the L/R pan control
 */
void CreatePan(w_parent)
    Widget   w_parent;
{
    Widget   w_panLabel, w_panVal, w_pan;
    void     CBSliderMoved();

    /*
     * Build the current value window using a caption widget and
     * a static text widget.
     */
    w_panLabel = XtCreateWidget(
        "panLabel",
```

```
            captionWidgetClass,
            w_parent,
            tmpArg,
            TmpArgList(
                XtNlabel,    "Pan:",
                0
            )
    );
    w_panVal =
        XtCreateManagedWidget(
            "panValue",
            staticTextWidgetClass,
            w_panLabel,
            tmpArg,
            TmpArgList(
                XtNstring,   "0",
                0
            )
        );
    XtManageChild(w_panLabel);

    /*
     * Pan control is a simple slider.
     */
    w_pan =
        XtCreateManagedWidget(
            "pan",                  /* instance name */
            sliderWidgetClass,      /* widget class */
            w_parent,               /* parent widget */
            tmpArg,                 /* arg list */
            TmpArgList(
                XtNorientation,     OL_HORIZONTAL,
                XtNsliderMin,       -10,
                XtNsliderMax,       10,
                XtNsliderValue,     0,
                XtNgranularity,     1,
                XtNinitialDelay,    250,
                0
            )
        );
    XtAddCallback(
        w_pan,
        XtNsliderMoved,
        CBSliderMoved,
        w_panVal
    );

    return;
}
```

```
/*
 * CreateFader() - build the level fader
 */
void CreateFader(w_parent)
    Widget  w_parent;
{
    Widget  w_faderLabel, w_faderVal, w_fader;
    void    CBSliderMoved();

    /*
     * Build the current value window
     */
    w_faderLabel = XtCreateWidget(
        "faderLabel",
        captionWidgetClass,
        w_parent,
        tmpArg,
        TmpArgList(
            XtNlabel,    "Level:",
            0
        )
    );
    w_faderVal =
        XtCreateManagedWidget(
            "faderValue",
            staticTextWidgetClass,
            w_faderLabel,
            tmpArg,
            TmpArgList(
                XtNstring,   "-10",
                0
            )
        );
    XtManageChild(w_faderLabel);

    /*
     * Build the fader
     */
    w_fader =
        XtCreateManagedWidget(
            "fader",                /* instance name */
            sliderWidgetClass,      /* widget class */
            w_parent,               /* parent widget */
            tmpArg,                 /* arg list */
            TmpArgList(
                XtNorientation,     OL_VERTICAL,
                XtNheight,          200,
                XtNsliderMin,       -10,
                XtNsliderMax,       5,
                XtNsliderValue,     -10,
                XtNgranularity,     5,
```

165

```
                XtNinitialDelay,    250,
                0
            )
        );
    XtAddCallback(
        w_fader,
        XtNsliderMoved,
        CBSliderMoved,
        w_faderVal
    );

    return;
}


/*
 * CBSliderMoved() - update the current value windows
 */
void CBSliderMoved(wid, client_data, call_data)
    Widget  wid;
    caddr_t client_data;
    caddr_t call_data;
{
    char    str[10];

    sprintf(str, "%d", *((int *) call_data));/* show in window */
    SetValue((Widget) client_data, XtNstring, str);

    return;
}
```

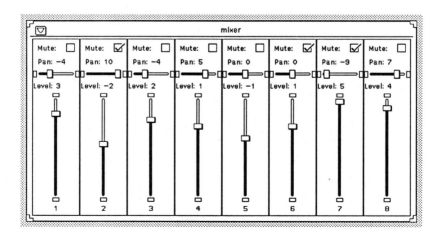

Figure 5.13 A simple audio mixer

Another example, panel.c, demonstrates a simple Control Area containing a single row of Oblong Buttons. These buttons have graphic labels, courtesy of the utility library function XYBitmapImageFromData, and semantics, provided by the callback CBButtonLogic. Figure 5.14 shows the Pause and Play buttons depressed.

```
/*
 * Demonstrate the OPEN LOOK Control Area widget
 * @(#) sccs/s.panel.c 1.3 last delta 2/18/90 13:04:14
 */
#include <X11/Intrinsic.h>
#include <X11/StringDefs.h>
#include <Xol/OpenLook.h>
#include <Xol/ControlAre.h>
#include <Xol/OblongButt.h>
#include <stdio.h>
#include "xtutil.h"

#define play_width 16
#define play_height 16
static char play_bits[] = {
    0x03, 0x00, 0x0f, 0x00, 0x3f, 0x00, 0xff, 0x00,
    0xff, 0x03, 0xff, 0x0f, 0xff, 0x3f, 0xff, 0xff,
    0xff, 0xff, 0xff, 0x3f, 0xff, 0x0f, 0xff, 0x03,
    0xff, 0x00, 0x3f, 0x00, 0x0f, 0x00, 0x03, 0x00};

#define pause_width 16
#define pause_height 16
static char pause_bits[] = {
    0x00, 0x00, 0x3c, 0x3c, 0x3c, 0x3c, 0x3c, 0x3c,
    0x3c, 0x3c, 0x3c, 0x3c, 0x3c, 0x3c, 0x3c, 0x3c,
    0x3c, 0x3c, 0x3c, 0x3c, 0x3c, 0x3c, 0x3c, 0x3c,
    0x3c, 0x3c, 0x3c, 0x3c, 0x3c, 0x3c, 0x00, 0x00};

#define stop_width 16
#define stop_height 16
static char stop_bits[] = {
    0x00, 0x00, 0xfe, 0x7f, 0xfe, 0x7f, 0xfe, 0x7f,
    0xfe, 0x7f, 0xfe, 0x7f, 0xfe, 0x7f, 0xfe, 0x7f,
    0xfe, 0x7f, 0xfe, 0x7f, 0xfe, 0x7f, 0xfe, 0x7f,
    0xfe, 0x7f, 0xfe, 0x7f, 0xfe, 0x7f, 0x00, 0x00};

#define ff_width 16
#define ff_height 16
static char ff_bits[] = {
    0x02, 0x01, 0x06, 0x03, 0x0e, 0x07, 0x1e, 0x0f,
    0x3e, 0x1f, 0x7e, 0x3f, 0x7e, 0x7f, 0x7e, 0xff,
```

```
    0x7e, 0x7f, 0x7e, 0x3f, 0x3e, 0x1f, 0x1e, 0x0f,
    0x0e, 0x07, 0x06, 0x03, 0x02, 0x01, 0x00, 0x00};

#define rew_width 16
#define rew_height 16
static char rew_bits[] = {
    0x80, 0x40, 0xc0, 0x60, 0xe0, 0x70, 0xf0, 0x78,
    0xf8, 0x7c, 0xfc, 0x7e, 0xfe, 0x7e, 0xff, 0x7e,
    0xfe, 0x7e, 0xfc, 0x7e, 0xf8, 0x7c, 0xf0, 0x78,
    0xe0, 0x70, 0xc0, 0x60, 0x80, 0x40, 0x00, 0x00};

typedef struct _FRONT_PANEL {
    Widget        play;
    Widget        stop;
    Widget        ff;
    Widget        rew;
    Widget        pause;
    Pixel         fg;
    Pixel         bg;
    unsigned int     state;
} FRONT_PANEL;
FRONT_PANEL frontPanel;

#define STOP     0
#define PAUSE    (1<<0)
#define PLAY     (1<<1)
#define REWIND   (1<<2)
#define FORWARD  (1<<3)


Widget CreateInitialWidgets(w_parent)
{
    Widget                w_control, CreateImageButton();
    void                  CBButtonLogic();
    extern FRONT_PANEL    frontPanel;
    extern Pixmap         busy;

    w_control =
        XtCreateWidget(
            "frontPanel",
            controlAreaWidgetClass,
            w_parent,
            tmpArg,
            TmpArgList(
                XtNlayoutType,  OL_FIXEDROWS,
                XtNmeasure,     1,
                0
            )
        );

    frontPanel.rew =
```

```
        CreateImageButton(
            w_control,
            rew_bits,
            rew_width,
            rew_height
        );

    frontPanel.stop =
        CreateImageButton(
            w_control,
            stop_bits,
            stop_width,
            stop_height
        );

    frontPanel.pause =
        CreateImageButton(
            w_control,
            pause_bits,
            pause_width,
            pause_height
        );

    frontPanel.play =
        CreateImageButton(
            w_control,
            play_bits,
            play_width,
            play_height);

    frontPanel.ff =
        CreateImageButton(
            w_control,
            ff_bits,
            ff_width,
            ff_height
        );

    XtGetValues(
        frontPanel.play,      /* each button could be different */
        tmpArg,
        TmpArgList(
            XtNforeground,   &frontPanel.fg,
            XtNbackground,   &frontPanel.bg,
            0
        )
    );

    XtAddCallback(
        frontPanel.rew, XtNselect, CBButtonLogic, REWIND);
    XtAddCallback(
```

```
            frontPanel.stop, XtNselect, CBButtonLogic, STOP);
    XtAddCallback(
            frontPanel.pause, XtNselect, CBButtonLogic, PAUSE);
    XtAddCallback(
            frontPanel.play, XtNselect, CBButtonLogic, PLAY);
    XtAddCallback(
            frontPanel.ff, XtNselect, CBButtonLogic, FORWARD);

    XtManageChild(w_control);
    return(w_control);
}


Widget CreateImageButton(w_parent, pBits, width, height)
    Widget      w_parent;
    char        *pBits;
    Dimension   width, height;
{
    Widget      w_button;
    XImage      *image;

    image =
        XYBitmapImageFromData(      /* Utility Library routine */
            w_parent,
            pBits,
            width,
            height
        );

    w_button =
        XtCreateManagedWidget(
            "imageButton",                /* instance name */
            oblongButtonWidgetClass,      /* widget class */
            w_parent,                     /* parent widget */
            tmpArg,                       /* arglist */
            TmpArgList(
                XtNlabelType,  OL_IMAGE,
                XtNlabelImage, image,
                XtNlabelTile,  FALSE,
                0
            )
        );

    return(w_button);
}


/*
 * CBButtonLogic() - user has pressed a button, so figure
 * out what the panel state should be.  Operation is the
 * same as any standard tape transport:
```

```
        - pressing PAUSE suspends REWIND, FAST FORWARD, and PLAY
        - pressing STOP clears all buttons
        - pressing REWIND, FAST FORWARD, and PLAY clears any
            other mode, but leaves PAUSE unchanged

 * New buttons (e.g. RECORD, REVERSE PLAY, NEXT, PREV) and
 * their logic can be added easily, using the existing
 * buttons as examples.  An interesting enhancement to this
 * program would be making certain buttons different
 * colors, such as a red RECORD button.
 *
 */
void CBButtonLogic(wid, client_data, call_data)
    Widget  wid;
    caddr_t client_data;
    caddr_t call_data;
{
    int     action = (int) client_data;
    void    UpdatePanel();

    switch(action) {
    case REWIND:
        frontPanel.state = REWIND | (frontPanel.state & PAUSE);
        break;
    case STOP:
        frontPanel.state = STOP;
        break;
    case PAUSE:
        frontPanel.state ^= PAUSE;
        break;
    case PLAY:
        frontPanel.state = PLAY | (frontPanel.state & PAUSE);
        break;
    case FORWARD:
        frontPanel.state = FORWARD | (frontPanel.state & PAUSE);
        break;
    default:
        OlWarning("Unknown action in CBButtonLogic()\n");
        break;
    }

    UpdatePanel();

    return;
}

/*
 * UpdatePanel() - update the panel's graphic representation,
 * highlighting and unhighlighting buttons as necessary.
 * This routine must be separate from the button callback,
```

```
 * since the application may need to modify the panel state in
 * response to other events, like reaching the end of the
 * tape.
 */
void UpdatePanel()
{
    extern FRONT_PANEL  frontPanel;
    static unsigned int last = STOP;
    unsigned int        set, unset, changed;
    void                HighlightButton();

    /*
     * determine which buttons have been changed (set or unset)
     */
    set = frontPanel.state & ~last;
    unset = ~frontPanel.state & last;
    changed = set | unset;


    /*
     * Set/Unset buttons that have changed.  Note that each
     * button could have its own foreground/background color
     * combination.
     */
    if (changed & REWIND) {
        HighlightButton(
            frontPanel.rew,            /* widget */
            frontPanel.state & REWIND, /* set? */
            frontPanel.fg,             /* foreground color */
            frontPanel.bg              /* background color */
        );
    }

    if (changed & PAUSE) {
        HighlightButton(
            frontPanel.pause,          /* widget */
            frontPanel.state & PAUSE,  /* set? */
            frontPanel.fg,             /* foreground color */
            frontPanel.bg              /* background color */
        );
    }

    if (changed & PLAY) {
        HighlightButton(
            frontPanel.play,           /* widget */
            frontPanel.state & PLAY,   /* set? */
            frontPanel.fg,             /* foreground color */
            frontPanel.bg              /* background color */
        );
    }
```

```
    if (changed & FORWARD) {
        HighlightButton(
            frontPanel.ff,                /* widget */
            frontPanel.state & FORWARD,   /* set? */
            frontPanel.fg,                /* foreground color */
            frontPanel.bg                 /* background color */
        );
    }

    last = frontPanel.state;              /* save state */
    return;
}


void HighlightButton(w_button, set, fg, bg)
    Widget      w_button;
    Boolean     set;
    Pixel       fg, bg;
{
    if (set) {
        XtSetValues(
            w_button,
            tmpArg,
            TmpArgList(
                XtNforeground,  bg, /* reverse */
                XtNbackground,  fg,
                0
            )
        );
    } else {
        XtSetValues(
            w_button,
            tmpArg,
            TmpArgList(
                XtNforeground,  fg, /* normal */
                XtNbackground,  bg,
                0
            )
        );
    }
    return;
}
```

Figure 5.14 A simple control panel

5.2.9 Exclusive Settings

The Exclusive Settings widget class arranges Rectangle Button children in a row/column format similar to Control Area. Additionally, it manages the set/unset state of its children such that only one button may be set at any time.

The example, exclusiv.c, creates an Exclusives container and adds several Rectangular Button children. Clicking SELECT on a button sets it and unsets the previously selected button. In Figure 5.15, the Mooney button is set.

```
/*
 * Demonstrate the OPEN LOOK Exclusives widget
 * @(#) sccs/s.exclusiv.c 1.6 last delta 2/9/90 10:55:55
 */
#include <X11/Intrinsic.h>
#include <X11/StringDefs.h>
#include <Xol/OpenLook.h>
#include <Xol/Exclusives.h>
#include <Xol/RectButton.h>
#include "xtutil.h"


Widget CreateInitialWidgets(w_parent)
    Widget  w_parent;
{
    Widget  w_choiceContainer, AddChoice();

    /*
     * Create the exclusive container - but don't manage it
     * until we have added the rectangular buttons.
     */
    w_choiceContainer =
       XtCreateWidget(
           "choices",              /* instance name */
           exclusivesWidgetClass,  /* class name */
           w_parent,               /* parent widget */
           NULL,                   /* arg list */
           0                       /* arg count */
       );

    /*
     * Add buttons as children of the Exclusive widget
     */
    AddChoice(w_choiceContainer, "Piper");
```

```
    AddChoice(w_choiceContainer, "Cessna");
    AddChoice(w_choiceContainer, "Beechcraft");
    AddChoice(w_choiceContainer, "Mooney");
    AddChoice(w_choiceContainer, "Grumman");
    AddChoice(w_choiceContainer, "Aerospatiale");

    XtManageChild(w_choiceContainer);
    return(w_choiceContainer);
}


Widget AddChoice(w_parent, label)
    Widget  w_parent;
    String  label;
{
    Widget  w_button;
    void    CBButtonChanged();

    w_button =
        XtCreateManagedWidget(
            label,                  /* instance name */
            rectButtonWidgetClass,  /* widget class */
            w_parent,               /* parent widget */
            tmpArg,                 /* arg list */
            TmpArgList(
                XtNlabel,   label,
                0
            )
        );
    XtAddCallback(w_button, XtNselect, CBButtonChanged, NULL);
    XtAddCallback(w_button, XtNunselect, CBButtonChanged, NULL);

    return(w_button);
}


static void CBButtonChanged(wid, client_data, call_data)
    Widget  wid;
    caddr_t client_data;
    caddr_t call_data;
{
    Boolean val;
    String  label;

    /*
     * get resource values from the widget
     */
    val = (Boolean) GetValue(wid, XtNset);
    label = (String) GetValue(wid, XtNlabel);

    dbg(
```

175

```
        "%s button: %s\n",
        label,
        val ? "SET" : "UNSET"
    );

    return;
}
```

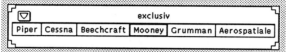

Figure 5.15 *The Exclusive Settings widget class*

As an option, setting the Exclusives resource XtNnoneSet to TRUE allows the user to set *at most* one button, rather than exactly one button. With this option, clicking SELECT on a set button unsets it.

5.2.10 Nonexclusive Settings

The Nonexclusive Settings widget class is similar to Exclusive Settings, except that it

- implements many-of-many instead of one-of-many choices
- allows Checkbox children in addition to Rectangular Button children

The example, nonexclu.c, lays out a grid of delicatessen sandwich choices and prints out a message when a choice is set or unset. In AddChoice, notice that since XtNlabel is not explicitly set, the label defaults to the widget instance name. Also, note that defining USE_CHECK_BOXES changes a single line of code to create Checkboxes instead of Rectangular Buttons.

```
/*
 * Demonstrate the OPEN LOOK Nonexclusives widget
 * @(#) sccs/s.nonexclu.c 1.8 last delta 4/22/90 18:15:41
 */
#include <X11/Intrinsic.h>
#include <X11/StringDefs.h>
#include <Xol/OpenLook.h>
#include <Xol/Nonexclusi.h>
#include <Xol/RectButton.h>
#include <Xol/CheckBox.h>
#include "xtutil.h"


Widget CreateInitialWidgets(w_parent)
    Widget  w_parent;
{
    Widget  w_frame, AddChoice(), AddCheckBox();

    /*
     * Create the container - but don't manage it until
     * we have added the rectangular buttons.
     */
    w_frame =
        XtCreateWidget(
            "sandwich",                       /* instance name */
            nonexclusivesWidgetClass,    /* widget class */
            w_parent,                         /* parent widget */
            tmpArg,                           /* arg list */
            TmpArgList(
                XtNlayoutType,      OL_FIXEDROWS,
                XtNmeasure,         5,
                0
            )
        );

    AddChoice(w_frame, "Ham");
    AddChoice(w_frame, "Roast Beef");
    AddChoice(w_frame, "Turkey");
    AddChoice(w_frame, "Pastrami");
    AddChoice(w_frame, "Tuna");

    AddChoice(w_frame, "Cheddar");
    AddChoice(w_frame, "Swiss");
    AddChoice(w_frame, "Cream");
    AddChoice(w_frame, "Provolone");
    AddChoice(w_frame, "Jack");

    AddChoice(w_frame, "Mayo");
    AddChoice(w_frame, "Mustard");
    AddChoice(w_frame, "Dijon");
    AddChoice(w_frame, "Oil");
```

177

```
        AddChoice(w_frame,  "Vinegar");

        AddChoice(w_frame,  "Lettuce");
        AddChoice(w_frame,  "Tomato");
        AddChoice(w_frame,  "Pickle");
        AddChoice(w_frame,  "Onion");
        AddChoice(w_frame,  "Sprouts");

        XtManageChild(w_frame);

        return(w_frame);
}


Widget AddChoice(w_parent, label)
        Widget   w_parent;
        String   label;
{
        Widget   w_button;
        void     CBPrintStatus();

        w_button =
            XtCreateManagedWidget(
                label,                  /* instance name */
#ifdef USE_CHECK_BOXES
                checkBoxWidgetClass,    /* class name */
#else
                rectButtonWidgetClass,  /* class name */
#endif
                w_parent,               /* parent widget */
                NULL,                   /* arg list */
                0
            );

        XtAddCallback(w_button, XtNselect, CBPrintStatus, NULL);
        XtAddCallback(w_button, XtNunselect, CBPrintStatus, NULL);

        return(w_button);
}


static void CBPrintStatus(w, client_data, call_data)
        Widget   w;
        caddr_t  client_data;
        caddr_t  call_data;
{
        Boolean val=0;
        String  label=NULL;

        XtGetValues(
            w,
```

```
        tmpArg,
        TmpArgList(
            XtNlabel,    &label,
            XtNset,      &val,
            0
        )
    );

    dbg(
        "%s button: %s\n",
        label ? label : "NULL",
        val ? "SET" : "UNSET"
    );

    return;
}
```

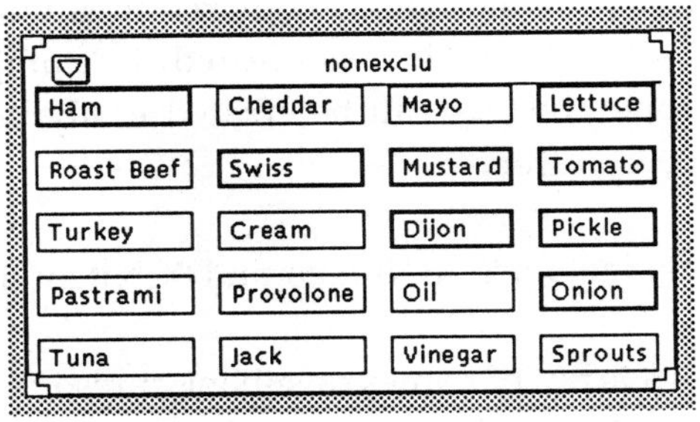

Figure 5.16   The Nonexclusive Setting widget class, managing Rectangular Buttons

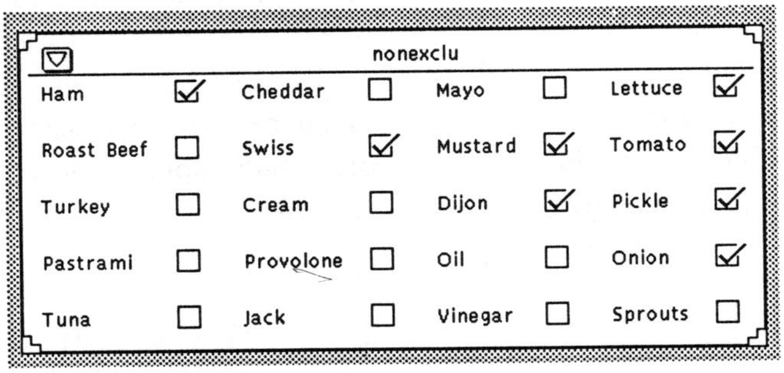

Figure 5.17   The Nonexclusive Setting widget class, managing Checkboxes

179

5.2.11 Flat Widgets

For applications that need large, homogeneous arrays of Exclusive or Nonexclusive Settings, the OPEN LOOK widget set provides *flat widgets*. Rather than managing a collection of discrete Rectangular Buttons or Checkboxes, flat widgets implement the choice functionality directly. Currently, there are three flat widgets in the OPEN LOOK Toolkit: Flat Checkbox, Flat Exclusives, and Flat Nonexclusives. All three will be covered in this section.

Using flat widgets is a bit more complicated than using normal widgets, but it is also more efficient, especially for large arrays. The main difference is that using flat widgets requires more planning but little to no work after the widget is created; by comparison, normal Exclusives and Nonexclusives can be created easily but require additional work to add children.

The keys to flat widgets are XtNitems and XtNitemFields:

XtNitemFields—An array of names of subobject resources (for example, XtNlabel) you wish to specify for each choice item. Unspecified resources inherit their values from the flat widget container object.

XtNitems—An array of structures containing resource values to match XtNitemFields.

In flatwidg.c, we specify only the trivial case of subobject resources (the label string), although we could easily specify additional resources without changing the code structure.

```
/*
 * Demonstrate the OPEN LOOK Flat Widgets
 * @(#) 1.7 last delta 2/18/90 09:20:17
 */
#include <X11/Intrinsic.h>
#include <X11/StringDefs.h>
#include <Xol/OpenLook.h>
#include <Xol/Nonexclusi.h>
#include <Xol/RectButton.h>
#include <Xol/FCheckBox.h>
#include <Xol/FNonexclus.h>
#include <Xol/FExclusive.h>
#include "xtutil.h"

/*
 * ensure that one of these is defined
 */
#ifdef USE_CHECKBOX
#define FOOBAR   static dummy;
#endif
#ifdef USE_NONEXCLUSIVES
#define FOOBAR   static dummy;
#endif
#ifdef USE_EXCLUSIVES
#define FOOBAR   static dummy;
#endif

FOOBAR

/*
 * itemFields[] -  array of choice item resource names
 */
String  itemFields[] = {
    XtNlabel,
};
#define NR_ITEM_FIELDS  \
    (sizeof(itemFields) / sizeof(itemFields[0]))

/*
 * item[] - array of choice item resources
 */
typedef struct _Item {
    String      label;
} Item;
Item    items[] = {
    { "Ham",      },
    { "Roast Beef", },
    { "Turkey", },
    { "Pastrami",    },
    { "Tuna",     },
```

```
        { "Cheddar",     },
        { "Swiss",  },
        { "Cream",  },
        { "Provolone",   },
        { "Jack",   },

        { "Mayo",   },
        { "Mustard",     },
        { "Dijon",  },
        { "Oil",    },
        { "Vinegar",     },

        { "Lettuce",     },
        { "Tomato", },
        { "Pickle", },
        { "Onion",  },
        { "Sprouts",     },
};
#define NR_ITEMS     (sizeof(items) / sizeof(items[0]))



Widget CreateInitialWidgets(w_parent)
    Widget   w_parent;
{
    Widget   w_sandwich;
    void     CBSet(), CBUnset();


    w_sandwich =
        XtCreateManagedWidget(
            "sandwich",                      /* instance name */
#ifdef USE_CHECKBOX
            flatCheckBoxWidgetClass,         /* widget class */
#endif
#ifdef USE_NONEXCLUSIVES
            flatNonexclusivesWidgetClass,    /* widget class */
#endif
#ifdef USE_EXCLUSIVES
            flatExclusivesWidgetClass,       /* widget class */
#endif
            w_parent,           /* parent widget */
            tmpArg,             /* arg list */
            TmpArgList(
                XtNlayoutType,      OL_FIXEDROWS,
                XtNmeasure,         5,
                XtNitems,           items,
                XtNnumItems,        NR_ITEMS,
                XtNitemFields,      itemFields,
                XtNnumItemFields,   NR_ITEM_FIELDS,
#ifdef USE_CHECKBOX
```

```
                    XtNlabelJustify,     OL_RIGHT,
#else
                    XtNlabelJustify,     OL_LEFT,
#endif
                    XtNselectProc,       CBSet,
                    XtNunselectProc,     CBUnset,
                    0
            )
        );

    return(w_sandwich);
}


/*
 * CBSet() - demonstrate indirect way to get
 * sub-object resource values
 */
static void CBSet(wid, client_data, call_data)
    Widget  wid;
    caddr_t client_data;
    caddr_t call_data;
{
    OlFlatCallData  *ol_flat_call_data =
                                (OlFlatCallData *) call_data;
    String       label;

    /*
     * Get the resource value from the sub-object
     */
    OlFlatGetValues(
        wid,                               /* widget */
        ol_flat_call_data->item_index,     /* item_index */
        tmpArg,                            /* args */
        TmpArgList(
            XtNlabel,    &label,
            0
        )
    );

    dbg("set %s\n", label);

    return;
}
/*
 * CBUnset() - use direct access to sub-object resources.
 * (The sub-object data is actually maintained here in the
 * application.)
 */
static void CBUnset(w, client_data, call_data)
```

```
    Widget  w;
    caddr_t client_data;
    caddr_t call_data;
{
    OlFlatCallData  *ol_flat_call_data =
                                (OlFlatCallData *) call_data;
    extern Item items[]; /* same we used to create flat widget */

    dbg(
        "unset = %s\n",
        items[ol_flat_call_data->item_index].label
    );
    return;
}
```

The array itemFields contains just one element, XtNlabel. Following that, items contains an Item structure for each subobject.

5.2.11.1 Adding Subobject Resources

To specify additional resources, we would:

- add the resource name to itemFields
- add a field to Item that matched the resource type
- add an entry in each Item structure in items to specify the resources value for that subobject

For example, to specify subobject specific client_data, add the resource name to itemFields:

```
String itemFields[] = {
    XtNlabel,
    XtNclientData,
};
```

Add a field to Item:

```
typedef struct _Item {
    String label;
    XtPointer    client_data;
} Item;
```

And add the value entries in the item array:

```
Item    items[] = {
        { "Ham",              (XtPointer) 785,           },
        { "Roast Beef"        (XtPointer) roastBeef,     },
...
```

5.2.11.1.1 Flat Callbacks

Flat widgets handle callbacks differently than normal widgets. For one thing, they call a single callback procedure, rather than a callback list, and this callback applies to all subobjects. The flat widgets provide two callback resources: XtNselectProc and XtNunselectProc, which are set using standard resource techniques rather than XtAddCallback.

The callbacks are handed a pointer to an OlFlatCallData structure, which contains the items and itemFields data we passed to XtCreateManagedWidget, as well as the index of the subobject item initiating the callback. In flatwidg.c, the two callbacks, CBSet and CBUnset, demonstrate two different techniques for deriving subobject information.

CBSet calls the special *get-values* routine OlFlatGetValues, which is identical to XtGetValues except that it takes the subobject index as an additional parameter. We can change the value of a subobject's resource by using the complementary function, OlFlatSetValues. We cannot, however, change subobject resources that were not provided in XtNitemFields.

By contrast, CBUnset looks directly at the items data we pass to XtCreateManagedWidget when creating the flat widget. This is perfectly valid, as the widget shares this data directly with the application—it does not copy it. We are also free to directly change the data, as long as we notify the container object when we are done by setting XtNitemsTouched to TRUE.

The following frames show the Flat Checkbox, Flat Exclusive Settings, and Flat Nonexclusive Settings using the deli-sandwich dataset from the previous section.

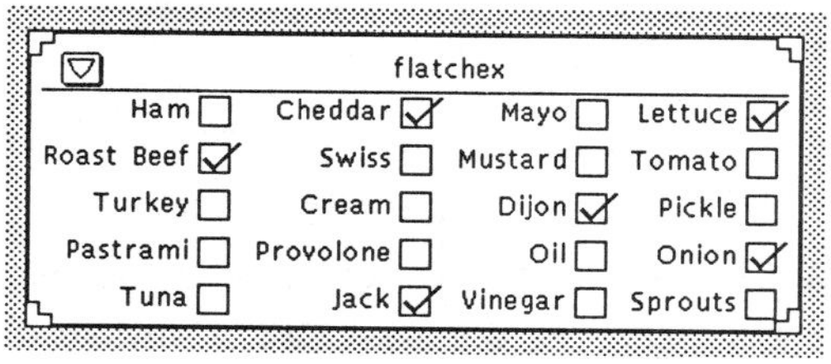

Figure 5.18 The Flat Checkbox widget class

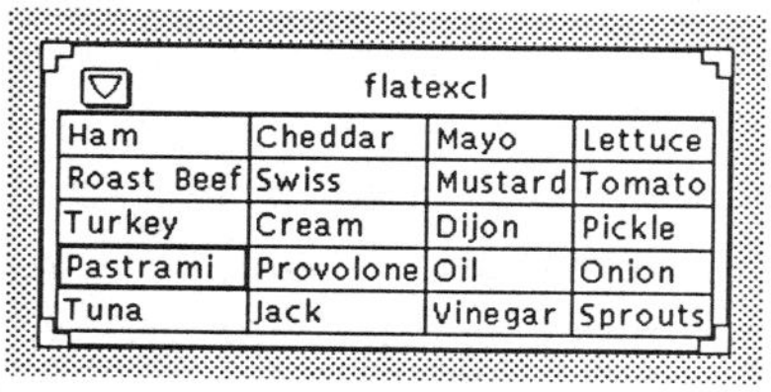

Figure 5.19 The Flat Exclusive Settings widget class

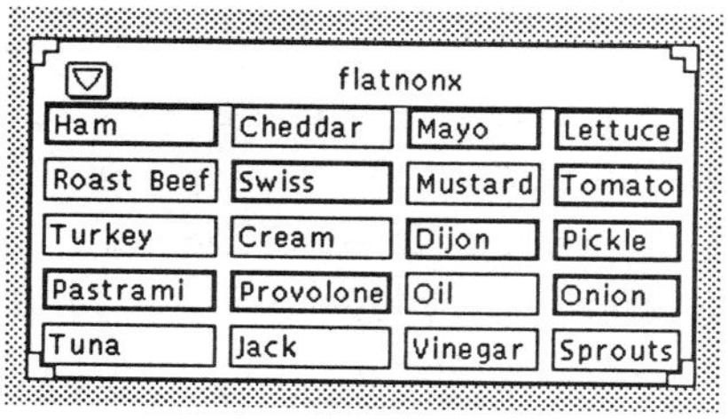

Figure 5.20 The Flat Nonexclusive Settings widget class

5.2.12 Bulletin Board

If you need absolute control over widget layout, use the Bulletin Board. Using this widget class, the application assumes responsibility for calculating child widget sizes and placement. Bulletin Board knows only how to adjust its own geometry, according to the following layout modes:

OL_MINIMIZE—Maintains size just large enough to contain all children.

OL_IGNORE—Ignores children's extents.

OL_MAXIMIZE—Grows to encompass all children, but never shrinks automatically.

In the example, bboard.c, we create a Bulletin Board and add several children, manually calculating their positions. The most complicated of these is in the placement of the Oblong Button, labeled Takeoff. Of course, we could manually position each of the items in the checklist, too, but rather than be masochistic, we use a Nonexclusive Settings widget, instead.

```
/*
 * Demonstrate the OPEN LOOK Bulletin Board widget
 * @(#) sccs/s.bboard.c 1.8 last delta 2/9/90 10:11:53
 */
#include <X11/Intrinsic.h>
#include <X11/StringDefs.h>
#include <Xol/OpenLook.h>
#include <Xol/BulletinBo.h>
#include <Xol/OblongButt.h>
#include <Xol/Nonexclusi.h>
#include <Xol/CheckBox.h>
#include <Xol/StaticText.h>
#include "xtutil.h"

#define PAD 4


Widget CreateInitialWidgets(w_parent)
    Widget  w_parent;
{
    extern Widget    AddTakeoffButton();
    extern Widget    AddCheckList(), AddComm();
    Widget           w_cockpit, w_button;
    Widget           w_checklist, w_comm;
    Dimension        commWidth, commHeight;
    Dimension        checklistWidth, checklistHeight;
```

```
    Dimension         buttonWidth, buttonHeight;

    /*
     * Create the Bulletin Board container - but don't
     * tell its parent to manage it until we have added
     * the children.
     */
    w_cockpit =
        XtCreateWidget(
            "cockpit",                  /* instance name */
            bulletinBoardWidgetClass,   /* class name */
            w_parent,                   /* parent widget */
            tmpArg,
            TmpArgList(
                XtNlayout,          OL_MINIMIZE,
                0
            )
        );

    /*
     * Add the Communications Radio window.
     */
    w_comm =
        AddComm(
            w_cockpit,      /* parent widget */
            0,              /* x position */
            PAD             /* y position */
        );
    XtGetValues(
        w_comm,
        tmpArg,
        TmpArgList(
            XtNheight,      &commHeight,
            XtNwidth,       &commWidth,
            0
        )
    );

    /*
     * Add the checklist controls
     */
    w_checklist =
        AddCheckList(
            w_cockpit,              /* parent widget */
            0,                      /* x position */
            commHeight + (2 * PAD)  /* y position */
        );
    XtGetValues(
        w_checklist,
        tmpArg,
        TmpArgList(
```

```
                XtNheight,         &checklistHeight,
                XtNwidth,          &checklistWidth,
                0
        )
    );

    /*
     * Add the takeoff button and position it relative to the
     * other controls.
     */
    w_button =
        AddTakeoffButton(
            w_cockpit,            /* parent widget */
            checklistWidth,       /* x position */
            commHeight            /* y position */
        );
    XtGetValues(
        w_button,
        tmpArg,
        TmpArgList(
            XtNheight,         &buttonHeight,
            XtNwidth,          &buttonWidth,
            0
        )
    );

    SetValue(
        w_button,
        XtNx,
        ((commWidth - checklistWidth) / 2)
            + checklistWidth
            - (buttonWidth / 2)
    );

    SetValue(
        w_button,
        XtNy,
        (checklistHeight / 2) + commHeight
            - (buttonHeight / 2)
    );


    XtManageChild(w_cockpit);    /* add widget to parent's list */
    return(w_cockpit);
}

Widget AddTakeoffButton(w_parent, x, y)
    Widget      w_parent;
    Position    x, y;
{
    Widget  w_button;
```

```
    extern  exit();

    w_button =
        XtCreateManagedWidget(
            "takeoffButton",
            oblongButtonWidgetClass,
            w_parent,
            tmpArg,
            TmpArgList(
                XtNlabel,    "Takeoff",
                XtNx,        x,
                XtNy,        y,
                0
            )
        );

    XtAddCallback(w_button, XtNselect, exit, 0);

    return(w_button);
}


Widget AddCheckList(w_parent, x, y)
    Widget       w_parent;
    Position     x, y;
{
    Widget  w_frame, AddCheckBox();

    /*
     * Create the container - but don't manage it until
     * we have added the rectangular buttons.
     */
    w_frame =
        XtCreateWidget(
            "checkList",                 /* instance name */
            nonexclusivesWidgetClass,    /* widget class */
            w_parent,                    /* parent widget */
            tmpArg,                      /* arg list */
            TmpArgList(
                XtNlayoutType,  OL_FIXEDCOLS,
                XtNmeasure,     1,
                XtNx,           x,
                XtNy,           y,
                0
            )
        );


    AddCheckBox(w_frame, "Mixture: rich");
    AddCheckBox(w_frame, "Trim: takeoff");
    AddCheckBox(w_frame, "Carb Heat: cold");
```

190

```
        AddCheckBox(w_frame, "Flaps: 15 degrees");
        AddCheckBox(w_frame, "Throttle: full");

        XtManageChild(w_frame);

        return(w_frame);
}


Widget AddCheckBox(w_parent, label)
        Widget   w_parent;
        String   label;
{
        Widget   w_button;
        void     PrintStatus();

        w_button =
            XtCreateManagedWidget(
                label,                  /* instance name */
                checkBoxWidgetClass,    /* class name */
                w_parent,               /* parent widget */
                tmpArg,                 /* arg list */
                TmpArgList(
                    XtNlabel,    label,
                    0
                )
            );

        return(w_button);
}


#define MESSAGE \
    "Tower: Barnburner eight-zero-whiskey, cleared for takeoff."

Widget AddComm(w_parent, x, y)
        Widget       w_parent;
        Position     x, y;
{
        Widget   w_comm;

        w_comm =
            XtCreateManagedWidget(
                "radioText",            /* instance name */
                staticTextWidgetClass,  /* widget class */
                w_parent,               /* parent widget */
                tmpArg,                 /* arg list */
                TmpArgList(
                    XtNstring,           MESSAGE,
                    XtNx,                x,
                    XtNy,                y,
```

```
            XtNborderWidth,      1,
               0
         )
      );

   return(w_comm);
}
```

```
 ┌────────────────────────────────────────────┐
 │ ┌──┐                   bboard                │
 │ │▽ │                                         │
 │ └──┘                                         │
 │ ┌─────────────────────────────────────────┐ │
 │ │Tower: Barnburner eight−zero−whiskey, cleared for takeoff.│ │
 │ └─────────────────────────────────────────┘ │
 │  Mixture: rich        ☑                      │
 │                                              │
 │  Trim: takeoff        ☑                      │
 │                                              │
 │  Carb Heat: cold      ☑        ( Takeoff )   │
 │                                              │
 │  Flaps: 15 degrees    ☑                      │
 │                                              │
 │  Throttle: full       ☑                      │
 └────────────────────────────────────────────┘
```

Figure 5.21 The Bulletin Board widget class

5.2.13 Text Fields

Text Fields prompt the user for a single line of text input, providing basic line-editing functions and horizontal scrolling.

Text Fields sharing a common Control Area, Bulletin Board, or Form ancestor (not necessarily the parent) can have that widget manage the input focus among the Text Fields. The ancestor maintains a list of all descendents requesting input focus and traverses this list when the user presses the NEXTFIELD and PREVFIELD keys.[4]

The following example creates a Control Area and three Text Field widgets with Caption parents. The Control Area has its XtNtraversalManager resource set to TRUE, so it will be looking for

---

[4]The default settings for these keys is Tab and Shift Tab, respectively, but they can be remapped by the user from the Workspace Manager's Properties menu.

Text or Text Field descendents with XtNtraversalOn resources set TRUE.

```
/*
 * Demonstrate OPEN LOOK Text Field widget and
 * Input Focus management
 * @(#) sccs/s.txtfield.c 1.8 last delta 2/9/90 15:55:35
 */
#include <X11/Intrinsic.h>
#include <X11/StringDefs.h>
#include <Xol/OpenLook.h>
#include <Xol/TextField.h>
#include <Xol/Caption.h>
#include <Xol/ControlAre.h>
#include "xtutil.h"


Widget CreateInitialWidgets(w_parent)
    Widget  w_parent;
{
    Widget  w_control, w_name, w_address, w_phone;
    Widget  CreateCaptionedTextField();

    w_control =
        XtCreateWidget(
            "namePanel",
            controlAreaWidgetClass,
            w_parent,
            tmpArg,
            TmpArgList(
                XtNalignCaptions,       TRUE,
                XtNlayoutType,          OL_FIXEDCOLS,
                XtNmeasure,             1,
                XtNtraversalManager,    TRUE,
                0
            )
        );

    w_name = CreateCaptionedTextField(w_control, "Name:");
    w_address = CreateCaptionedTextField(w_control, "Address:");
    w_phone = CreateCaptionedTextField(w_control, "Phone:");

    XtManageChild(w_control);

    return(w_control);
}

Widget CreateCaptionedTextField(w_parent, label)
    Widget  w_parent;
    String  label;
```

193

```
{
    Widget       w_caption, w_textField;
    void         CBVerifyTextField();

    /*
     * Create the Caption for the text field
     */
    w_caption =
        XtCreateManagedWidget(
            "fieldLabel",        /* instance name */
            captionWidgetClass,  /* widget class */
            w_parent,            /* parent widget */
            tmpArg,              /* arg list */
            TmpArgList(
                XtNlabel,        label,
                0
            )
        );


    /*
     * Create the Text Field itself
     */
    w_textField =
        XtCreateManagedWidget(
            "textField",          /* instance name */
            textFieldWidgetClass, /* widget class */
            w_caption,            /* parent widget */
            tmpArg,               /* arg list */
            TmpArgList(
                XtNwidth,        200,
                XtNtraversalOn,  TRUE,
                0
            )
        );
    XtAddCallback(
        w_textField, XtNverification, CBVerifyTextField, NULL);

    return(w_caption);
}

static void CBVerifyTextField(wid, client_data, call_data)
    Widget  wid;
    caddr_t client_data;
    caddr_t call_data;
{
    OlTextFieldVerify    *verify =
                            (OlTextFieldVerify *) call_data;

    dbg("string value: %s\n", verify->string);
    return;
}
```

The callback, CBVerifyTextField, is invoked whenever the input focus leaves a Text Field (as in the case when the user presses NEXTFIELD or PREVFIELD, or clicks SELECT on another client) or the user presses Return.

In Figure 5.22, notice the left and right scroll arrows on the Address line.

Figure 5.22 The Text Field widget class

5.2.14 Text

The Text widget class provides multi-line text editing, with a variety of user-interface and programmatic-interface options. In addition to keyboard input-focus traversal (mentioned previously in the "Text Fields" section), the Text widget class has the following options:

- horizontal and vertical scrollbars
- read-only text
- use a disk file as source text
- grow horizontally and/or vertically to accommodate text input
- automatic word wrap to next line
- programmatic interface to the text buffer
- callbacks for input focus leave, insert cursor motion, text modification

The example program, text.c, creates a single Text widget and adds callbacks that get called when:

- the input focus leaves the widget (the same as seen previously in the Text Fields section)
- the text insert point has moved
- text has been inserted, deleted, replaced, or otherwise modified

```
/*
 * Demonstrate the OPEN LOOK Text widget
 * @(#) sccs/s.text.c 1.7 last delta 2/9/90 16:34:03
 */
#include <X11/Intrinsic.h>
#include <X11/StringDefs.h>
#include <Xol/OpenLook.h>
#include <Xol/Text.h>
#include "xtutil.h"
#include <stdio.h>


#define MESSAGE \
"Now is the time for all good men to come \
to the aid of the party.  The quick brown fox \
jumped over the lazy dog.  All men are created equal. \
We, the people, in order to form a more perfect union...."

char    buf[BUFSIZ];      /* edit buffer */

Widget CreateInitialWidgets(w_parent)
    Widget  w_parent;
{
    Widget  w_text;
    void    CBLeaveVerify();     /* forward declaration */
    void    CBMotionVerify();    /* forward declaration */
    void    CBModifyVerify();    /* forward declaration */

    /*
     * stuff some text into our read/write edit buffer
     */
    strncpy(buf, MESSAGE, min(sizeof(buf), sizeof(MESSAGE)));

    w_text =
        XtCreateManagedWidget(
            "textPane",          /* instance name */
            textWidgetClass,     /* widget class */
            w_parent,            /* parent widget */
```

```
            tmpArg,                 /* argument list */
            TmpArgList(
                XtNeditType,        OL_TEXT_EDIT,
                XtNgrow,            OL_GROW_OFF,
                XtNhorizontalSB,    FALSE,
                XtNmaximumSize,     sizeof(buf),
                XtNrecomputeSize,   FALSE,
                XtNsourceType,      OL_STRING_SOURCE,
                XtNstring,          buf,
                XtNverticalSB,      TRUE,
                XtNwrap,            TRUE,
                XtNwrapBreak,       OL_WRAP_WHITE_SPACE,
                0
            )
        );
    XtAddCallback(
        w_text, XtNleaveVerification, CBLeaveVerify, NULL);
    XtAddCallback(
        w_text, XtNmotionVerification, CBMotionVerify, NULL);
    XtAddCallback(
        w_text, XtNmodifyVerification, CBModifyVerify, NULL);

    return(w_text);
}

static void CBLeaveVerify(w, client_data, call_data)
    Widget  w;
    caddr_t client_data;
    caddr_t call_data;
{
    OlTextVerifyPtr pTextVerify = (OlTextVerifyPtr) call_data;

    if (pTextVerify->doit == FALSE)
        return;             /* another callback gave thumbs down */

    fprintf(stdout,
        "leaveVerificaton\n");
    fprintf(stdout,
        "\tcurrInsert = %d\n", pTextVerify->currInsert);

    pTextVerify->doit = TRUE;   /* okay the action */

    return;
}

static void CBMotionVerify(w, client_data, call_data)
    Widget  w;
    caddr_t client_data;
    caddr_t call_data;
{
    OlTextVerifyPtr pTextVerify = (OlTextVerifyPtr) call_data;
```

197

```
        fprintf(stdout,
            "MotionVerificaton\n");
        fprintf(stdout,
            "\tcurrInsert = %d\n", pTextVerify->currInsert);
        fprintf(stdout,
            "\tnewInsert = %d\n", pTextVerify->newInsert);

        return;
}

static void CBModifyVerify(w, client_data, call_data)
    Widget  w;
    caddr_t client_data;
    caddr_t call_data;
{
        OlTextVerifyPtr pTextVerify = (OlTextVerifyPtr) call_data;

        fprintf(stdout,
            "ModifyVerificaton\n");
        fprintf(stdout,
            "\tcurrInsert = %d\n", pTextVerify->currInsert);
        fprintf(stdout,
            "\tstartPos = %d\n", pTextVerify->startPos);
        fprintf(stdout,
            "\tendPos = %d\n", pTextVerify->endPos);
        fprintf(stdout,
            "\ttext = \n");
        fprintf(stdout,
            "\t\tfirstPos = %d\n", pTextVerify->text->firstPos);
        fprintf(stdout,
            "\t\tlength = %d\n", pTextVerify->text->length);
        fprintf(stdout,
            "\t\tptr = ");
        write(
            fileno(stdout),              /* get fd of output stream */
            pTextVerify->text->ptr,      /* text to write */
            pTextVerify->text->length    /* character count */
        );
        fputc('\n', stdout);

        return;
}
```

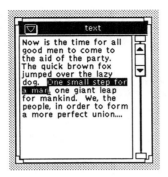

Figure 5.23 The Text widget class

5.2.15 Menu Button

Menu Buttons are Oblong Buttons with built-in menu semantics: if the "power-user" option is on,[5] clicking MENU on a Menu Button pops up its associated menu, while clicking SELECT activates the default item in that menu. If the "power-user" option is off, clicking either SELECT or MENU on a Menu Button pops up the menu.

To the application, the menu pane looks just like another Control Area. Applications obtain the Menu Pane widget (which is automatically created when you create the Menu Button) by inquiring the value of XtNmenuPane after creating the Menu Button. To the user, the menu pane behaves much like any other pop-up menu.

The following example, menubutt.c, creates a Menu Button, gets the value of XtNmenuPane, and adds several Oblong Buttons to it.

---

[5]To set the "power-user" option, bring up the Miscellaneous property sheet from the Workspace Manager and set "SELECT Mouse Press" to "Displays Default."

```c
/*
 * Demonstrate the OPEN LOOK Menu Button widget and gadget
 * @(#) sccs/s.menubutt.c 1.9 last delta 2/9/90 17:52:43
 */
#include <X11/Intrinsic.h>
#include <X11/StringDefs.h>
#include <Xol/OpenLook.h>
#include <Xol/OblongButt.h>
#include <Xol/MenuButton.h>
#include "xtutil.h"

#define USE_GADGETS

Widget CreateInitialWidgets(w_parent)
    Widget  w_parent;
{
    Widget  w_menuButton, w_controlArea, w_button, AddItem();

    w_menuButton =
        XtCreateWidget(
            "editMenuButton",            /* instance name */
#ifdef USE_GADGETS
            menuButtonGadgetClass,       /* widget class */
#else
            menuButtonWidgetClass,       /* widget class */
#endif
            w_parent,            /* parent widget */
            tmpArg,              /* arglist */
            TmpArgList(
                XtNlabel,           "Edit",
                XtNtitle,           "Edit",
                XtNpushpin,         OL_OUT,
                XtNrecomputeSize,   FALSE,
                0
            )
        );

    w_controlArea = (Widget) GetValue(w_menuButton, XtNmenuPane);

    (void)  AddItem(w_controlArea, "Cut");
    (void)  AddItem(w_controlArea, "Copy");
    (void)  AddItem(w_controlArea, "Paste");
    w_button = AddItem(w_controlArea, "Undo");
    SetValue(w_button, XtNdefault, TRUE);
    (void)  AddItem(w_controlArea, "Again");

    XtManageChild(w_menuButton);
    return(w_menuButton);
}
```

```
Widget AddItem(w_parent, label)
    Widget   w_parent;
    String   label;
{
    Widget   w_button;

    w_button =
        XtCreateManagedWidget(
            label,                         /* instance name */
#ifdef USE_GADGETS
            oblongButtonGadgetClass,       /* widget class */
#else
            oblongButtonWidgetClass,       /* widget class */
#endif
            w_parent,                      /* parent widget */
            NULL,
            0
        );

    return(w_button);
}
```

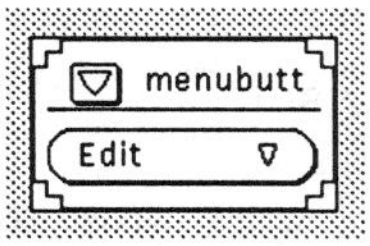

Figure 5.24 The Menu Button widget class

Figure 5.25 A Menu Button with the menu popped up

One especially handy OPEN LOOK GUI feature is the optional menu
pushpin. Clicking SELECT on a pushpin changes the menu from a pop-
up to a stay-up, at which point it remains on the screen until the pin

201

is pulled out by again clicking SELECT. In addition, the user can relocate stay-up menus anywhere on the screen.

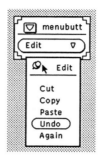

Figure 5.26 A pinned pop-up menu

5.2.16 Menu

Use the Menu widget class to create pop-up menus. Menus have nearly the same characteristics as Menu Buttons except that:

- they do not have the default-item preview capability, as there is nowhere to display it. Instead, when the menu is popped up, the cursor is positioned next to the default item.

- the menu title is always displayed, even as a pop-up, whereas the title of Menu Button menus is only displayed when the menu is pinned into a stay-up.

In the following example, menu.c, we create a Menu as the child of a Static Text widget. Note that as subclasses of Shell, Menus are created with XtCreatePopupShell, rather than XtCreateWidget, and can be pop-up children of primitive widgets, such as Static Text. To this Menu we add several items, including a Menu Button, several Oblong Buttons, and a new widget class, Stub. We will look at the Stub widget class in more detail later, but this example shows how it can be used to visually separate items in a Menu.

```
/*
 * Demonstrate the OPEN LOOK MenuShell Widget
 * @(#) sccs/s.menu.c 1.7 last delta 2/9/90 18:37:13
 */
#include <X11/Intrinsic.h>
#include <X11/StringDefs.h>
#include <Xol/OpenLook.h>
#include <Xol/MenuButton.h>
#include <Xol/OblongButt.h>
#include <Xol/StaticText.h>
#include <Xol/Stub.h>
#include <Xol/Menu.h>
#include "xtutil.h"


Widget CreateInitialWidgets(w_parent)
    Widget  w_parent;
{
    Widget  w_frame;
    Widget  AddMainMenu();

    w_frame =
        XtCreateManagedWidget(
            "frame",
            staticTextWidgetClass,
            w_parent,
            tmpArg,
            TmpArgList(
                XtNstring,   "Press MENU button in here",
                0
            )
        );

    AddMainMenu(w_frame);

    return(w_frame);
}

Widget AddMainMenu(w_parent)
    Widget  w_parent;
{
    Widget  w_menu, w_controlArea, w_button;
    Widget  AddOblongButton(), AddCutMenuButton();

    w_menu =
        XtCreatePopupShell(
            "menu",                       /* instance name */
            menuShellWidgetClass,         /* widget class */
            w_parent,                     /* parent widget */
            tmpArg,                       /* arglist */
            TmpArgList(
```

```
                        XtNtitle,        "Selection",
                        XtNpushpin,      OL_OUT,
                        0
                )
        );

    w_controlArea = (Widget) GetValue(w_menu, XtNmenuPane);

    w_button = AddCutMenuButton(w_controlArea, "Cut");
    w_button = AddOblongButton(w_controlArea, "Copy");
    SetValue(w_button, XtNdefault, TRUE);
    w_button = AddOblongButton(w_controlArea, "Paste");

    /*
     * space between the previous menu items and the next ones
     */
    XtCreateManagedWidget(
        "menuSpacer",
        stubWidgetClass,
        w_controlArea,
        tmpArg,
        TmpArgList(
            XtNheight,      10,
            XtNwidth,       1,  /* must have non-zero width */
            XtNborderWidth, 0,
            0
        )
    );

    w_button = AddOblongButton(w_controlArea, "Undo");
    w_button = AddOblongButton(w_controlArea, "Again");

    return(w_menu);
}


Widget AddOblongButton(w_parent, label)
    Widget  w_parent;
    String  label;
{
    Widget  w_button;

    w_button =
        XtCreateManagedWidget(
            label,                      /* instance name */
            oblongButtonWidgetClass,    /* widget class */
            w_parent,                   /* parent widget */
            tmpArg,                     /* arglist */
            TmpArgList(
                XtNlabel,   label,
                0
```

```
            )
        );

    return(w_button);
}


Widget AddCutMenuButton(w_parent)
    Widget   w_parent;
{
    Widget w_menu, w_button, w_control, AddOblongButton();

    w_menu =
        XtCreateWidget(
            "cutMenu",                    /* instance name */
            menuButtonGadgetClass,        /* widget class */
            w_parent,                     /* parent widget */
            tmpArg,                       /* arglist */
            TmpArgList(
                XtNlabel,         "Cut",
                XtNpushpin,       OL_NONE,
                0
            )
        );

    w_control = (Widget) GetValue(w_menu, XtNmenuPane);

    w_button = AddOblongButton(w_control, "Append Clipboard");
    w_button = AddOblongButton(w_control, "Replace Clipboard");
    SetValue(w_button, XtNdefault, TRUE);

    XtManageChild(w_menu);
    return(w_menu);
}
```

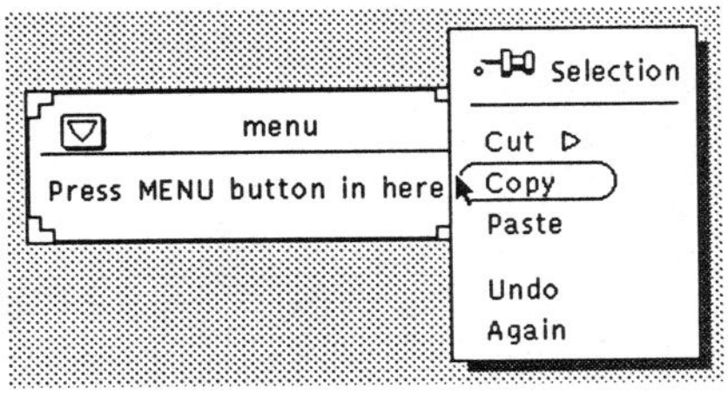

Figure 5.27 The Menu widget class

5.2.17 Abbreviated Menu Button

The Abbreviated Menu Button offers yet another way to access menus, this one with the added feature of an optional display window to view the current selection and preview the default. The Abbreviated Menu Button widget handles the previewing, but the application is responsible for creating the preview-window widget and updating its contents when the user chooses a new item from the menu.

The example program, abbrev.c, presents a font-family choice as an Abbreviated Menu Button, with a Caption-like label and a preview window.

```
/*
 * Demonstrate the OPEN LOOK Abbreviated Menu Button widget
 * @(#) sccs/s.abbrev.c 1.1 last delta 4/5/90 20:41:18
 */
#include <X11/Intrinsic.h>
#include <X11/StringDefs.h>
#include <Xol/OpenLook.h>
#include <Xol/AbbrevMenu.h>
#include <Xol/ControlAre.h>
#include <Xol/FExclusive.h>
#include <Xol/RectButton.h>
#include <Xol/StaticText.h>
#include "xtutil.h"

static Widget   w_currentSelection;

typedef struct _Item {
    String      label;
} Item;

static String itemFields[] = {
    XtNlabel,
};
#define NR_ITEM_FIELDS  \
    (sizeof(itemFields) / sizeof(itemFields[0]))

static Item items[] = {
    { "Avant Garde",    },
    { "Bookman",        },
    { "Courier",        },
    { "Garamound",      },
    { "Goudy Old Style",},
    { "Helvetica",      },
```

```
    { "Lubalin Graph",  },
    { "Lucida",         },
    { "Optima",         },
    { "Times Roman",    },
    { "Univers",        },
    { "Zapf Chancery",  },
};

#define NR_ITEMS    (sizeof(items) / sizeof(items[0]))
#define DEFAULT_ITEM   10


Widget CreateInitialWidgets(w_parent)
    Widget  w_parent;
{
    Widget  w_label, w_control, w_menuButton;
    Widget  AddLabel();
    Widget  AddAbbrevMenuButton(), AddCurrentSelection();

    /*
     * Create the controlArea, but don't manage it until we
     * have attached the child.
     */
    w_control =
        XtCreateWidget(
            "fontSelect",         /* instance name */
            controlAreaWidgetClass, /* widget class */
            w_parent,             /* parent widget */
            tmpArg,               /* arg list */
            TmpArgList(
                XtNlayoutType,    OL_FIXEDROWS,
                XtNmeasure,       1,
                XtNrecomputeSize, FALSE,
                0
            )
        );

    /*
     * Three parts to a complete abbrev button:
     * the label, the button itself, and the preview window.
     */

    w_label =                          /* Abbrev Button label */
        XtCreateManagedWidget(
            "label",              /* instance name */
            staticTextWidgetClass, /* widget class */
            w_control,            /* parent widget */
            tmpArg,
            TmpArgList(
                XtNstring,        "Font Family:",
                XtNborderWidth,   0,
```

207

```
                    0
                )
            );

    w_menuButton = AddAbbrevMenuButton(w_control);

    w_currentSelection =               /* Preview Window */
        XtCreateManagedWidget(
            "currentSelection",        /* instance name */
            staticTextWidgetClass,     /* widget class */
            w_control,                 /* parent widget */
            tmpArg,
            TmpArgList(
                XtNwidth,          200,
                XtNrecomputeSize,  FALSE,
                XtNgravity,        NorthWestGravity,
                XtNborderWidth,    1,
                XtNstring,         items[DEFAULT_ITEM].label,
                0
            )
        );

    /*
     * tell the abbrev menu button about the preview widget
     */
    SetValue(w_menuButton, XtNpreviewWidget, w_currentSelection);

    XtManageChild(w_control);
    return(w_control);
}

Widget AddAbbrevMenuButton(w_parent)
    Widget  w_parent;
{
    Widget  w_menuButton, w_controlArea, w_choice;
    void    CBselect();

    /*
     * Create the abbreviated menu button
     */
    w_menuButton =
        XtCreateWidget(
            "fontFamily",                    /* instance name */
            abbrevMenuButtonWidgetClass,     /* widget class */
            w_parent,                        /* parent widget */
            tmpArg,                          /* arglist */
            TmpArgList(
                XtNtitle,      "Font Family",
                XtNpushpin,    OL_OUT,
                0
            )
```

```
        );

    /*
     * Add items to the button's menu
     */
    w_controlArea = (Widget) GetValue(w_menuButton, XtNmenuPane);
    w_choice =
        XtCreateWidget(
            "choice",
            flatExclusivesWidgetClass,
            w_controlArea,
            tmpArg,
            TmpArgList(
                XtNlayoutType,      OL_FIXEDCOLS,
                XtNmeasure,         3,
                XtNitems,           items,
                XtNnumItems,        NR_ITEMS,
                XtNitemFields,      itemFields,
                XtNnumItemFields,   NR_ITEM_FIELDS,
                XtNselectProc,      CBselect,
                0
            )
        );

    /*
     * Set the default button
     */
    OlFlatSetValues(
        w_choice,
        DEFAULT_ITEM,           /* sub-item to modify */
        tmpArg,                 /* ArgList */
        TmpArgList(
            XtNdefault,     TRUE,
            XtNset,         TRUE,
            0
        )
    );

    XtManageChild(w_choice);
    XtManageChild(w_menuButton);
    return(w_menuButton);
}


/*
 * CBselect() - update the preview widget with the
 * item selected from the Abbreviated Menu Buttons menu.
 */
void CBselect(wid, client_data, call_data)
    Widget  wid;
    caddr_t client_data;
```

```
    caddr_t call_data;
{
    extern Widget    w_currentSelection;
    OlFlatCallData   *ol_flat_call_data =
                        (OlFlatCallData *) call_data;
    String       label;

    /*
     * Get the string label of the chosen sub-object
     */
    OlFlatGetValues(
        wid,
        ol_flat_call_data->item_index,
        tmpArg,
        TmpArgList(
            XtNlabel,    &label,
            0
        )
    );

    /*
     * Display the string in the preview window
     */
    SetValue(w_currentSelection, XtNstring, label);

    return;
}
```

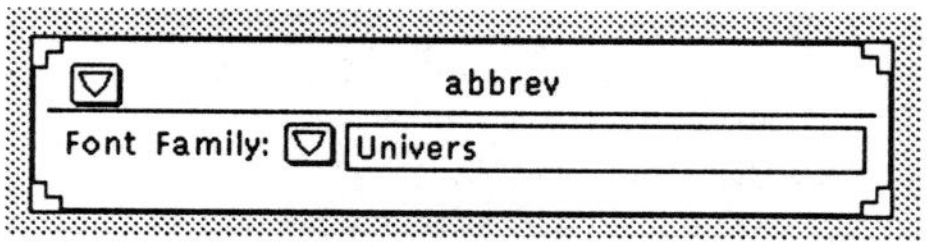

Figure 5.28 The Abbreviated Menu Button widget class

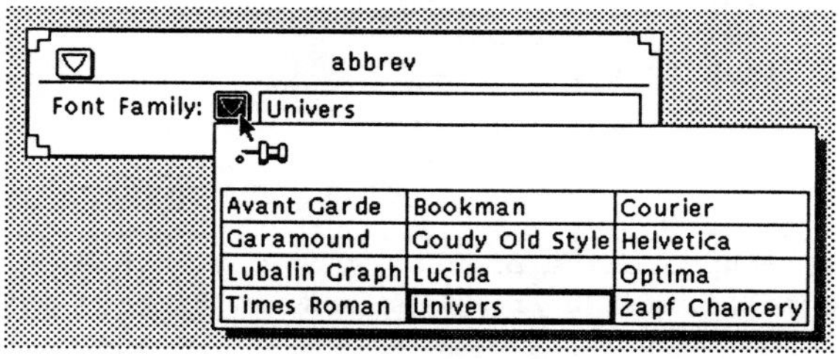

Figure 5.29 An Abbreviated Menu Button with the menu popped up

First, we create a Control Area to hold three widgets: the Static Text label, the Abbreviated Menu Button, and the Static Text preview window.[6] Then, we create the label and call AddAbbrevMenuButton to create the Abbreviated Menu Button and add a Flat Exclusive Settings widget as the menu.

Next, we create the Static Text preview widget, setting the initial value of XtNstring to the label of the default item. As the final step, we identify the preview widget by setting the Abbreviated Menu Button's XtNpreviewWidget resource to its value.

5.2.18 Form

The Form widget class is a "container" widget like Control Area, but rather than simply managing children in rows and columns, Form controls layout according to spatial relationships specified by each of the children. With this information, Forms maintain the relative sizes and placement of their children, even after the Form is resized.

Control Area and other manager widgets maintain their layout information internally (using for example, XtNlayoutType), but Form augments each child with *constraint resources* through which each child specifies its own layout requirements. Constraint resources define the widget's spatial relationship to the Form parent and to a peer *reference widget* in X and Y. Form augments each child with the following constraint resources:

XtNxRefWidget, XtNyRefWidget—Widget ID of the reference widget.

XtNxRefName, XtNyRefName—Instance name of the reference widget, as an alternate to specifying the widget ID.

------

[6]By using an editable Text or Text Field widget for the preview window, we could easily implement a type-in menu choice.

XtNxAddWidth, XtNyAddHeight—If TRUE, add the width/height of the reference widget to the widget's position.

XtNxOffset, XtNyOffset—Add this many pixels to the reference widget's origin to determine this widget's position.

XtNxAttachRight, XtNyAttachBottom—If TRUE, position the widget along the right or bottom of the Form.

XtNxAttachOffset, XtNyAttachOffset—If TRUE, adjust padding against the right and bottom edges of the Form when the widget is attached.

XtNxResizable, XtNyResizable—If TRUE, the widget can be resized.

XtNxVaryOffset, XtNyVaryOffset—If TRUE, it is okay to adjust the space between the widget and the reference widget when the Form is resized.

In the example program, form.c, we create a Form widget and several children with various constraints. Notice that we do not need to specify any resources when creating the Form. All of the constraint resources are specified when creating the children.

```
/*
 * Demonstrate the OPEN LOOK Form widget
 * @(#) sccs/s.form.c 1.7 last delta 2/10/90 18:30:34
 */
#include <X11/Intrinsic.h>
#include <X11/StringDefs.h>
#include <Xol/OpenLook.h>
#include <Xol/Form.h>
#include <Xol/OblongButt.h>
#include <Xol/StaticText.h>
#include <Xol/Slider.h>
#include <Xol/Text.h>
#include "xtutil.h"


Widget CreateInitialWidgets(w_parent)
    Widget  w_parent;
```

```
{
    Widget  w_form, w_oblong1, w_oblong2, w_text, w_slider;

    /*
     * Create a plain-vanilla form widget
     */
    w_form =
        XtCreateWidget(
            "form",
            formWidgetClass,
            w_parent,
            NULL,
            0
        );

    /*
     * Add a simple Oblong Button
     */
    w_oblong1 =
        XtCreateManagedWidget(
            "button1",
            oblongButtonWidgetClass,
            w_form,
            NULL,
            0
        );

    /*
     * Add a text widget, offset by the width and height
     * of w_oblong1
     */
    w_text =
        XtCreateManagedWidget(
            "text",
            textWidgetClass,
            w_form,
            tmpArg,
            TmpArgList(
                XtNwidth,        250,
                XtNheight,       200,
                XtNxAddWidth,    TRUE,
                XtNyAddHeight,   TRUE,
                XtNxOffset,      4,
                XtNyOffset,      4,
                XtNxRefWidget,   w_oblong1,
                XtNyRefWidget,   w_oblong1,
                XtNxResizable,   TRUE,
                XtNyResizable,   TRUE,
                XtNxVaryOffset,  TRUE,
                XtNyVaryOffset,  TRUE,
                0
```

```
                )
            );

        /*
         * Add another Oblong Button, offset in X by w_text,
         * attached to the right side of w_form.
         */
        w_oblong2 =
            XtCreateManagedWidget(
                "button2",
                oblongButtonWidgetClass,
                w_form,
                tmpArg,
                TmpArgList(
                    XtNxAddWidth,        TRUE,
                    XtNxAttachRight,     TRUE,
                    XtNxOffset,          4,
                    XtNxRefWidget,       w_text,
                    0
                )
            );

        /*
         * Finally, create a Slider, offset in Y by w_text,
         * attached to the bottom and spanning across the
         * Form to the right side.
         */
        w_slider =
            XtCreateManagedWidget(
                "slider",
                sliderWidgetClass,
                w_form,
                tmpArg,
                TmpArgList(
                    XtNorientation,      OL_HORIZONTAL,
                    XtNyAddHeight,       TRUE,
                    XtNxAttachRight,     TRUE,
                    XtNyAttachBottom,    TRUE,
                    XtNyOffset,          4,
                    XtNyRefWidget,       w_text,
                    XtNxResizable,       TRUE,
                    XtNxVaryOffset,      FALSE,
                    XtNyVaryOffset,      TRUE,
                    0
                )
            );


        XtManageChild(w_form);
        return(w_form);
}
```

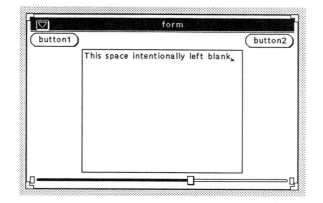

Figure 5.30 The Form widget class

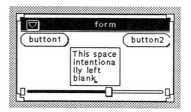

Figure 5.31 The Form after resizing

The first child, w_oblong1, is a simple Oblong Button. Since it doesn't specify any constraints, it is positioned at (0, 0).

Next, we add a Text widget, w_text, which identifies w_oblong1 as its reference widget in both X and Y. Among its constraints, it lists XtNxAddWidth and XtNyAddHeight, and so is positioned off of the lower-right corner of w_oblong1.

We then create another Oblong Button, attaching it to the right of the Form and offset four pixels right of its reference widget, w_text.

Last, we add a Slider widget, positioned below four pixels below w_text and attached to the bottom and right sides of the Form. Since XtNxVaryOffset is FALSE, the Slider spans the width of the Form.

5.2.19 Footer Panel

The Footer Panel is a convenient container for application messages, per the OPEN LOOK Specification. The widget manages a top and bottom child, giving the bottom child priority.

The example program, footer.c, defines the AddFooter function, which creates four general-purpose application footer areas using the Footer Panel, Form, and Static Text widget classes. After calling AddFooter to create the message areas, CreateInitialWidgets uses each of them to display a sample message.

```
/*
 * Demonstrate the OPEN LOOK Footer Panel widget
 * @(#) sccs/s.footer.c 1.6 last delta 2/10/90 16:42:18
 */
#include <X11/Intrinsic.h>
#include <X11/StringDefs.h>
#include <Xol/OpenLook.h>
#include <Xol/FooterPane.h>
#include <Xol/Form.h>
#include <Xol/StaticText.h>
#include "xtutil.h"

/*
 * These widgets are globally-available static text widgets
 * for displaying messages.
 */
Widget  w_footerLongTermL, w_footerLongTermR;
Widget  w_footerShortTerm, w_footerMediumTerm;

Widget CreateInitialWidgets(w_parent)
    Widget  w_parent;
{
    Widget  w_footer, AddFooter();

    w_footer = AddFooter(w_parent); /* create the footer panel */

    /*
     * Examples of how the message areas can be used.
     * Note that the bottom messages have size priority
```

```
     * over the top (by virtue of the footerPanel widget)
     * and that left messages have priority
     * over right message (by virtue of the form widget).
     */
    SetValue(w_footerLongTermL, XtNstring, "myprog.c");
    SetValue(w_footerLongTermR, XtNstring, "[Modified]");
    SetValue(w_footerShortTerm, XtNstring, "Saving...");
    SetValue(w_footerMediumTerm, XtNstring, "line 297");

    return(w_footer);
}


Widget AddFooter(w_parent)
    Widget  w_parent;
{

    Widget  w_footer;
    Widget  AddFooterTop(), AddFooterBottom();

    /*
     * simple call to instantiate a footer panel
     */
    w_footer =
        XtCreateWidget(
            "footer",
            footerPanelWidgetClass,
            w_parent,
            NULL,
            0
        );

    /*
     * a footer panel can have at most two children, with the 2nd
     * child having higher priority.
     */
    AddFooterTop(w_footer);
    AddFooterBottom(w_footer);

    XtManageChild(w_footer);

    return(w_footer);
}


static Widget AddFooterTop(w_parent)
    Widget  w_parent;
{
    Widget          w_form;
    extern Widget   w_footerLongTermL, w_footerLongTermR;
```

217

```
    /*
     * use a form widget so we can lock the two static
     * text panes in the corners.
     */
    w_form =
        XtCreateWidget(
            "footerTop",
            formWidgetClass,
            w_parent,
            tmpArg,
            TmpArgList(
                0
            )
        );

    /*
     * NOTE that the XtNxVaryOffset is a
     * form constraint resource.
     */
    w_footerLongTermL =
        XtCreateManagedWidget(
            "longTermL",
            staticTextWidgetClass,
            w_form,
            tmpArg,
            TmpArgList(
                XtNgravity,         NorthWestGravity,
                XtNxVaryOffset,     TRUE,
                0
            )
        );

    w_footerLongTermR =
        XtCreateManagedWidget(
            "longTermR",
            staticTextWidgetClass,
            w_form,
            tmpArg,
            TmpArgList(
                XtNgravity,         NorthEastGravity,
                XtNxAddWidth,       TRUE,
                XtNxAttachRight,    TRUE,
                XtNxRefWidget,      w_footerLongTermL,
                XtNxVaryOffset,     TRUE,
                0
            )
        );

    XtManageChild(w_form);
    return(w_form);
}
```

```
static Widget AddFooterBottom(w_parent)
    Widget   w_parent;
{

    Widget          w_form;
    extern Widget   w_footerShortTerm, w_footerMediumTerm;

    w_form =
        XtCreateWidget(
            "footerBottom",
            formWidgetClass,
            w_parent,
            tmpArg,
            TmpArgList(
                0
            )
        );

    w_footerShortTerm =
        XtCreateManagedWidget(
            "shortTerm",
            staticTextWidgetClass,
            w_form,
            tmpArg,
            TmpArgList(
                XtNgravity,         SouthWestGravity,
                XtNxVaryOffset,     TRUE,
                0
            )
        );

    w_footerMediumTerm =
        XtCreateManagedWidget(
            "mediumTerm",
            staticTextWidgetClass,
            w_form,
            tmpArg,
            TmpArgList(
                XtNgravity,         SouthEastGravity,
                XtNxAddWidth,       TRUE,
                XtNxAttachRight,    TRUE,
                XtNxRefWidget,      w_footerShortTerm,
                XtNxVaryOffset,     TRUE,
                0
            )
        );

    XtManageChild(w_form);
    return(w_form);
}
```

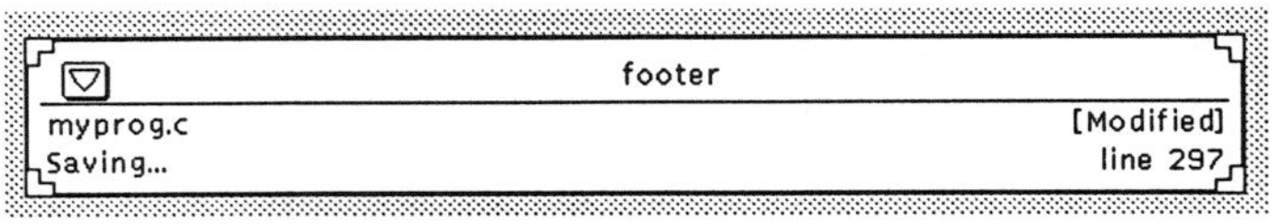

```
┌──────────────────────────────────────────────┐
│ ▽              footer                          │
├────────────────────────────────────────────────┤
│ myprog.c                            [Modified] │
│ Saving...                           line 297   │
└──────────────────────────────────────────────┘
```

Figure 5.32 The Footer Panel widget class

5.2.20 Stub and Scrolled Window

In the example programs we have seen so far, the widgets draw themselves on the screen according to the resource state set by the application. The Stub widget class does not draw itself; instead, it provides hooks for the application to draw in its window. Applications use Stub in conjunction with the Scrolled Window widget class to affect a scrollable graphics pane.

The key to using Stub as a graphics pane is its XtNexpose resource. This resource holds a pointer to an application function that is to be invoked whenever the Stub's window receives an Expose event from the X server. Recall from Chapter 2 that Expose events specify areas of an application's window that need repainting. It is standard X programming practice to put all of the drawing code for a window in the routine that receives its Expose events.

The Scrolled Window pans its child widget relative to its own origin. Since child windows are clipped to their parent's extents, this affects the child's horizontal and vertical scrolling. If the size of the Scrolled Window is large enough to display the entire child, the scrollbars are not displayed.

The example program, scrwin.c, demonstrates the Scrolled Window and Stub widget classes, creating a scrollable graphics pane and filling it with a bitmap image.

```
/*
 * Demonstrate the OPEN LOOK Scrolled Window widget
 * @(#) sccs/s.scrwin.c 1.7 last delta 2/18/90 17:27:29
 */
#include <X11/Intrinsic.h>
#include <X11/StringDefs.h>
#include <X11/Xutil.h>
#include <Xol/OpenLook.h>
#include <Xol/ScrolledWi.h>
#include <Xol/Stub.h>
#include "xtutil.h"

#define BITMAP_FILE "tiger.xbm"


Widget CreateInitialWidgets(w_parent)
    Widget  w_parent;
{
    void        DrawPicture();
    Widget      w_scrolledWindow, w_content;

    /*
     * Create a Scrolled Window.
     *
     * The Stub child does not know what size it will be
     * after the bitmap file is read, so we turn off the
     * size recomputes here to start up with the
     * Scrolled Window size defaults, rather than using
     * the inital size the child.
     */
    w_scrolledWindow =
        XtCreateWidget(
            "scrolledWindow",            /* instance name */
            scrolledWindowWidgetClass,   /* widget class */
            w_parent,                    /* parent widget */
            tmpArg,
            TmpArgList(
                XtNrecomputeHeight, FALSE,
                XtNrecomputeWidth,  FALSE,
                0
            )
        );

    /*
     * Create a Stub as a child of the Scrolled Window to
     * affect a scrollable graphics pane.  The actual size
     * of this widget is set in the first call to our
     * Expose proc.
     */
    w_content =
        XtCreateManagedWidget(
```

```
                "content",
                stubWidgetClass,
                w_scrolledWindow,
                tmpArg,
                TmpArgList(
                    XtNexpose,   DrawPicture,
                    XtNwidth,    1,      /* specify non-zero */
                    XtNheight,   1,      /* specify non-zero */
                    0
                )
            );

    XtManageChild(w_scrolledWindow);
    return(w_scrolledWindow);
}

void DrawPicture(wid, event, region)
    Widget   wid;
    XEvent   *event;
    Region   region;
{
    XExposeEvent     *expose = &event->xexpose;
    extern Display   *ourDisplay;        /* main.c */
    static Pixmap    bitmap;
    static GC        gc;
    static Boolean   inited = FALSE;

    /*
     * The first time we get called, read in the bitmap
     * and initialize a graphics context for drawing the image.
     */
    if (inited == FALSE) {
        XGCValues       xgc;
        Status          status;
        unsigned int    width, height;
        int             xhot, yhot;


        /*
         * Read in a X11 bitmap file to display in the window
         */
        status =
            XReadBitmapFile(
                ourDisplay,            /* display */
                XtWindow(wid),         /* any drawable */
                BITMAP_FILE,           /* file name */
                &width,                /* returns width */
                &height,               /* returns height */
                &bitmap,               /* returns bitmap */
                &xhot,                 /* returns x hotspot */
                &yhot                  /* returns y hotspot */
```

```
        );
    if (status != BitmapSuccess)
        BitmapFailure(status);

    /*
     * Adjust the size of the Stub widget
     * to accomodate our picture.
     */
    XtSetValues(
        wid,
        tmpArg,
        TmpArgList(
            XtNwidth,    width,
            XtNheight,   height,
            0
        )
    );

    /*
     * Create a Graphics Context with the drawing
     * attributes we want
     */
    xgc.foreground = XWhitePixelOfScreen(XtScreen(wid));
    xgc.background = XBlackPixelOfScreen(XtScreen(wid));
    gc = XCreateGC(
        ourDisplay,                     /* display */
        XtWindow(wid),                  /* drawable */
        GCForeground | GCBackground,    /* values to set */
        &xgc                            /* values */
    );

    inited = TRUE;
}

/*
 * Update the picture
 */
XCopyPlane(
    ourDisplay,      /* display */
    bitmap,          /* bitmap */
    XtWindow(wid),   /* drawable */
    gc,              /* graphics context */
    expose->x,       /* src x */
    expose->y,       /* src y */
    expose->width,   /* width */
    expose->height,  /* height */
    expose->x,       /* dst x */
    expose->y,       /* dst y */
    1                /* plane mask */
);
```

```
    return;
}

BitmapFailure(status)
    int status;
{
    extern  errno;

    switch (status) {
    case BitmapOpenFailed:
        OlError("Cannot open bitmap file\n");
        break;
    case BitmapFileInvalid:
        OlError("Invalid bitmap data\n");
        break;
    case BitmapSuccess:
        OlError(
            "Bitmap is okay, but BitmapFailure() was called\n"
        );
        break;
    case BitmapNoMemory:
        OlError("Not enough memory for bitmap\n");
        break;
    default:
        OlError("unknown bitmap error\n");
        break;
    }

    exit(errno);
}
```

In CreateInitialWidgets, we create the Scrolled Window and a Stub child. Notice how simple it is to use the Scrolled Window: Create it and forget it. Use it to viewport *any* widget simply by using the Scrolled Window as the widget's parent.

The expose-handler for the Stub, DrawPicture, displays a bitmap image in its window, updating only the regions that are newly exposed. If the procedure is being called for the first time, it also reads the bitmap file, adjusts the size of the Stub, and creates an X Graphics Context.

The Xlib procedure XReadBitmapFile allocates and fills an X bitmap with the monochrome image data contained in a disk file.[7] Upon successful completion, we adjust the size resources of our Stub widget to reflect the size of the bitmap. The Scrolling widget uses this information to adjust the sizes and proportions of the scrollbars. As the last part of the initialization, we create an X Graphics Context with the drawing attributes we wish to use for the image.

Drawing the image is trivial. Since we created the bitmap and the window the same size, the Expose event fully describes the region to paint, without any extra translation.

Figure 5.33   The Scrolled Window widget class with horizontal and vertical scrollbars

---

[7]The bitmap file tiger.xbm was created by the X window dump program *xwd*, modified to use XWriteBitmapFile. Because of its size (136,539 bytes) the contents of tiger.xbm are not listed here. If you do not have the program disk, substitute a large bitmap file created with the X bitmap editor bitmap or an image converted to the X11 bitmap format with pbm.

Figure 5.34 The Scrolled Window widget class without scrollbars

5.2.21 Scrolling List

The Scrolling List widget class is a visual list editor. Using Scrolling Lists, applications display a list of string items, letting the user choose and optionally edit items.

Scrolling List is unique in defining class methods above and beyond those normally available through Xt Intrinsics (i.e., XtCreateWidget, XtSetValues, XtGetValues, etc.). Applications use these additional methods for adding, deleting, or editing items in the list, as well as for controlling access or visibility of items. After creating the widget, the application obtains the entry points for the Scrolling List methods through XtGetValues.

Our example program, scrlist.c, displays a list of the 50 states in the United States and allows the user to choose, add, edit, and delete items from this list. Items are maintained as elements of a linked list of application-defined State structures:

```
typedef struct _State {
        struct _State          *next;
        OlListToken            token;
        String                 label;
} State;
```

The Scrolling List generates the token field to uniquely identify an item when it is added to the list. All further communication between the widget and the application regarding this item uses this token.

```
/*
 * Demonstrate the OPEN LOOK ScrollingList widget
 * @(#) sccs/s.scrlist.c 1.10 last delta 4/5/90 20:44:16
 */

#include <X11/Intrinsic.h>
#include <X11/StringDefs.h>
#include <Xol/OpenLook.h>
#include <Xol/ControlAre.h>
#include <Xol/OblongButt.h>
#include <Xol/ScrollingL.h>
#include <Xol/TextField.h>
#include "xtutil.h"


static OlListToken   (*ScrollingListAddItem)();
static void          (*ScrollingListDeleteItem)();
static void          (*ScrollingListEditClose)();
static void          (*ScrollingListEditOpen)();
static void          (*ScrollingListTouchItem)();
static void          (*ScrollingListUpdateView)();
static void          (*ScrollingListViewItem)();
static Widget        w_scrollingList;    /* the Scrolling List */
static Widget        w_textField;        /* edit field in list */

OlListToken     AddState();
void            EditState(), DeleteState();

#define NO_ITEM      (OlListToken) 0
static OlListToken   selectedToken = NO_ITEM;

String  itemLabels[] = {
    "Alabama", "Alaska", "Arizona", "Arkansas",
    "California", "Colorado", "Connecticut",
```

```
        "Delaware", "District of Columbia",
        "Florida",
        "Georgia",
        "Hawaii",
        "Idaho", "Illinois", "Indiana", "Iowa",
        "Kansas", "Kentucky",
        "Louisianna",
        "Maine", "Massachusetts", "Maryland", "Michigan",
        "Minnesota", "Missisipi", "Missouri", "Montana",
        "Nebraska", "Nevada", "New Hampshire", "New Jersey",
        "New Mexico", "New York", "North Carolina", "North Dakota",
        "Ohio", "Oregon", "Oklahoma",
        "Pennsylvania",
        "Rhode Island",
        "South Carolina", "South Dakota",
        "Texas",
        "Utah",
        "Vermont", "Virginia",
        "Washington", "West Virginia", "Wisconsin", "Wyoming"
};
#define NR_ITEMS    (sizeof(itemLabels) / sizeof(String))

/*
 * State: linked-list of application-specific data items.
 */
typedef struct _State {
    struct _State   *next;  /* pointer to next in linked list */
    OlListToken token;      /* magic cookie from ScrollingList */
    /*
     * Application data
     */
    String      label;
} State;

State   *pFirst=NULL, *pLast=NULL;  /* linked list head/tail */


Widget CreateInitialWidgets(w_parent)
    Widget  w_parent;
{
    Widget  w_frame, CreateScrollingList(), CreateButtons();

    w_frame =
        XtCreateWidget(
            "states",
            controlAreaWidgetClass,
            w_parent,
            tmpArg,
            TmpArgList(
                XtNlayoutType,      OL_FIXEDCOLS,
                XtNmeasure,         1,
```

```
                    0
                )
        );

    (void) CreateScrollingList(w_frame);   /* create state list */
    (void) CreateButtons(w_frame);         /* add edit buttons */

    XtManageChild(w_frame);
    return(w_frame);
}


Widget CreateScrollingList(w_parent)
    Widget   w_parent;
{
    void                CBSelectItem(), CBCutItems();
    void                CBTextVerification();
    register unsigned int   count;
    OlListItem          item;

    w_scrollingList =
        XtCreateWidget(
            "scrollingList",            /* instance name */
            scrollingListWidgetClass,   /* widget class */
            w_parent,                   /* parent widget */
            tmpArg,                     /* arg list */
            TmpArgList(
                XtNselectable,      FALSE,
                XtNrecomputeWidth,  TRUE,
                XtNviewHeight,      10,
                0
            )
        );

    /*
     * Get instance methods from the ScrollingList widget
     * so we can modify the List.  We also get the widget ID
     * of the editable text field.
     */
    XtGetValues(
        w_scrollingList,
        tmpArg,
        TmpArgList(
            XtNapplAddItem,     &ScrollingListAddItem,
            XtNapplDeleteItem,  &ScrollingListDeleteItem,
            XtNapplEditClose,   &ScrollingListEditClose,
            XtNapplEditOpen,    &ScrollingListEditOpen,
            XtNapplTouchItem,   &ScrollingListTouchItem,
            XtNapplUpdateView,  &ScrollingListUpdateView,
            XtNapplViewItem,    &ScrollingListViewItem,
            XtNtextField,       &w_textField,
```

```
                0
            )
        );

        /*
         * Add callback routines:
         *   CBSelectItem() is called when an item is selected
         *   CBCutItems() is called to cut/delete from the list
         *   CBTextVerification() is called to get text field input
         */
        XtAddCallback(
            w_scrollingList, XtNuserMakeCurrent, CBSelectItem, NULL);
        XtAddCallback(
            w_scrollingList, XtNuserDeleteItems, CBCutItems, NULL);
        XtAddCallback(
            w_textField, XtNverification, CBTextVerification, NULL);

        /*
         * Add items to the list
         */
        for (count = 0; count < NR_ITEMS; count++) {
            AddState(itemLabels[count]);
        }

        XtManageChild(w_scrollingList);
        return(w_scrollingList);
}


Widget CreateButtons(w_parent)
    Widget  w_parent;
{
    Widget  w_control, w_add, w_edit, w_delete;
    void    CBAddState(), CBEditState(), CBDeleteState();

    w_control =
        XtCreateWidget(
            "buttonArea",
            controlAreaWidgetClass,
            w_parent,
            tmpArg,
            TmpArgList(
                XtNlayoutType,  OL_FIXEDROWS,
                XtNmeasure,     1,
                0
            )
        );

    w_add =
        XtCreateManagedWidget(
            "Add",
```

```
                oblongButtonWidgetClass,
                w_control,
                NULL,
                0
            );
        XtAddCallback(w_add, XtNselect, CBAddState, NULL);

        w_edit =
            XtCreateManagedWidget(
                "Edit",
                oblongButtonWidgetClass,
                w_control,
                NULL,
                0
            );
        XtAddCallback(w_edit, XtNselect, CBEditState, NULL);

        w_delete =
            XtCreateManagedWidget(
                "Delete",
                oblongButtonWidgetClass,
                w_control,
                NULL,
                0
            );
        XtAddCallback(w_delete, XtNselect, CBDeleteState, NULL);

        XtManageChild(w_control);
        return(w_control);
}


/**************  Scrolling List callbacks ******************/

static void CBSelectItem(w, client_data, call_data)
    Widget  w;
    caddr_t client_data;
    caddr_t call_data;
{
    OlListItem  *pItem = OlListItemPointer(call_data);
    OlListToken token = (OlListToken) call_data;

    if (selectedToken == token) {
        dbg("already selected: %s\n", pItem->label);
    } else {
        dbg("selected: %s\n", pItem->label);

        /*
         * Mark the item as selected or current by setting a bit
         * in its attribute field.  Notify the widget that
         * we have touched an item.
```

```
     */
    pItem->attr |= OL_LIST_ATTR_CURRENT;
                                   /* set current attr */
    (*ScrollingListTouchItem)(w, token);    /* tell list */

    /*
     * Make sure the item is viewable
     */
    (*ScrollingListViewItem)(w, token);

    /*
     * If there was a previously selected item, unselect by
     * clearing the CURRENT attribute bit.  Again,
     * since we have modified an item, we must notify
     * the widget.
     */
    if (selectedToken != NO_ITEM) {
        pItem = OlListItemPointer(selectedToken);
                                         /* get item */
        pItem->attr &= ~OL_LIST_ATTR_CURRENT;/* unselect */
        (*ScrollingListTouchItem)(w, selectedToken);
    }

    selectedToken =  token;    /* remember the current item */
    }
    return;
}

/*
 * CBCutItems() - Callback routine to "cut" (delete) items
 * from a scrolling list.  This routine decides which items
 * are actually deleted; the input list merely contains those
 * items which were selected at the time of the "cut" operation.
 */
static void CBCutItems(w, client_data, call_data)
    Widget  w;           /* ScrollingList widget */
    caddr_t client_data;
    caddr_t call_data;  /* pointer to OlDeleteList struct */
{
    OlListDelete    *deleteList = (OlListDelete *) call_data;
    Cardinal        nTokens = deleteList->num_tokens;
    OlListToken     *pTokens = deleteList->tokens;  /* -> list */

    dbg("deleting %d item(s):\n", deleteList->num_tokens);

    while (nTokens--) {
        /*
         * if the currently selected item is being deleted,
         * there won't be a current selection.
         */
        if (*pTokens == selectedToken) {
```

```
                    selectedToken = NO_ITEM;
            }

            dbg("\t%s\n", (OlListItemPointer(*pTokens))->label);

            /*
             * Use the widget instance method to actually
             * delete the item.  NOTE that we were not
             * obligated to delete any items.
             */
            (*ScrollingListDeleteItem)(w, *pTokens++);
    };
    return;
}


/********* Action button and Text Field callbacks ***********/

/*
 * CBAddState() - user wants to insert a new item.
 */
static void CBAddState(wid, client_data, call_data)
    Widget  wid;
    caddr_t client_data;
    caddr_t call_data;
{

    OlListItem  *pItem;

    /*
     * Scrolling List edit "Insert" isn't implemented yet, so we
     * do it ourselves:
     *  - unselect current item
     *  - Add a NULL item
     *  - Open it for edit
     *  - select new item
     */
    if (selectedToken != NO_ITEM) {
        pItem = OlListItemPointer(selectedToken);/* get item */
        pItem->attr &= ~OL_LIST_ATTR_CURRENT;    /* unselect */
        (*ScrollingListTouchItem)
            (w_scrollingList, selectedToken);
    }

    selectedToken = AddState("");
    (*ScrollingListEditOpen)
        (w_scrollingList, FALSE, selectedToken);

    pItem = OlListItemPointer(selectedToken);
    pItem->attr |= OL_LIST_ATTR_CURRENT;
    (*ScrollingListTouchItem)(w_scrollingList, selectedToken);
```

```
        return;
}

/*
 * CBEditState() - user wants to edit the current item.
 */
static void CBEditState(wid, client_data, call_data)
    Widget  wid;
    caddr_t client_data;
    caddr_t call_data;
{
    /*
     * Open the window, overwriting the current item
     */
    (*ScrollingListEditOpen)
        (w_scrollingList, FALSE, selectedToken);

    return;
}

/*
 * CBTextVerification() - get string input from the
 * Text Field widget.
 */
static void CBTextVerification(wid, client_data, call_data)
    Widget  wid;
    caddr_t client_data;
    caddr_t call_data;
{
    OlTextFieldVerify   *olTextFieldVerify =
                            (OlTextFieldVerify *) call_data;

    EditState(selectedToken, olTextFieldVerify->string);
    (*ScrollingListEditClose)(w_scrollingList);

    return;
}

/*
 * CBDeleteState() - user wants to delete the current item.
 */
static void CBDeleteState(wid, client_data, call_data)
    Widget  wid;
    caddr_t client_data;
    caddr_t call_data;
{
    DeleteState(selectedToken);
    return;
}

/********************  List routines  ********************/
```

```
/*
 * AddState() - add an item to the linked list AND
 * the Scrolling List
 */
OlListToken AddState(label)
    String   label;
{
    register State  *pThis;
    extern State    *pFirst, *pLast;
    OlListItem      item;

    /*
     * Add items to the list by:
     *  - malloc'ing an State struct
     *  - adding it to the Scrolling List
     *  - adding to our linked list
     */
    pThis = (State *) malloc(sizeof(State));
    if (pThis == NULL) {
        Error("couldn't malloc an State in AddState\n");
    }
    pThis->next = NULL;
    pThis->label = (String) malloc(strlen(label) + 1);
    if (pThis->label == NULL)
        Error("AddState malloc\n");
    strcpy(pThis->label, label);

    /*
     * Add to Scrolling List widget's list
     */
    item.label_type = OL_STRING;
    item.label = pThis->label;
    item.attr = 0;
    pThis->token =
        (*ScrollingListAddItem)(
            w_scrollingList,    /* ScrollingList instance */
            0,                  /* zero for future use */
            selectedToken,      /* where to insert */
            item                /* OlListItem to add */
        );

    /*
     * Add to our linked list
     */
    if (pFirst == NULL) {       /* first one */
        pFirst = pLast = pThis;
    } else {
        pLast->next = pThis;    /* chain into list */
        pLast = pThis;          /* new last element */
    }
```

```
        return(pThis->token);
}

/*
 * EditState() - edit an item in the linked list AND
 * the Scrolling List
 */
void EditState(token, label)
    OlListToken token;
    String      label;        /* new label */
{
    register State  *pThis;
    extern State    *pFirst, *pLast;
    OlListItem      *pItem;

    /*
     * try to match the token, and if we do, modify the data
     * and then tell the Scrolling List that we have touched it.
     */
    for (pThis = pFirst; pThis != NULL; pThis = pThis->next) {
        if (pThis->token == token) {
            /*
             * free the old label and malloc/copy the new
             */
            free(pThis->label);
            pThis->label = (String) malloc(strlen(label) + 1);
            if (pThis->label == NULL)
                Error("EditState malloc\n");
            strcpy(pThis->label, label);

            /*
             * tell Scrolling List widget about it
             */
            pItem = OlListItemPointer(token);
            pItem->label = pThis->label;
            (*ScrollingListTouchItem)(w_scrollingList, token);
        }
    }
    return;
}

/*
 * DeleteState() - delete an item from the linked list AND
 * the Scrolling List
 */
void DeleteState(token)
    OlListToken token;
{
    register State  *pPrev, *pThis;
    extern State    *pFirst, *pLast;
    OlListItem  *pItem;
```

```
    /*
     * try to match the token, and if we do, delete the item from
     * the Scrolling List and from our linked list
     */
    for (
        pPrev = NULL,
        pThis = pFirst;

        pThis != NULL;

    ) {
        if (pThis->token != token) {      /* nope */
            pPrev = pThis;
            pThis = pThis->next;
            continue;
        } else {
            /*
             * Delete from Scrolling List
             */
            pItem = OlListItemPointer(token);      /* get item */
            pItem->attr &= ~OL_LIST_ATTR_CURRENT;/* unselect */
            (*ScrollingListTouchItem)(w_scrollingList, token);
            (*ScrollingListDeleteItem)(w_scrollingList, token);
            selectedToken = NO_ITEM;

            /*
             * Delete from linked list
             */
            if (pThis == pFirst) {
                if (pFirst == pLast)    /* only one */
                    pLast = NULL;
                pFirst = pThis->next;   /* point at 2nd */
                free(pThis);            /* free 1st */
                pThis = pFirst;         /* point at new 1st */
            } else {
                pPrev->next = pThis->next;
                if (pThis == pLast)
                    pLast = pPrev;
                free(pThis);
                pThis = pPrev->next;
            }
        }
    }
    return;
}
```

In CreateScrollingList, we create the Scrolling List and get the Text Field edit widget and the entry points for the Scrolling List class methods. We then add three callbacks. The first callback is invoked when the user chooses an item, the second when the user cuts items,[8] and the third to get character input from the Text Field widget. Finally, we add all the items in the list, manage the Scrolling List widget, and return.

To add items to the list, we call AddState with the string to use as the item's label. In AddState, we allocate a State structure, fill it, and invoke a Scrolling List class method to add the item to the widget's list. We then chain the new item into our application's list and return.

It is important to note that the application's list and the widget's list are two separate entities. The widget keeps a list of OlListItem structures, and the application keeps whatever it needs; in this case, a linked list of State structures. The application can access the widget's OlListItem structure for a particular item by using the macro OlListItemPointer with the item's token.

---

[8]For the time being, we have disabled *cut* and *copy* operations on the list by specifying XtNselectable as FALSE. This functionality is demonstrated in the "Selections" section in Chapter 6.

Back in CreateInitialWidgets, we call CreateButtons to add the Add, Edit, and Delete buttons below the Scrolling List. We'll look at the callbacks for these buttons after covering the rest of the Scrolling List functionality.

5.2.21.1 Choosing Items

We have now completely initialized our application, and, after main calls XtMainLoop, have a window that looks like this:

Figure 5.35 The Scrolling List widget class

Scroll down and click SELECT on Hawaii. The widget draws a 1-point box around the label and calls the XtNuserMakeCurrent callback, CBSelectItem.

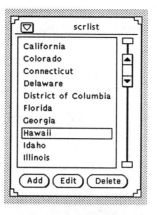

Figure 5.36 The Scrolling List widget class with Hawaii as the current item

In CBSelectItem, the callback

1. Prints the item label.

2. Makes the item current.

3. Brings the item into view.

4. Unselects the previous item.

5. Globally registers the new current item.

Several of these operations involve modifying the Scrolling List widget's data structure for this item. The widget class allows us to do this, as long as we notify it afterwards with the XtNapplTouchItem method.

Users may choose items from the keyboard, also. Make sure that the keyboard focus is on the scrlist window and type "O" twice to see this effect:

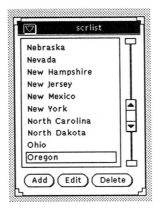

Figure 5.37 Choosing Scrolling List items from the keyboard

5.2.21.2 Adding Items

Our example program allows users to add items to the list. To see how this works, choose Florida and click SELECT on the Add button, which invokes the CBAddState callback. This code unselects the current item (Florida), adds a null item (using AddItem), and calls the Scrolling List class method XtNapplEditOpen to edit the label of the new item.[9] The window now looks like this:

---

[9]Early versions of the OPEN LOOK X Toolkit Release 2.0 may print a warning message complaining about the size of the Text Field window; this message may be ignored.

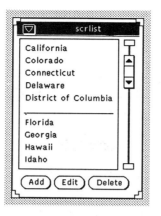

Figure 5.38 Adding an item to the Scrolling List

Type the string "Fantasy Island," followed by a Tab or Carriage Return to trigger the Text Field's XtNverification callback, CBTextVerification. This routine calls EditState to replace the previously null item label with the string you typed. Before returning, CBTextVerification invokes its XtNapplEditClose method, which tells the Scrolling List that you're done with the Text Field. The finished result:

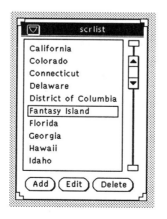

Figure 5.39 The Scrolling List after adding an item

5.2.21.3 Editing Items

Editing an item is similar to adding an item (described above). To see how this works, choose District of Columbia and click SELECT on the Edit button. Select the entire line for edit by triple-clicking anywhere in the string. The window now looks like this:

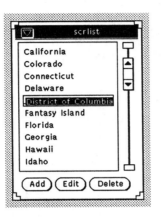

Figure 5.40 Editing an existing Scrolling List item

Type "Washington, D.C." then Tab or Return to complete the edit:

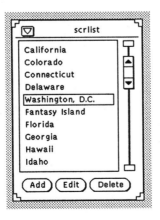

Figure 5.41 The Scrolling List after editing

5.2.21.4 Deleting Items

To delete an item, the CBDeleteState simply calls DeleteState to do the work. This routine looks for a matching label, and if it finds one, the routine deletes the item from the Scrolling List with the XtNapplDeleteItem method and frees the corresponding application structure from its linked list.

To the user, this is as simple as choosing the item and clicking SELECT on the Delete button. Choose Fantasy Island and click Delete:

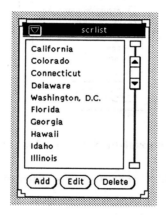

Figure 5.42 The Scrolling List after deleting Fantasy Island

5.2.22 Notice

Applications use Notices to alert users of serious conditions or to confirm nonreversible actions.

When an application displays a Notice, it generally requires that the user make a decision before it can proceed. The Notice enables this *application modal* behavior by busying the rest of application while it is popped-up.

Unfortunately, the asynchronous callback architecture of the Toolkit makes it difficult for a callback to get user input through other callbacks. For example, the callback for a Quit button might want to use a Notice to prompt the user for confirmation before exiting. Instantiating the Notice and its buttons is straightforward, but how do you return to the Quit button's callback from the Notice buttons callbacks?[10] How does the Quit callback know what the user chose?

Xtutil solves this problem with the Notice function. It temporarily usurps X event dispatching while the Notice is displayed, returning only after the user chooses a button from the Notice. This allows the application to make a single, synchronous function call to display a Notice and receive the user's choice.

Calls to Notice pass the widget that caused the Notice (known as the *emanate widget*), a string message, and a variable-length list of button labels with the value to return if that button is clicked:

```
caddr_t Notice(
     Widget wid;              /* emanate widget */
     String message;
     String button_label_1;
     caddr_t      button_return_1;
     ...
     String button_label_N;
     caddr_t      button_return_N;
     int          0           /* terminate button list */
)
```

---

[10]Remember that it is not permissible to *longjmp* out of a callback.

The example program, notice.c, calls Notice in the Quit button call-back, CBQuit, and gives the user three choices: Save and quit, Quit without saving, and Cancel.

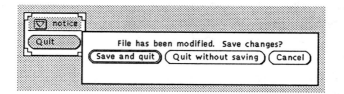

Figure 5.43 The Notice widget class

```
/*
 * Demonstrate the OPEN LOOK Notice Shell widget
 * @(#) sccs/s.notice.c 1.7 last delta 2/18/90 20:36:25
 */
#include <X11/Intrinsic.h>
#include <X11/StringDefs.h>
#include <Xol/OpenLook.h>
#include <Xol/OblongButt.h>
#include <Xol/Notice.h>
#include "xtutil.h"


Widget CreateInitialWidgets(w_parent)
    Widget  w_parent;
{
    Widget      w_save;
    extern void CBQuit();

    /*
     * Create the quit button
     */
    w_save =
        XtCreateManagedWidget(
            "quit",                    /* instance name */
            oblongButtonWidgetClass,   /* widget class */
            w_parent,                  /* parent widget */
            tmpArg,                    /* arg list */
            TmpArgList(
                XtNlabel,              "Quit",
                XtNrecomputeSize,      FALSE,
                0
            )
        );
```

```
    /*
     * Add callbacks
     */
    XtAddCallback(w_save, XtNselect, CBQuit, NULL);

    return(w_save);
}

/*
 * CBQuit() - use has clicked the Quit button.
 *  This example assumes that the application has file
 *  state to save.  Prompt the user for the appropriate
 *  action, using the Utility Library function, Notice().
 */
void CBQuit(wid, client_data, call_data)
    Widget  wid;
    caddr_t client_data;
    caddr_t call_data;
{
    enum {
        CANCEL,
        NOSAVE,
        SAVE,
    } choice;

    choice =
        Notice(
            wid,                                  /* emanate widget */
            "File has been modified.  Save changes?", /* msg */
            "Save and quit",             /* button label */
            SAVE,                        /* return value */
            "Quit without saving",       /* button label */
            NOSAVE,                      /* return value */
            "Cancel",                    /* button label */
            CANCEL,                      /* return value */
            0                            /* terminate list */
        );

    switch (choice) {
    case CANCEL:
        return;
    case SAVE:
        /* insert save code here */
        /* note no break */
    case NOSAVE:
        exit(0);
    }
}
```

5.2.23 Pop-up Window Shell

Pop-up Window Shells are used to implement OPEN LOOK Command Windows and Property Windows. Command Windows get user input for actions, such as the name of a file to edit or the string to search for. Property Windows let users adjust an application's settings and attributes.

5.2.23.1 Command Windows

In our first Pop-up Window Shell example, cmdwin.c, we create a Command Window to implement the "Save as..." function of a hypothetical word processor. The callback of an Oblong Button (labeled "Save as...") in the application's BaseWindowShell window prompts the user for the name of the output file by creating and popping up a PopupWindowShell as a Command Window. The callback for the Save button in the Command Window opens this file and writes out the data.

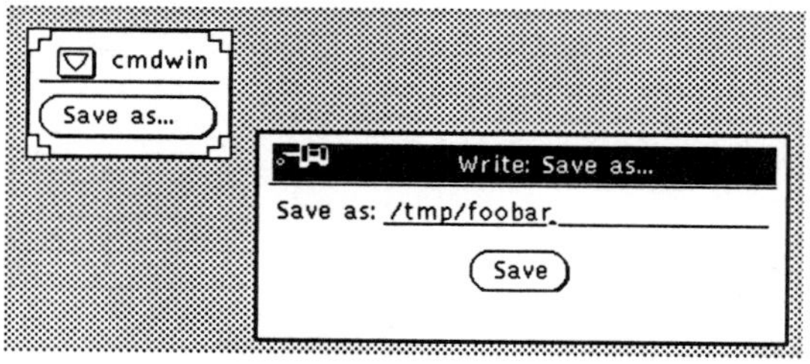

Figure 5.44 The Pop-up Shell widget class as a Command Window

```
/*
 * Demonstrate the PopupWindowShell widget as
 * an OPEN LOOK Command Window for a hypothetical word processor.
 *
 * @(#) sccs/s.cmdwin.c 1.2 last delta 4/8/90 23:53:07
 */
#include <X11/Intrinsic.h>
#include <X11/StringDefs.h>
#include <Xol/OpenLook.h>
#include <Xol/Caption.h>
```

```
#include <Xol/OblongButt.h>
#include <Xol/PopupWindo.h>
#include <Xol/StaticText.h>
#include <Xol/TextField.h>
#include "xtutil.h"

Widget CreateInitialWidgets(w_parent)
    Widget  w_parent;
{
    Widget  w_saveAs;
    void    CBSaveAs();

    /*
     * Create a button to pop up the Command Window
     */
    w_saveAs =
        XtCreateManagedWidget(
            "save",                        /* instance name */
            oblongButtonWidgetClass,       /* widget class */
            w_parent,                      /* parent widget */
            tmpArg,                        /* arglist */
            TmpArgList(
                XtNlabel,          "Save as...",
                XtNrecomputeSize,  FALSE,
                0
            )
        );

    XtAddCallback(w_saveAs, XtNselect, CBSaveAs, NULL);

    return(w_saveAs);
}

typedef struct _CommandWindow_SaveAs {
    Widget  w_commandWindow;    /* command window */
    Widget  w_textInput;        /* data input */
    Widget  w_save;             /* action button */
    Widget  w_message;          /* footer message area */
    Boolean okay;               /* okay to pop-down window */
} CommandWindow_SaveAs;

/*
 * CBSaveAs - the user requests that we save state
 * to a file, so here we pop-up a Command Window to
 * get the target filename.
 */
void CBSaveAs(wid, client_data, call_data)
    Widget  wid;
    caddr_t client_data;
    caddr_t call_data;
{
```

```
static CommandWindow_SaveAs cmdwin;
static Boolean             inited=FALSE;
Widget              w_upper, w_lower, w_caption, w_footer;
void                Verify(), Save();
static XtCallbackRec    verifyList[] = {
    { (XtCallbackProc) Verify, (caddr_t) &cmdwin },
    { NULL, NULL },
};

if (inited)
    goto popup;      /* already built the Command Window */
else
    inited = TRUE;  /* for next time */

/*
 * Instantiate a PopupWindowShell widget as a pop-up
 * child of the button.  Notice that pop-up children
 * are created using XtCreatePopupShell, as opposed to
 * XtCreateManagedWidget, which creates a normal child.
 *
 * NOTE 1: Normal children require their parent to be
 * a subclass of Composite.
 *
 * NOTE 2: Gadgets cannot have pop-up children.
 *
 * For the title string, we concatenated our
 * function, "Save as..." to the name of the
 * application, "Write" and separated them with
 * a colon.
 */
cmdwin.w_commandWindow =
    XtCreatePopupShell(
        "commandWindow",
        popupWindowShellWidgetClass,
        wid,
        tmpArg,
        TmpArgList(
            XtNverify,   verifyList,
            XtNtitle,    "Write: Save as...",
            0
        )
    );

XtGetValues(                    /* get control areas */
    cmdwin.w_commandWindow,
    tmpArg,
    TmpArgList(
        XtNupperControlArea,    &w_upper,
        XtNlowerControlArea,    &w_lower,
        XtNfooterPanel,         &w_footer,
        0
```

```
        )
    );

    /*
     * 1. Add a captioned text field area to get the filename
     * 2. Add an action button to perform the save
     */

    /*
     * Create a captioned text field for filename input
     */
    w_caption =
        XtCreateManagedWidget(
            "fieldLabel",              /* instance name */
            captionWidgetClass,        /* widget class */
            w_upper,                   /* parent widget */
            tmpArg,                    /* arg list */
            TmpArgList(
                XtNlabel,    "Save as:",
                0
            )
        );
    cmdwin.w_textInput =
        XtCreateManagedWidget(
            "textField",               /* instance name */
            textFieldWidgetClass,      /* widget class */
            w_caption,                 /* parent widget */
            tmpArg,                    /* arg list */
            TmpArgList(
                XtNwidth,        200,
                XtNtraversalOn,  TRUE,
                0
            )
        );


    /*
     * Create the "Save" action button and attach
     * a callback to do the work.
     */
    cmdwin.w_save =
        XtCreateManagedWidget(
            "Save",
            oblongButtonWidgetClass,
            w_lower,
            NULL,
            0
        );
    XtAddCallback(
        cmdwin.w_save,
        XtNselect,
```

```
            Save,
            (caddr_t) &cmdwin
    );

    /*
     * Create error-message text area in the
     * Command Window's footer panel
     */
    cmdwin.w_message =
        XtCreateManagedWidget(
            "errorMessage",
            staticTextWidgetClass,
            w_footer,
            tmpArg,
            TmpArgList(
                XtNalignment,   OL_LEFT,
                XtNgravity, SouthWestGravity,
                0
            )
        );

popup:
    XtPopup(cmdwin.w_commandWindow, XtGrabNone);
    return;
}


/*
 * Verify - is it okay to pop-down the Command Window?
 */
void Verify(wid, client_data, call_data)
    Widget  wid;
    caddr_t client_data;
    caddr_t call_data;
{
    Boolean                 *pOkay = (Boolean *) call_data;
    CommandWindow_SaveAs    *cmdwin =
                            (CommandWindow_SaveAs *) client_data;

    if (*pOkay != FALSE) {          /* if not veto'd already, */
        *pOkay = cmdwin->okay;      /* set the current state */
    }
    return;
}



/*
 * Save - save stuff to file
 */
void Save(wid, client_data, call_data)
    Widget  wid;
    caddr_t client_data;
```

```
    caddr_t call_data;
{
    extern char             *sys_errlist[]; /* error strings */
    extern int              errno;          /* error code */
    CommandWindow_SaveAs    *cmdwin =
                            (CommandWindow_SaveAs *) client_data;
    String                  filename;
    int                     fd;

    /*
     * Clear any displayed error message
     */
    SetValue(cmdwin->w_message, XtNstring, "");

    /*
     * Try to open the filename in the text field
     */
    filename = (String) GetValue(cmdwin->w_textInput, XtNstring);
    fd = open(filename, O_WRONLY | O_CREAT, 0644);

    if (fd < 0) {                           /* open failed */
        char    buf[80];

        cmdwin->okay = FALSE;               /* don't pop down */

        /*
         * Ring bell
         */
        XBell(XtDisplay(cmdwin->w_message), 100);

        /*
         * display error message in footer
         */
        sprintf(buf, "error: %s", sys_errlist[errno]);
        SetValue(cmdwin->w_message, XtNstring, buf);
    } else {
        cmdwin->okay = TRUE;                /* okay to pop down */
#ifdef notdef
        /*
         * Add code to save state to file
         */
        write(fd, stuff, sizeof(stuff));
#endif
        close(fd);
    }
    return;
}
```

The structure CommandWindow_SaveAs keeps a record of the widgets in the Command Window (including the Command Window itself) and a status flag (checked by the PopupWindowShell's pop-down verify callback) to authorize or veto the Command Window pop-down when the user initiates an action in the window.

The "Save as..." button's callback, CBSaveAs, creates the Popup Window Shell widget using XtCreatePopupShell and then retrieves the implicitly created area managers: the upper and lower Control Areas and the Footer Panel. To these areas, it adds a Caption plus Text Field for filename entry, an Oblong Button to initiate the Save action, and a Static Text area for any error message. Finally, the Command Window is popped up by calling XtPopup.

In the Save callback, we get the current value of the Command Window's Text Field and use it as the name of the file to open. If the open succeeds, we write out the data, close the file, and return. Otherwise, we indicate the failure in cmdwin->okay and display an error string in the Static Text area of the Command Window's Footer Panel.

If the Verify callback sets *pOkay to FALSE, the Popup Window Shell keeps the Command Window popped-up to let the user see the error message and try a different filename. Note that Verify is not called if the user unpins the window or dismisses it through the window menu.

5.2.23.2 Property Windows

Property Windows are more complex that Command Windows to implement fully, due to the complexity of the user interface. The OPEN LOOK GUI stipulates that users may choose between four Property Window actions to determine how the settings in the window affect the current settings:

Apply—Accepts the values displayed in the Property Window.

Set Defaults—Remembers the current settings as the "factory defaults."

Reset—Cancels changes made since the last Apply action.

Reset To Factory—Reverts to the factory default settings.

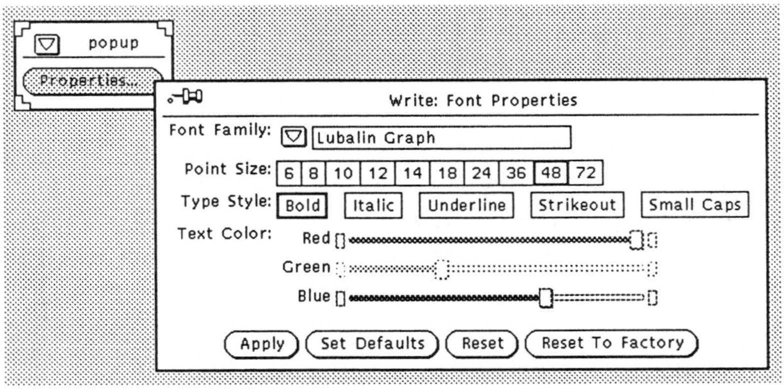

Figure 5.45 The Pop-up Shell widget class as a Property Window

For a very small number of controls, the Property Window button callbacks can implement their Apply, Set Defaults, Reset, and Reset To Factory functions by directly manipulating the control widgets, reading and writing their values as appropriate. With more than one or two controls, however, this approach quickly becomes unwieldy.

Our example program, propwin.c, implements a more extensible approach. Here, each control (Slider, Exclusive Setting, and Nonexclusive Setting) is treated as a fully encapsulated object that knows how to handle a small set of commands, or messages, such as NEW (create yourself), GET (return your current value), and SET (set your current value). The code implementing the Property Window needs only to manage a collection of control objects, which at this level all have the same semantics. The Property Window code does not know (or need to know) the implementation details of the controls, only their data type for saving/setting their values.

The example program, propwin.c, implements a Property Window for setting font attributes in a hypothetical word processor or paint program. It demonstrates control objects of various data types, including String, int, a bitmask, and struct. Every object knows how to create itself, return its current value, set a new value, and update its current value from its widget callbacks. The Property Window code manages the control objects for Font Family, Point Size, Type Style, and Text Color, according to the user's input on the Apply, Set Defaults, Reset, and Reset to Factory buttons.

As you look through the example code, note the differences and similarities between each of the control objects.[11] Also note the simplicity of the Property Window code, which is essentially contained in the two routines, CreatePropertyWindow and HandleButtonAction.

```
/*
 * @(#) sccs/s.propwin.c 1.14 last delta 4/8/90 23:53:09
 * Demonstrate the PopupWindowShell widget as an
 * OPEN LOOK Property Window
 */
#include <X11/Intrinsic.h>
#include <X11/StringDefs.h>
#include <Xol/OpenLook.h>
```

---

[11] At over 1,200 lines, this example is, by far, the longest in the book. However, since practically any OPEN LOOK application will need to implement at least one Property Window, the length and completeness of the example are justified.

```c
#include <Xol/AbbrevStac.h>
#include <Xol/Caption.h>
#include <Xol/ControlAre.h>
#include <Xol/Exclusives.h>
#include <Xol/Nonexclusi.h>
#include <Xol/OblongButt.h>
#include <Xol/PopupWindo.h>
#include <Xol/RectButton.h>
#include <Xol/Slider.h>
#include <Xol/StaticText.h>
#include <stdio.h>
#include "xtutil.h"

/*
 * Bit masks for typeStyle
 */
#define NORMAL          0
#define BOLD            1
#define ITALIC          2
#define UNDERLINE       4
#define STRIKEOUT       8
#define SMALLCAPS       16

/*
 * Property Window actions.
 */
#define APPLY           1
#define RESET           2
#define RESETFACTORY    3
#define SETDEFAULTS     4

/*
 * Control-object messages.
 */
#define NEW             1
#define SET             2
#define GET             3
#define DIM             4
#define UNDIM           5
#define DEFAULT         6
#define SELECT          7
#define UNSELECT        8
#define VERIFY          9
#define UPDATE_RED      10
#define UPDATE_GREEN    11
#define UPDATE_BLUE     12

/*
 * RGB - simple, unencumbered RGB specification.
 */
typedef struct _RGB {
```

```
        unsigned int    red;
        unsigned int    green;
        unsigned int    blue;
} RGB;

/*
 * textDefaults - initial defaults.
 * textAttrs - global record of text attributes set
 *    in this module.
 */
typedef struct _TextAttributes {
    String      fontFamily;     /* font name string */
    unsigned int    pointSize;  /* size, in points */
    unsigned int    typeStyle;  /* bitmask of style attributes */
    RGB         textColor;      /* RGB */
} TextAttributes;

static TextAttributes   textDefaults = {
    "Lucida",       /* fontFamily */
    10,             /* pointSize */
    NORMAL,         /* typeStyle */
    { 0, 0, 0 },    /* (black) */
};
TextAttributes  textAttrs;



/*
 * CreateInitialWidgets() - create a "Properties..." button to
 * popup an OPEN LOOK Property Window.
 */
Widget CreateInitialWidgets(w_parent)
    Widget  w_parent;
{
    Widget  w_propertyButton, w_propertyWindow;
    Widget  CreatePropertyWindow();
    void    CBPopupPropertyWindow(), CBUnbusyButton();

    /*
     * Create a button to trigger popping up the property window
     */
    w_propertyButton =
        XtCreateManagedWidget(
            "propertyButton",
            oblongButtonWidgetClass,
            w_parent,
            tmpArg,
            TmpArgList(
                XtNlabel,           "Properties",
                XtNlabelType,       OL_POPUP,
                XtNrecomputeSize,   FALSE,
```

```
                  0
              )
          );

      /*
       * Create the property window
       */
      w_propertyWindow = CreatePropertyWindow(w_propertyButton);

      /*
       * When the property button is pressed,
       * pop up the property window
       */
      XtAddCallback(
          w_propertyButton,
          XtNselect,
          CBPopupPropertyWindow,
          w_propertyWindow
      );

      /*
       * When the property window is popped down,
       * unbusy the property button
       */
      XtAddCallback(
          w_propertyWindow,
          XtNpopdownCallback,
          CBUnbusyButton,
          w_propertyButton
      );

      return(w_propertyButton);
}

void CBPopupPropertyWindow(wid, client_data, call_data)
    Widget  wid;
    caddr_t client_data;
    caddr_t call_data;
{
    Widget  w_propertyWindow = (Widget) client_data;

    SetValue(wid, XtNbusy, TRUE);   /* busy property button */
    XtPopup(w_propertyWindow, XtGrabNone);  /* popup window */
    return;
}

void CBUnbusyButton(wid, client_data, call_data)
    Widget  wid;
    caddr_t client_data;
    caddr_t call_data;
{
```

```
        SetValue((Widget) client_data, XtNbusy, FALSE); /* unbusy */
        return;
}

/*
 * Property Window routines:  This code demonstrates techniques
 * for creating a Property Window and managing its controls.
 * Note the use of messaging to partition the work between
 * the Property Window, which knows how to APPLY and RESET
 * (tasks which apply to all controls), and the control
 * items which have more rudimentary and tasks which
 * pertain only to them, like NEW, SET value, and GET value.
 */
Widget CreatePropertyWindow(w_parent)
    Widget  w_parent;
{
    Widget  w_prop, w_controlTop, w_controlBottom, w_footerPanel;
    void    HandleButtonAction();
    caddr_t ObjFontFamily(), ObjPointSize();
    caddr_t ObjTypeStyle(), ObjTextColor();

    /*
     * The PopupWindowShell automatically creates buttons
     * for Apply, Reset, Reset to Factory, and Set Defaults,
     * but ONLY if you specify the callbacks when the widget
     * is created.  This is a bit of a hassle, but of course,
     * you can always skip this and create the buttons yourself.
     *
     * A Callback list is a null-terminated list of
     * CallbackProc + call_data
     */
    static XtCallbackRec    apply[] = {
        { (XtCallbackProc) HandleButtonAction, (caddr_t) APPLY },
        { NULL, NULL },
    };

    static XtCallbackRec    reset[] = {
        { (XtCallbackProc) HandleButtonAction, (caddr_t) RESET },
        { NULL, NULL },
    };

    static XtCallbackRec    resetFactory[] = {
        { (XtCallbackProc) HandleButtonAction,
                                    (caddr_t) RESETFACTORY },
        { NULL, NULL },
    };

    static XtCallbackRec    setDefaults[] = {
        { (XtCallbackProc) HandleButtonAction,
                                    (caddr_t) SETDEFAULTS },
        { NULL, NULL },
```

```
};

/*
 * create the popup window widget
 */
w_prop =
    XtCreatePopupShell(
        "fontProperties",               /* instance name */
        popupWindowShellWidgetClass,    /* widget class */
        w_parent,                       /* parent widget */
        tmpArg,                         /* arglist */
        TmpArgList(
            XtNtitle,           "Write: Font Properties",
            XtNpushpin,         OL_OUT,
            XtNapply,           apply,
            XtNreset,           reset,
            XtNresetFactory,    resetFactory,
            XtNsetDefaults,     setDefaults,
            0
        )
    );

/*
 * retrieve the widget IDs of the control areas
 * and the footer panel
 */
XtGetValues(
    w_prop,
    tmpArg,
    TmpArgList(
        XtNupperControlArea,    &w_controlTop,
        XtNlowerControlArea,    &w_controlBottom,
        XtNfooterPanel,         &w_footerPanel,
        0
    )
);

/*
 * Add property items to the popup.  Each object has its own
 * unique entry point where you send action messages such as
 * NEW, SET, and GET.  The Apply, Reset, ResetToFactory, and
 * Set Defaults actions are handled at this level, above
 * those objects.
 */
ObjFontFamily(NEW, w_controlTop);
ObjPointSize(NEW, w_controlTop);
ObjTypeStyle(NEW, w_controlTop);
ObjTextColor(NEW, w_controlTop);

/*
 * set initial values to default by copying the defaults and
```

```
     * forcing a RESET
     */
    textAttrs = textDefaults;
    HandleButtonAction(w_prop, RESETFACTORY, NULL);

    return(w_prop);
}


/*
 * HandleButtonAction() - manages events that effect
 * the state of the entire Property Window.
 */
void HandleButtonAction(wid, client_data, call_data)
    Widget  wid;
    caddr_t client_data;
    caddr_t call_data;
{
    int action = (int) client_data;
    caddr_t ObjFontFamily(), ObjPointSize();
    caddr_t ObjTypeStyle(), ObjTextColor();

    switch (action) {

    case APPLY:
        textAttrs.pointSize = (unsigned) ObjPointSize(GET, 0);
        textAttrs.fontFamily   = (String) ObjFontFamily(GET, 0);
        textAttrs.typeStyle = (unsigned) ObjTypeStyle(GET, 0);
        ObjTextColor(GET, &textAttrs.textColor);
        break;

    case RESET:
        ObjFontFamily(SET,   textAttrs.fontFamily);
        ObjPointSize(SET,    textAttrs.pointSize);
        ObjTypeStyle(SET,    textAttrs.typeStyle);
        ObjTextColor(SET,    &textAttrs.textColor);
        break;

    case RESETFACTORY:
        ObjFontFamily(SET,   textDefaults.fontFamily);
        ObjPointSize(SET,    textDefaults.pointSize);
        ObjTypeStyle(SET,    textDefaults.typeStyle);
        ObjTextColor(SET,    &textDefaults.textColor);
        break;

    case SETDEFAULTS:
        textDefaults.pointSize  = (unsigned) ObjPointSize(GET,0);
        textDefaults.fontFamily = (String) ObjFontFamily(GET,0);
        textDefaults.typeStyle  = (unsigned) ObjTypeStyle(GET,0);
        ObjTextColor(GET, &textDefaults.textColor);
        break;
```

```
    default:
        Warning(
            "HandleButtonAction: Unknown action %d\n",
            action
        );
        break;
    }

    return;
}



/************ Property Window Control Objects ***************/


/* ################## Font Family ######################### */

typedef struct _FamilyItem {
    Widget      wid;
    String      label;
    String      value;
} FamilyItem;

static FamilyItem families[] = {
    { NULL, "Avant Garde",      "Avant-Garde" },
    { NULL, "Bookman",          "Bookman" },
    { NULL, "Courier",          "Courier" },
    { NULL, "Garamound",        "Garamound" },
    { NULL, "Goudy Old Style",  "Goudy-Old-Style" },
    { NULL, "Helvetica",        "Helvetica" },
    { NULL, "Lubalin Graph",    "Lubalin-Graph" },
    { NULL, "Lucida",           "Lucida" },
    { NULL, "Optima",           "Optima" },
    { NULL, "Times Roman",      "Times-Roman" },
    { NULL, "Univers",          "Univers" },
    { NULL, "Zapf Chancery",    "Zapf-Chancery" },
};
#define NR_FAMILIES (sizeof(families) / sizeof(FamilyItem))

caddr_t ObjFontFamily(message, param)
    int message;
    caddr_t param;
{
    static Widget       w_display;  /* displays current font */
    static Widget       w_choices;  /* rect butt container */
    static FamilyItem   *current = &families[0];

    switch (message) {
    case NEW: {
```

```
/*
 * NEW: create the object from scratch
 *
 *   INPUT: param == parent widget
 *   RETURN: parent's child (highest level created here)
 */
Widget      AddCaption(), AddRectButton();
Widget      w_caption, w_control, w_stack, w_menuPane;
Widget      w_parent = (Widget) param;
void        CBFontFamily();
register int    loop;

/*
 * Create the caption widget, which will serve as the
 * top-level container widget for this object.
 */
w_caption = AddCaption(w_parent, "Font Family:");

/*
 * Add the control area to hold the abbrev button stack
 * and its display-current-value widget.
 */
w_control =
    XtCreateWidget(
        "control",
        controlAreaWidgetClass,
        w_caption,
        tmpArg,
        TmpArgList(
            XtNlayoutType,  OL_FIXEDROWS,
            XtNmeasure, 1,
            0
        )
    );

/*
 * Create the abbreviated button stack widget as a
 * child of control
 */
w_stack =
    XtCreateWidget(
        "buttonStack",
        abbrevStackWidgetClass,
        w_control,
        tmpArg,
        TmpArgList(
            XtNtitle,    "Font Family",
            XtNpushpin, OL_OUT,
            XtNborderWidth, 0,
            0
        )
```

```
    );

/*
 * Create the static text widget to display the
 * current setting of the button stack.  Also a
 * child of control.
 */
w_display =
    XtCreateManagedWidget(
        "selection",            /* instance name */
        staticTextWidgetClass,  /* widget class */
        w_control,              /* parent widget */
        tmpArg,
        TmpArgList(
            XtNwidth,           200,
            XtNrecomputeSize,   FALSE,
            XtNgravity,         NorthWestGravity,
            XtNborderWidth,     1,
            0
        )
    );

/*
 * Tell the button stack widget about w_display so it
 * can use it as a preview area for the default
 * selection. (i.e., when the user holds down
 * the SELECT button on the abbrev widget, it
 * should display the default in w_display
 */
SetValue(w_stack, XtNpreviewWidget, w_display);

/*
 * Add the exclusives container to the abbrev stack by
 * making it a child of the abbrev stack menuPane
 */
w_menuPane = (Widget) GetValue(w_stack, XtNmenuPane);
w_choices =
    XtCreateWidget(
        "size",
        exclusivesWidgetClass,
        w_menuPane,
        tmpArg,
        TmpArgList(
            XtNlayoutType,  OL_FIXEDCOLS,
            XtNmeasure,     3,
            0
        )
    );


/*
```

```
         * Add rectangular buttons as choices, children of the
         * exclusives widget
         */
        for (loop = 0; loop < NR_FAMILIES; loop++) {
            /*
             * Add rectangular button
             */
            families[loop].wid =
                AddRectButton(
                    w_choices,
                    families[loop].label
                );

            /*
             * chain in the select action callback
             */
            XtAddCallback(
                families[loop].wid,      /* widget ID */
                XtNselect,               /* SELECT button */
                CBFontFamily,            /* callback proc */
                &families[loop]          /* ptr to item */
            );
        }

    XtManageChild(w_choices);
    XtManageChild(w_stack);
    XtManageChild(w_control);
    return((caddr_t) w_caption);
}

case SET: {
    /*
     * SET: set the value of the object.  NOTE that this is
     * a forced set by our parent, the property window
     * object, as opposed to a direct use selection.
     *
     *  INPUT: param == value to set
     *  RETURN: value actually set
     */
    int      value = (int) param;
    FamilyItem  *pItem, *FindFamily();

    if ((int) current->value == value) {
        return((caddr_t) value);      /* already set */
    }

    pItem = FindFamily(value, families, NR_FAMILIES);
    if (pItem != NULL) {
        /*
         * set the new value and unset the old
         */
```

266

```
        SetValue(w_choices, XtNnoneSet, TRUE);/* allow */

        SetValue(pItem->wid, XtNset, TRUE);   /* set new */
        SetValue(current->wid, XtNset, FALSE);/* unset old */

        SetValue(w_choices, XtNnoneSet, FALSE);/* disallow */
        current = pItem;          /* remember new */

        /*
         * display in Current Selection widget
         */
        SetValue(w_display, XtNstring, current->label);
    }
    return((caddr_t) current->value);
}

case GET: {
    /*
     * GET: return the current value of the object
     *
     *  INPUT: param N/A
     *  RETURN: current value
     */
    return((caddr_t) current->value);
}

case SELECT: {
    /*
     * SELECT: One of our widgets become selected, so
     * remember which one it was so we can return
     * the value on GET.  NOTE that this message is
     * for use by the XtNselect callback
     * associated with the button widgets.
     *
     *  INPUT: param == pSizeItem of object
     *  RETURN: pSizeItem of object actually set.
     */
    current = (FamilyItem *) param;

    /*
     * display in Current Selection widget
     */
    SetValue(w_display, XtNstring, current->label);

    return((caddr_t) current);
}

default:
    Warning("ObjFontFamily: Unknown message %d\n", message);
    return((caddr_t) NULL);
}
```

```
}


static void CBFontFamily(wid, client_data, call_data)
    Widget   wid;
    caddr_t  client_data;
    caddr_t  call_data;
{
    ObjFontFamily(SELECT, client_data); /* send msg to obj */
    return;
}

static FamilyItem *FindFamily(value, list, count)
    String      value;
    FamilyItem  *list;
    register    count;
{
    register FamilyItem *pItem = list;

    for (; count--; pItem++) {
        if (!strcmp(value, pItem->value)) {
            return(pItem);
        }
    }
    Warning("ObjFontFamily: couldn't set value %d\n", value);
    return(NULL);
}

/* ################ Point Size ################### */

typedef struct _SizeItem {
    Widget      wid;
    String      label;
    unsigned    value;
} SizeItem;

static SizeItem sizes[] = {
    /* Widget ID    Label       Value */
    { NULL,         "6",        6  },
    { NULL,         "8",        8  },
    { NULL,         "10",       10 },
    { NULL,         "12",       12 },
    { NULL,         "14",       14 },
    { NULL,         "18",       18 },
    { NULL,         "24",       24 },
    { NULL,         "36",       36 },
    { NULL,         "48",       48 },
    { NULL,         "72",       72 },
};
#define NR_SIZES    (sizeof(sizes) / sizeof(SizeItem))
```

```
caddr_t ObjPointSize(message, param)
    int message;
    caddr_t param;
{
    static SizeItem     *current = &sizes[0];
    static Widget       w_choices;        /* button container */

    switch (message) {
    case NEW: {
        /*
         * NEW: create the object from scratch
         *
         *   INPUT: param == parent widget
         *   RETURN: parent's child (highest level created here)
         */
        Widget          w_caption;
        Widget          w_parent = (Widget) param;
        Widget          AddCaption(), AddRectButton();
        void            CBPointSize();
        register int    loop;

        /*
         * Create the caption widget, which will serve as the
         * top-level container widget for this object.
         */
        w_caption = AddCaption(w_parent, "Point Size:");

        /*
         * Add the exclusives area as the caption's child
         */
        w_choices =
            XtCreateWidget(
                "size",                 /* instance name */
                exclusivesWidgetClass,  /* class name */
                w_caption,              /* parent widget */
                tmpArg,                 /* arg list */
                TmpArgList(
                    XtNlayoutType,      OL_FIXEDROWS,
                    XtNmeasure,         1,
                    0
                )
            );

        /*
         * Add rectangular buttons as choices, children of the
         * exclusives widget
         */
        for (loop = 0; loop < NR_SIZES; loop++) {
            /*
             * Add rectangular button
             */
```

```
            sizes[loop].wid =
                AddRectButton(
                    w_choices,
                    sizes[loop].label
                );

            /*
             * chain in the select action callback
             */
            XtAddCallback(
                sizes[loop].wid,     /* widget ID */
                XtNselect,           /* SELECT button */
                CBPointSize,         /* callback proc */
                &sizes[loop]         /* ptr to item */
            );
        }

        /*
         * Manage the choice widget and return
         */
        XtManageChild(w_choices);
        return((caddr_t) w_caption);
    }

    case SET: {
        /*
         * SET: set the value of the object.  NOTE that this is
         * a forced set by our parent, the property window
         * object, as opposed to a direct use selection.
         *
         *   INPUT: param == value to set
         *   RETURN: value actually set
         */
        unsigned    value = (unsigned) param;
        SizeItem    *pItem, *FindSize();

        if (current->value == value) {
            return((caddr_t) value);     /* already set */
        }

        pItem = FindSize(value, sizes, NR_SIZES);
        if (pItem != NULL) {
            SetValue(w_choices, XtNnoneSet, TRUE);  /* allow */

            SetValue(pItem->wid, XtNset, TRUE);     /* set new */
            SetValue(current->wid, XtNset, FALSE);/* unset old */

            SetValue(w_choices, XtNnoneSet, FALSE); /*disallow*/
            current = pItem;                    /* remember new */
        }
        return((caddr_t) current->value);
```

```
        }

    case GET: {
        /*
         * GET: return the current value of the object
         *
         *   INPUT: param N/A
         *   RETURN: current value
         */
        return((caddr_t) current->value);
    }

    case SELECT: {
        /*
         * SELECT: One of our widgets become selected,
         * so remember which one it was so we can return
         * the value on GET. NOTE that this message is
         * for use by the XtNselect callback
         * associated with the button widgets.
         *
         *   INPUT: param == pSizeItem of object
         *   RETURN: pSizeItem of object actually set.
         */
        current = (SizeItem *) param;
        return((caddr_t) current);
    }

    default:
        Warning("ObjPointSize: Unknown message %d\n", message);
        return((caddr_t) NULL);
    }
}


static void CBPointSize(wid, client_data, call_data)
    Widget  wid;
    caddr_t client_data;
    caddr_t call_data;
{
    ObjPointSize(SELECT, client_data);  /* send msg to obj */
    return;
}


static SizeItem *FindSize(value, list, count)
    unsigned    value;
    SizeItem    *list;
    register    count;
{
    register SizeItem   *pItem = list;
```

```
    for (; count--; pItem++) {
        if (pItem->value == value) {
            return(pItem);
        }
    }
    Warning("FindSize: couldn't find value %d\n", value);
    return(NULL);
}

/* ################### Type Style #################### */

typedef struct _StyleItem {
    Widget      wid;
    String      label;
    unsigned    value;
} StyleItem;

static StyleItem    styles[] = {
    /* Widget ID      Label           Value */
    { NULL,          "Bold",          BOLD },
    { NULL,          "Italic",        ITALIC },
    { NULL,          "Underline",     UNDERLINE },
    { NULL,          "Strikeout",     STRIKEOUT },
    { NULL,          "Small Caps",    SMALLCAPS },
};
#define NR_STYLES   (sizeof(styles) / sizeof(StyleItem))

caddr_t ObjTypeStyle(message, param)
    int message;
    caddr_t param;
{
    static unsigned     current = 0;
                            /* bitmask of current styles */
    static Widget       w_choices;      /* button container */

    switch (message) {
    case NEW: {
        /*
         * NEW: create the object from scratch
         *
         *  INPUT: param == parent widget
         *  RETURN: parent's child (highest level created here)
         */
        Widget          w_caption;
        Widget          w_parent = (Widget) param;
        Widget          AddCaption(), AddRectButton();
        void            CBTypeStyleSelect();
        void            CBTypeStyleUnselect();
        register int    loop;

        /*
```

```
 * Create the caption widget, which will serve as the
 * top-level container widget for this object.
 */
w_caption = AddCaption(w_parent, "Type Style:");

/*
 * Add the exclusives area as the caption's child
 */
w_choices =
    XtCreateWidget(
        "style",
        nonexclusivesWidgetClass,
        w_caption,
        tmpArg,
        TmpArgList(
            XtNlayoutType,   OL_FIXEDROWS,
            XtNmeasure,      1,
            0
        )
    );

/*
 * Add rectangular buttons as children of the
 * nonexclusives widget
 */
for (loop = 0; loop < NR_STYLES; loop++) {
    /*
     * Add rectangular button
     */
    styles[loop].wid =
        AddRectButton(
            w_choices,
            styles[loop].label
        );

    /*
     * chain in the select action callback
     */
    XtAddCallback(
        styles[loop].wid,        /* widget ID */
        XtNselect,               /* SELECT button */
        CBTypeStyleSelect,       /* callback */
        styles[loop].value       /* value, not ptr */
    );

    /*
     * chain in the unselect action callback
     */
    XtAddCallback(
        styles[loop].wid,        /* widget ID */
        XtNunselect,             /* UNSELECT button */
```

273

```
                    CBTypeStyleUnselect,     /* callback */
                    styles[loop].value       /* value, not ptr */
                );
        }

        /*
         * Manage the choice widget and return
         */
        XtManageChild(w_choices);
        return((caddr_t) w_caption);
    }

    case SET: {
        /*
         * SET: set the value of the object.  NOTE that this is
         * a forced set by our parent, the property window
         * object, as opposed to a direct use selection.
         *
         * INPUT: param == value to set
         * RETURN: value actually set
         */
        unsigned    value = (unsigned) param;
        unsigned    set, unset, loopCount;
        StyleItem   *pItem;


        if (current == value) {
            return((caddr_t) value);    /* already set */
        }

        /*
         * determine which buttons to set and unset based on the
         * requested and current state.
         */
        set = value & ~current;
        unset = current & ~value;

        current = set;              /* remember set state */

        /*
         * loop through style choices and set or unset,
         * as requested
         */
        for (
            pItem = styles,
            loopCount = NR_STYLES;

            loopCount--;

            pItem++
        ) {
```

```
                if (pItem->value & set) {
                    SetValue(pItem->wid, XtNset, TRUE);
                } else if (pItem->value & unset) {
                    SetValue(pItem->wid, XtNset, FALSE);
                }
            }

        return((caddr_t) current);     /* return current value */
    }

    case GET: {
        /*
         * GET: return the current value of the object
         *
         *  INPUT: param N/A
         *  RETURN: current value
         */
        return((caddr_t) current);
    }

    case SELECT: {
        /*
         * SELECT: One of our widgets become selected, so
         * remember which one it was so we can return the
         * value on GET.  NOTE that this message is for use
         * by the XtNselect callback associated with the
         * button widgets.
         *
         *  INPUT: param == bit of selected style
         *  RETURN: mask of current selected styles
         */
        current |= ((unsigned) param);
        return((caddr_t) current);
    }

    case UNSELECT: {
        /*
         * UNSELECT: One of our widgets become unselected,
         * so remember which one it was so we can return
         * the value on GET.  NOTE that this message is
         * for use by the XtNselect callback associated with
         * the button widgets.
         *
         *  INPUT: param == bit of unselected style
         *  RETURN: mask of current selected styles
         */
        current &= ~((unsigned) param);
        return((caddr_t) current);
    }

    default:
```

```
        Warning("ObjTypeStyle: Unknown message %d\n", message);
        return((caddr_t) NULL);
    }
}


static void CBTypeStyleSelect(wid, client_data, call_data)
    Widget  wid;
    caddr_t client_data;
    caddr_t call_data;
{
    ObjTypeStyle(SELECT, client_data);  /* send msg to obj */
    return;
}

static void CBTypeStyleUnselect(wid, client_data, call_data)
    Widget  wid;
    caddr_t client_data;
    caddr_t call_data;
{
    ObjTypeStyle(UNSELECT, client_data);    /* send msg to obj */
    return;
}

/* ##################### Text Color ######################### */

caddr_t ObjTextColor(message, param)
    int message;
    caddr_t param;
{
    static Widget   w_red, w_green, w_blue;
    static RGB      current;

    switch (message) {
    case NEW: {
        /*
         * NEW: create the object from scratch
         *
         *   INPUT: param == parent widget
         *   RETURN: parent's child (highest level created here)
         */
        Widget          w_caption, w_control;
        Widget          w_parent = (Widget) param;
        Widget          AddCaption(), CreateSlider();
        void            CBSliderMoved();

        /*
         * Create the caption widget, which will serve as the
         * top-level container widget for this object.
         */
        w_caption = AddCaption(w_parent, "Text Color:");
```

```
            w_control =
                XtCreateWidget(
                    "controlArea",
                    controlAreaWidgetClass,
                    w_caption,
                    tmpArg,
                    TmpArgList(
                        XtNalignCaptions,    TRUE,
                        XtNlayoutType,       OL_FIXEDROWS,
                        XtNmeasure,          3,
                        0
                    )
                );

            w_red = CreateSlider(w_control, "Red", UPDATE_RED);
            w_green = CreateSlider(w_control, "Green", UPDATE_GREEN);
            w_blue = CreateSlider(w_control, "Blue", UPDATE_BLUE);

            /*
             * Manage control area and return
             */
            XtManageChild(w_control);
            return((caddr_t) w_caption);
    }

    case SET: {
        /*
         * SET: set the value of the object.  NOTE that this is
         * a forced set by our parent, the property window
         * object, as opposed to a direct user selection,
         * which is handled by the Slider widget directly.
         *
         *   INPUT: param == RGB values to set
         *   RETURN: values actually set
         */
        RGB *value = (RGB *) param;


        /*
         * set the slider values.  probably should do some
         * range checking here
         */
        if (current.red != value->red) {
            SetValue(w_red, XtNsliderValue, value->red);
        }

        if (current.green != value->green) {
            SetValue(w_green, XtNsliderValue, value->green);
        }
```

277

```
        if (current.blue != value->blue) {
            SetValue(w_blue, XtNsliderValue, value->blue);
        }

        current = *value;

        return((caddr_t) value);
    }

    case GET: {
        /*
         * GET: return the current value of the object
         *
         *  INPUT: *RGB to return values;
         *  RETURN: N/A
         */
        RGB *ret = (RGB *) param;

        *ret = current;
        return(NULL);
    }

    case UPDATE_RED: {
        /*
         *  INPUT: current value of slider
         *  RETURN: N/A
         */
        current.red = ((unsigned) param);
        return(NULL);
    }

    case UPDATE_GREEN: {
        /*
         *  INPUT: current value of slider
         *  RETURN: N/A
         */
        current.green = ((unsigned) param);
        return(NULL);
    }

    case UPDATE_BLUE: {
        /*
         *  INPUT: current value of slider
         *  RETURN: N/A
         */
        current.blue = ((unsigned) param);
        return(NULL);
    }

    default:
        Warning("ObjTextColor: Unknown message %d\n", message);
```

```
            return((caddr_t) NULL);
    }
}


static void CBSliderMoved(wid, client_data, call_data)
    Widget  wid;
    caddr_t client_data;
    caddr_t call_data;
{
    /*
     * Send a message to the Text Color widget, telling it which
     * slider was moved and what the new value is
     */
    ObjTextColor(client_data, *call_data);
    return;
}

static Widget CreateSlider(w_parent, colorName, updateMessage)
    Widget  w_parent;
    String  colorName;
    int updateMessage;
{
    Widget  w_caption, w_slider;
    XColor  actualColor, exactColor;

    /*
     * Create the caption for this slider
     */
    w_caption = AddCaption(w_parent, colorName);

#define COLOR
#ifdef COLOR
    /*
     * Allocate a sharable color cell for the slider.
     */
    XAllocNamedColor(
        XtDisplay(w_caption),
        XDefaultColormapOfScreen(XtScreen(w_caption)),
        colorName,
        &actualColor,
        &exactColor
    );
#endif

    w_slider =
        XtCreateManagedWidget(
            colorName,
            sliderWidgetClass,
            w_caption,
            tmpArg,
```

```
            TmpArgList(
                XtNorientation, OL_HORIZONTAL,
                XtNwidth,    250,
                XtNborderWidth, 0,
#ifdef COLOR
                XtNforeground,  actualColor.pixel,
#endif
                0
            )
        );

    /*
     * The callback gets called when the slider moved.
     * It sends a message to the TextColor object
     * detailing which slider moved (updateMessage)
     * and what its new value is.
     */
    XtAddCallback(
        w_slider,
        XtNsliderMoved,
        CBSliderMoved,
        updateMessage
    );

    return(w_slider);
}


/******************** Helper routines ********************/

/*
 * AddCaption() - create a caption widget with a label string
 */
Widget AddCaption(w_parent, string)
    Widget  w_parent;
    String  string;
{
    Widget  w_label;

    w_label =
        XtCreateManagedWidget(
            "label",
            captionWidgetClass,
            w_parent,
            tmpArg,
            TmpArgList(
                XtNalignment,   OL_TOP,
                XtNborderWidth, 0,
                XtNlabel,       string,
                XtNposition,    OL_LEFT,
                0
```

```
                )
            );

        return(w_label);
}


/*
 * AddRectButton() - create a rect button with a string label
 */
Widget AddRectButton(w_parent, label)
    Widget  w_parent;
    String  label;
{
    Widget  w_button;

    w_button =
        XtCreateManagedWidget(
            label,                  /* instance name */
            rectButtonWidgetClass,  /* widget class */
            w_parent,               /* parent widget */
            tmpArg,                 /* arg list */
            TmpArgList(
                XtNlabel,   label,
                0
            )
        );
    return(w_button);
}
```

Chapter 6

Building Applications

At this point, you know how to develop programs using the OPEN
LOOK Intrinsic Toolkit. This chapter tells you how to turn those
programs into fully functional applications. Specifically, you'll learn
how to:

- use the Resource Manager to get user-specified options and defaults.
- maintain ICCCM window properties to cooperate with an
  ICCCM-compliant Window Manager and Session Manager.
- utilize the OPEN LOOK File Manager as an extension of your
  application to add file browse and drag-and-drop
  capabilities.
- use the OPEN LOOK Workspace Manager to execute commands and add or delete resources.
- exchange data with other clients, using properties and selections.
- provide context-sensitive help.

Finally, the last part of this chapter gives a few suggestions for going
further.

6.1 Using the X Resource Manager

The previous chapter shows how resource values control widget behavior. Up to now, we have either used the resource defaults or explicitly specified their values during creation or with XtSetValues.
While this is acceptable for demo-type programs, better applications
allow users to customize resource values with a configuration file and
command-line options. The section shows how to use the *X Resource
Manager* (Xrm) to implement flexible, configurable applications.

6.1.1 The Resource Database

The X Resource Manager maintains a database of resource name and value strings that widgets (and other resource consumers) query to determine the initial values of their resources. Unlike a traditional database, in which the user makes imprecise queries to match precise data, as in "Which buttons are red?," Xrm users make precise queries on imprecise data, as in "What color is this button?"

Xrm satisfies queries by matching a fully qualified request string to the list of expression strings in the database. If a match is found, Xrm returns its corresponding value. The expression syntax is fairly simple: Strings match exact spelling, with fields separated by a tight-binding period (.) or an asterisk (*) wildcard that matches any number of intermediate fields.

To see how this works, let's use examples from the UNIX file system. Pretend for the moment that UNIX file attributes are a function of directory name, and an administrative file keeps an expression list of these attributes. Using the Xrm syntax, an excerpt from this file might look like this:

```
*owner:public
*group:other
*permission:0666
*bin.permission:a+x
*bob*owner:bob
*bob*group:eng
*bob*permission:g-w,o-w
*bob*project1.doc.permission:g+w
usr.bob.memos.confidential.permission:0600
*project1*backup:always
*tmp.backup:never
*backup:3
```

When a user opens a file, the operating system queries this database to obtain the file's attributes. Using the above database, we see that:

- Unless otherwise specified, all files in the system are owned by public, have the group other, and are readable and writeable. Files in bin directories are also executable.
- Files in bob's directories are owned by bob, and are readable by everyone.
- Files in bob's subdirectory project1/doc are also writable by members of bob's group, eng.
- Bob doesn't want anyone else to read or write the files in /usr/bob/memos/confidential.
- Unless otherwise specified, files should be backed up at dump level 3.
- Files in tmp should never be backed up. Note that this does not apply to files in tmp subdirectories.
- All files under the directories named project1 should always be backed up, except those in tmp directories.

As you would expect, less ambiguous expressions have higher precedence.

In X, the Resource Manager's database describes resources such as fontColor and string, rather than file attributes such as owner and permission. Instead of directory names, path expressions match widget names, of which each field can be either the widget's class name (such as StaticText, OblongButton, or Slider) or its instance name as given in the first parameter to XtCreateWidget (for example, message, quitButton, faderLevel).[1]

---

[1]Unlike directory or file names, however, fully qualified resource names are not required to be unique. This ambiguity is intentional (a feature, if you will) and is particularly relevant when using widget class names in resource expressions.

A fully qualified resource name is the concatenation of the following strings:

- the class or instance name of the application (provided to OlInitialize)
- the class or instance name of each widget from the child of the top-level shell down to the specified widget
- the class or instance name of the resource itself

For example, to identify the font color of the short-term message widget in footer.c from the last chapter, the resource's class name would be:

```
OlExamples.FooterPanel.Form.StaticText.FontColor
```

By comparison, the same resource's fully qualified instance name would be:

```
footer.footer.footerBottom.shortTerm.fontColor
```

OlExamples is the application class name we gave to OlInitialize. The program's name (argv[0]) is footer, and the Toolkit automatically uses this as the application instance name. We created a FooterPanel widget named footer as a child of the top-level shell widget, and its child, a Form, is named footerBottom. The Form has two children, StaticText widgets named shortTerm and mediumTerm. The string FontColor is the value of the resource class XtCFontColor, and font-Color is the string value of the resource name XtNfontColor.

When widgets are created, they query the Resource Manager to determine the initial values of their resources. For each query, Xrm attempts to match the fully qualified names of the resource to the expression strings in the database, and if it finds a match, it returns the corresponding value field (everything to the right of the colon (:)), after converting it from a string into the requested data type.

Resource expressions have varying degrees of ambiguity. For example, the class string given above to match shortTerm would also match mediumTerm, since it is a same-class sibling widget of shortTerm and is also a child of the Form. This level of ambiguity is a useful shortcut to specify attributes for all objects of a certain widget class.

Like widget classes, resource classes are also ambiguous. For example, XtNx and XtNy are both instances of the resource class XtCPosition. Therefore, the line

```
*Position : 10
```

accomplishes

```
*x : 10
*y : 10
```

and probably more.

6.1.2 Resource Files

The X Resource Manager builds its database when the Toolkit is initialized, taking its input from several sources in the following order:

1. Internal default values supplied by the widget or other resource consumer.

2. Resource files containing one resource expression per line. Each one of these files is read in turn, if they exist:

Application System Defaults—The file XAPPLOADDIR/classname, where XAPPLOADDIR is the system application defaults directory (for example, /usr/X/lib/app-defaults or /usr/lib/X11/app-defaults), and classname is the application class name supplied to OlInitialize.[2]

Application User Defaults—The file $XAPPLRESDIR/classname, where XAPPLRESDIR is a variable in the user's environment. If XAPPLRESDIR is not set, the user's home directory is used.

General User Defaults—The values of the RESOURCE_MANAGER property on the root window, or if this property is not set, the file .Xdefaults in the user's home directory.

On startup, the OPEN LOOK Workspace Manager sets the RESOURCE_MANAGER property to the contents of the user's .Xdefaults file. Users may also modify this property using the *xrdb* command.

Environment Defaults—The file specified by the environment variable XENVIRONMENT, or if this variable is not set, the file .Xdefaults-host, where host is the network host name of the machine running the client.

3. Command-line options. Applications can register options as resources with the Resource Manager, which takes care of command line parsing and data conversion.

4. Application-supplied values. Note that since this is the last step of the resource value-building process, any resources set explicitly by the application (as we have done in the previous example programs) cannot be tailored by the user.

---

[2]Early releases of OPEN LOOK 2.0 may not access this file properly. As a workaround, prepend a slash (/) to the application class name passed to OlInitialize. (for example, "/OlExample").

6.1.3 Command-Line options

The X Resource Manager allows users to modify the resource database from the application command line. Users may specify complete resource expression strings, as in

```
-xrm '*fontColor : red'
```

or use more intuitive options, as defined by the application:

```
-fontColor red
```

Several options are built in to the Toolkit,[3] and applications may add more of their own. Application-defined command-line options are passed as a table to OlInitialize. The format is an array of structures:

```
typedef struct {
    char            *option;        /* argv to match */
    char            *specifier;     /* resource specifier */
    XrmOptionKind   argKind;        /* arg parsing selector */
    caddr_t         value;          /* value if XrmoptionNoArg*/
} XrmOptionDescRec, *XrmOptionDescList;
```

---

[3]Even though X traditionally strives to provide functionality without setting policy, providing a basic set of command-line options was deemed important enough to be a standard part of the Toolkit. Although an application may override these standard options, doing so is frowned upon.

If the option string appears on the command line, the Resource Manager makes a name value entry in the database, using specifier as the name and the string selected by argKind as the value.

Legal values for argKind include:

XrmOptionKind	Action
XrmoptionNoArg	Value is specified in value.
XrmoptionIsArg	Value is option string itself.
XrmoptionStickyArg	Value is characters immediately following option, for example, -x5.
XrmoptionSepArg	Value is next argument in argv, for example, -x 5.
XrmoptionResArg	Resource and value is next argument in argv, for example, -xrm '*Font: fixed'.
XrmoptionSkipArg	Ignore this option and next argument in argv.
XrmoptionSkipLine	Ignore this option and rest of argv.

To demonstrate how this works, let's look at the program options.c:

```
/*
 * Demonstrate X Resource Manager option parsing
 * @(#) sccs/s.options.c 1.1 last delta 3/11/90 18:51:49
 */
#include <X11/Intrinsic.h>
#include <X11/StringDefs.h>
#include <X11/Shell.h>
#include <Xol/OpenLook.h>
#include <Xol/Text.h>
#include <stdio.h>
#include "xtutil.h"

static XrmOptionDescRec options[] = {
    { "-width", "*Text.width",  XrmoptionSepArg,(caddr_t) NULL },
    { "-height", "*Text.height",XrmoptionSepArg,(caddr_t) NULL },
};

void main(argc, argv)
    unsigned int argc;
    char *argv[];
{
    Widget  w_toplevel, w_text;
```

```
    w_toplevel = OlInitialize(
        NULL,                    /* app name */
        "OlExample",             /* app class */
        options,                 /* option table */
        XtNumber(options),       /* nr options in table */
        &argc,                   /* addr of main argc */
        argv                     /* main argv */
    );
    w_text =
        XtCreateManagedWidget(
            "Pane",
            textWidgetClass,
            w_toplevel,
            NULL,
            0,
            NULL
        );

    (void) XtRealizeWidget(w_toplevel);
    (void) XtMainLoop();
}
```

The options table allows the user to specify the width and height of
the Text pane on the command line:

```
options -width 500 -height 300
```

The options table provided by options.c augments the default options built into the Xt Intrinsics:

```
static XrmOptionDescRec opTable[] = {
{"+rv",          "*reverseVideo",XrmoptionNoArg, (caddr_t) "off"},
{"+synchronous","*synchronous", XrmoptionNoArg, (caddr_t) "off"},
{"-background", "*background",  XrmoptionSepArg, (caddr_t) NULL},
{"-bd",          "*borderColor", XrmoptionSepArg, (caddr_t) NULL},
{"-bg",          "*background",  XrmoptionSepArg, (caddr_t) NULL},
{"-bordercolor","*borderColor", XrmoptionSepArg, (caddr_t) NULL},
{"-borderwidth",".borderWidth", XrmoptionSepArg, (caddr_t) NULL},
{"-bw",          ".borderWidth", XrmoptionSepArg, (caddr_t) NULL},
{"-display",     ".display",    XrmoptionSepArg, (caddr_t) NULL},
{"-fg",          "*foreground", XrmoptionSepArg, (caddr_t) NULL},
{"-fn",          "*font",       XrmoptionSepArg, (caddr_t) NULL},
{"-font",        "*font",       XrmoptionSepArg, (caddr_t) NULL},
{"-foreground", "*foreground", XrmoptionSepArg, (caddr_t) NULL},
{"-geometry",    ".geometry",   XrmoptionSepArg, (caddr_t) NULL},
{"-iconic",      ".iconic",     XrmoptionNoArg,  (caddr_t) "on"},
{"-name",        ".name",       XrmoptionSepArg, (caddr_t) NULL},
{"-reverse",     "*reverseVideo",XrmoptionNoArg, (caddr_t) "on"},
{"-rv",          "*reverseVideo",XrmoptionNoArg, (caddr_t) "on"},
{"-selectionTimeout", ".selectionTimeout",
                                XrmoptionSepArg, (caddr_t) NULL},
{"-synchronous","*synchronous", XrmoptionNoArg,  (caddr_t) "on"},
{"-title",       ".title",      XrmoptionSepArg, (caddr_t) NULL},
{"-xrm",         NULL,          XrmoptionResArg, (caddr_t) NULL},
};
```

Thus, invoking the program with

```
options -width 500 -height 300 -font 9x15
```

is equivalent to specifying the following lines in a resource file:

```
        options*Text.width:500
        options*Text.height:300
        options*font:9x15
```

Had we explicitly set the width and height resources when we created the Text widget (by specifying XtNwidth and XtNheight in the argList), those values would take precedence over the database, and the above command-line options and resource file lines would have no effect.

As an application developer, you get to decide which resources you will allow users to customize. It is not necessary to provide command-line options for all of these resources, just the ones that a user might want to change for each invocation.

6.1.4 Application Resources

So far in this chapter we have considered resources only in terms of widgets, but we have hinted at the existence of other resource consumers. Applications, too, can use the Resource Manager to define their own internal resources. All that is required is a single subroutine call containing a table describing the application's resources. This table is an array of XtResource structures:

```
typedef        struct{
String         resource_name;
String         resource_class;
String         resource_type;
Cardinal       resource_size;
Cardinal       resource_offset;
String         default_type;
caddr_t        default_address;
} XtResource,  *XtResourceList;
```

The items in this structure define the parameters of the resource and specify a default value. Notice that resource consumers specify the resource's data type: Xrm keeps resource values (from resource files and command-line options) as strings[4] and converts the data to this type when the resource consumer queries the value.

XtResource Field	Description
resource_name	Name of the resource; first letter is lowercase, by convention
resource_class	Class of resource; first letter is capitalized, by convention
resource_type	Data type of the resource, specified as one of the XtR-prefixed resource representation strings defined in <X11/StringDefs.h>
resource_size	Size (in bytes) of the resource, usually calculated with sizeof
resource_offset	Relative or absolute address of the resource, added to the base address passed to XtGetApplicationResources
default_type	Data type of the default value, specified as a resource representation string
default_address	Address of default, or if default_type == XtRImmediate, the value of the default

The Resource Manager uses resource converters registered with the Xt Intrinsics to convert data into the form requested by resource_type. The Xt Intrinsics provide converters for most common types, and applications can define and register converters for other resource types.

---

[4]Actually, the strings are compiled (hashed) to an efficient internal representation called *quarks*.

The standard resource converters include:[5]

From	To
XtRString	XtRAcceleratorTable, XtRBoolean, XtRBool, XtRCursor, XtRDimension, XtRDisplay, XtRFile, XtRFloat, XtRFont, XtRFontStruct, XtRInt, XtRPixel, XtRPosition, XtRShort, XtRTranslationTable, XtRUnsignedChar
XtRInt	XtRBoolean, XtRBool, XtRColor, XtRDimension, XtRFloat, XtRFont, XtRPixel, XtRPixmap, XtRPosition, XtRShort, XtRUnsignedChar
XtRColor	XtRPixel
XtRPixel	XtRColor

In addition to the above types, default_type may specify one of two other resource representation strings:

XtRImmediate—Indicates that default_address contains the default value (rather than its address), so no conversion is necessary.

XtRCallProc—default_address contains an XtResourceDefaultProc (pointer to a function that sets the value).

---

[5]The type XtRFloat is documented but not implemented in Release 3.0 of the Xt Intrinsics.

The resource.c program demonstrates the use of application resources, including conversions to a few different types:

```
/*
 * Demonstrate Xrm Application Resources using
 * absolute resource_offsets
 * @(#) sccs/s.resource.c 1.5 last delta 3/11/90 19:10:28
 */
#include <X11/Intrinsic.h>
#include <X11/StringDefs.h>
#include <X11/Shell.h>
#include <Xol/OpenLook.h>
#include <Xol/Text.h>
#include <stdio.h>
#include "xtutil.h"

/*
 * application resource variables
 */
Boolean debug;
int     bufSize;
float   pi;
Pixel   alertColor;

/*
 * application resource list
 */
static XtResource    resources[] = {
    {
        "debug",                            /* resource name */
        "Debug",                            /* resource class */
        XtRBoolean,                         /* resource type */
        sizeof(Boolean),                    /* resource size */
        (Cardinal) &debug,                  /* resource offset */
        XtRImmediate,                       /* default type */
        (caddr_t) TRUE                      /* default */
    },
    {
        "bufSize",                          /* resource name */
        "BufSize",                          /* resource class */
        XtRInt,                             /* resource type */
        sizeof(int),                        /* resource size */
        (Cardinal) &bufSize,                /* resource offset */
        XtRImmediate,                       /* default type */
        (caddr_t) 1024                      /* default */
    },
    {
        "alertColor",                       /* resource name */
        "AlertColor",                       /* resource class */
        XtRPixel,                           /* resource type */
```

```
            sizeof(Pixel),                      /* resource size */
            (Cardinal) &alertColor,             /* resource offset */
            XtRString,                          /* default type */
            "red"                               /* default */
    },
#ifdef XtRFloat
    {
        "pi",                                   /* resource name */
        "Pi",                                   /* resource class */
        XtRFloat,                               /* resource type */
        sizeof(float),                          /* resource size */
        (Cardinal) &pi,                         /* resource offset */
        XtRString,                              /* default type */
        (caddr_t) "3.1416"                      /* default */
    }
#endif
};


/*
 * command line option table
 */
static XrmOptionDescRec options[] = {
/*  argv,          resource,        option type,       value, if NoArg */
{"-debug",        "*debug",        XrmoptionNoArg,  (caddr_t) "true" },
{"-bufSize",      ".bufSize",      XrmoptionSepArg, (caddr_t) NULL },
{"-pi",           ".pi",           XrmoptionSepArg, (caddr_t) NULL },
{"-alertColor",".alertColor",XrmoptionSepArg, (caddr_t) NULL },
};

void main(argc, argv)
    unsigned int argc;
    char *argv[];
{
    Widget      W_toplevel, W_text;
    XrmValue    from, to;

    W_toplevel = OlInitialize(
        NULL,               /* app name */
        "OlExample",        /* app class */
        options,            /* option table */
        XtNumber(options),  /* nr options in table */
        &argc,              /* addr of main argc */
        argv                /* main argv */
    );

    /*
     * Use XtGetApplicationResources to process our
     * resource list against the resource database
     * Xrm created from resource files and command
     * line options.
     */
```

```
XtGetApplicationResources(
    W_toplevel,             /* toplevel widget */
    NULL,                   /* resource data offset */
    resources,              /* resource list */
    XtNumber(resources),    /* # of resources */
    NULL,                   /* overriding ArgList */
    0                       /* # of overriding Arg's */
);

printf(
    "debug = %s, bufSize = %d, pi=%f, alertColor=%d\n",
    debug ? "TRUE" : "FALSE",
    bufSize,
    pi,
    alertColor
);

/*
 * Applications can use XtConvert to convert
 * arbitrary data.  Note that the converter
 * owns the space for the return data, so if we wanted
 * to keep it around we would have to copy it.
 */
from.size = sizeof(alertColor);
from.addr = (caddr_t) &alertColor;

XtConvert(W_toplevel, XtRPixel, &from, XtRColor, &to);

if (to.addr == NULL) {
    fprintf(stderr, "%s: XtConvert failed\n", argv[0]);
} else {
    XColor  *pColor;

    pColor = (XColor *) to.addr;   /* converter owns space */
    printf("pixel=%d, rgb=[0x%x,0x%x,0x%x]\n",
        pColor->pixel,
        pColor->red, pColor->green, pColor->blue
    );
}

exit(0);
}
```

The addresses of the global variables debug, bufSize, pi, and alert-Color are specified as resource_offset fields of the XtResource structures in the resources array. When the application calls XtGetApplicationResources, Xrm attempts to match each of the resources' name and class strings to the expressions in the database.

If a match is found, Xrm converts the database's corresponding value string to the data type specified by the resource_type field and writes it to (resource_offset + resource_data_offset), where resource_data_offset is the second parameter to XtGetApplicationResources. In this example, resource_data_offset is NULL, so the value of each resource_offset is an absolute address.

If the resource does not match any expression in Xrm's database, Xrm converts the data at default_address from the default_type to resource_type and writes it to resource_offset as described above. This example also demonstrates the use of XtRImmediate as default_type, in which default_address contains a value suitable for resource_offset without conversion.

Xrm constructs the fully qualified application resource instance-name and class-name strings by concatenating the resource_name and resource_class strings with the application name (argv[0]) and application class (the second parameter to OlInitialize), respectively. In resource.c, we have defined the resource instance names

```
resource.debug
resource.bufSize
resource.pi
resource.alertColor
```

and the resource class names[6]

```
OlExample.Debug
OlExample.BufSize
OlExample.Pi
OlExample.AlertColor
```

---

[6]As of this writing, the Toolkit matches "BaseWindowShell" for the application class name of all OPEN LOOK applications, rather than the name passed to OlInitialize. This and the app-defaults filename bug noted previously make it difficult to effectively use application classes for OPEN LOOK application resources. Fortunately, these problems will be fixed in the next release of the software. Until then, use the application's instance name.

Remember that resource expressions can use any combination of instance names and class names, so, for example, a user could specify yellow as the alert color with any of the following lines in a resource file:

```
resource.alertColor:yellow
resource.AlertColor:yellow
OlExample.alertColor:yellow
OlExample.AlertColor:yellow
```

We have also chosen to make each of these resources available as command-line options, using the techniques discussed in the previous section. Thus, the user could also specify yellow as the alert color with

```
-alertColor yellow
```

Note that wildcard in the -debug option's expression string causes it to effect any other resource named debug in this application. In particular, any widgets with a debug resource will match this value, unless explicitly overridden or matched by a less ambiguous expression.

Finally, the last section in resource.c demonstrates how to use the Xt Intrinsics' resource converters to convert between data types within an application. This example converts an integer pixel value into RGB.

In resource.c, we gave absolute addresses in the resource_offset field of the XtResource structures in the resources array. This was most convenient, since our variables debug, bufSize, pi, and alertColor were freestanding globals. As an alternative, resource variables can be specified relative to the base of a structure, as demonstrated in resourc2.c:

```
/*
 * Demonstrate Xrm Application Resources
 * (using relative addressing)
 * @(#) sccs/s.resourc2.c 1.5 last delta 3/11/90 19:10:27
 */
#include <X11/Intrinsic.h>
#include <X11/StringDefs.h>
```

```
#include <X11/Shell.h>
#include <Xol/OpenLook.h>
#include <Xol/Text.h>
#include <stdio.h>
#include "xtutil.h"

/*
 * application resource variables
 */
typedef struct _AppResources {
    Boolean    debug;
    int        bufSize;
    float      pi;
    Pixel      alertColor;
} AppResources, *AppResourcesPtr;

AppResources      appResources;

/*
 * application resource list
 */
static XtResource    resources[] = {
    {
        "debug",                                /* resource name */
        "Debug",                                /* resource class */
        XtRBoolean,                             /* resource type */
        sizeof(Boolean),                        /* resource size */
        XtOffset(AppResourcesPtr, debug),       /* resource offset */
        XtRImmediate,                           /* default type */
        (caddr_t) TRUE                          /* default */
    },
    {
        "bufSize",                              /* resource name */
        "BufSize",                              /* resource class */
        XtRInt,                                 /* resource type */
        sizeof(int),                            /* resource size */
        XtOffset(AppResourcesPtr, bufSize),     /* resource offset */
        XtRImmediate,                           /* default type */
        (caddr_t) 1024                          /* default */
    },
    {
        "alertColor",                           /* resource name */
        "AlertColor",                           /* resource class */
        XtRPixel,                               /* resource type */
        sizeof(Pixel),                          /* resource size */
        XtOffset(AppResourcesPtr, alertColor),  /* offset */
        XtRString,                              /* default type */
        "red"                                   /* default */
    },
#ifdef XtRFloat
    {
```

```
            "pi",                               /* resource name */
            "Pi",                               /* resource class */
            XtRFloat,                           /* resource type */
            sizeof(float),                      /* resource size */
            XtOffset(AppResourcesPtr, pi),      /* resource offset */
            XtRString,                          /* default type */
            (caddr_t) "3.1416"                  /* default */
    }
#endif
};

/*
 * command line option table
 */
static XrmOptionDescRec options[] = {
/*  argv,          resource,      option type,      value, if NoArg */
{"-debug",        "*debug",       XrmoptionNoArg,  (caddr_t) "true" },
{"-bufSize",      ".bufSize",     XrmoptionSepArg, (caddr_t) NULL },
{"-pi",           ".pi",          XrmoptionSepArg, (caddr_t) NULL },
{"-alertColor",".alertColor",XrmoptionSepArg, (caddr_t) NULL },
};

void main(argc, argv)
    unsigned int argc;
    char *argv[];
{
    Widget      W_toplevel, W_text;
    XrmValue    from, to;

    W_toplevel = OlInitialize(
        NULL,                   /* app name */
        "OlExample",            /* app class */
        options,                /* option table */
        XtNumber(options),      /* nr options in table */
        &argc,                  /* addr of main argc */
        argv                    /* main argv */
    );

    /*
     * Use XtGetApplicationResources to process our
     * resource list against the resource database
     * Xrm created from resource files and command
     * line options.
     */
    XtGetApplicationResources(
        W_toplevel,             /* toplevel widget */
        &appResources,          /* resource data offset */
        resources,              /* resource list */
        XtNumber(resources),    /* # of resources */
        NULL,                   /* overriding ArgList */
        0                       /* # of overriding Arg's */
```

```
    );

    printf(
        "debug = %s, bufSize = %d, pi=%f, alertColor=%d\n",
        appResources.debug ? "TRUE" : "FALSE",
        appResources.bufSize,
        appResources.pi,
        appResources.alertColor
    );

    /*
     * Applications can use XtConvert to convert
     * arbitrary data.  Note that the converter
     * owns the space for the return data, so if we wanted
     * to keep it around we would have to copy it.
     */
    from.size = sizeof(appResources.alertColor);
    from.addr = (caddr_t) &appResources.alertColor;

    XtConvert(W_toplevel, XtRPixel, &from, XtRColor, &to);

    if (to.addr == NULL) {
        fprintf(stderr, "%s: XtConvert failed\n", argv[0]);
    } else {
        XColor   *pColor;

        pColor = (XColor *) to.addr;   /* converter owns space */
        printf("pixel=%d, rgb=[0x%x,0x%x,0x%x]\n",
            pColor->pixel,
            pColor->red, pColor->green, pColor->blue
        );
    }

    exit(0);
}
```

Note that we use XtOffset to calculate the value of each of the resource_offset fields, and that we pass the address of the global structure appResources as the second parameter to XtGetApplicationResources instead of NULL.

6.1.5 Documenting the Application

Perhaps the best tool for documenting configurable resources is with an application system-defaults resource file, installed in the

app-defaults directory (typically in /usr/X/lib or /usr/lib/X11). This
file should

- have the same name as the application class passed to
  OlInitialize
- define functional defaults for resources such that users can run
  the application without modifying their own .Xdefaults file.
- optionally document valid value ranges for users to customize
  in their .Xdefaults file.
- optionally document command-line option flags and their ef-
  fects on the resources.

When designing command-line options, resources, and documentation,
consider that novice X users may not be accustomed to using the X
Resource Manager. Providing a comprehensive application system-defaults file will go a long way toward making your application more
usable and easier to tailor to the users' needs.

6.2 Communicating with Other Clients

Chapter 2 introduced the *Inter-Client Communication Conventions
Manual* (ICCCM), which defines proper behavior of clients and window managers in the X Window System. The OPEN LOOK GUI ex-
tends these conventions to allow clients access to the unique capabilities of the OPEN LOOK Window Manager, Workspace Manager, and
File Manager.

In this section, we will first look closer at properties, the heart of the
ICCCM conventions. Then we will see how applications using the
OPEN LOOK Intrinsic Toolkit and Xtutil comply with the ICCCM
and participate in the OPEN LOOK subprotocol.

As you read this section, remember that all inter-client communication
is by convention only. Applications are expected to conform to the
ICCCM and the subprotocol of its GUI, but it is important to note that
these conventions are merely hints: just because your application

writes a property doesn't mean that someone else is going to read it, let alone honor it.

Clients are subject to the window manager's layout policy, input focus model, icon style, etc., and conflicting requests are not likely to be honored. While this takes a slight amount of control away from the application, it ensures interface consistency for the user. Presumably, users choose a particular user-interface because they like the way it handles window layout, input focus, icons, etc.

6.2.1 Properties

The key to inter-client communication is *properties*. As mentioned in Chapter 2, a property is an arbitrary data packet associated with a window. Each property is a variable of a particular property type and can be assigned values of that type.

Applications communicate with each other by reading and writing properties, both on their own windows and other's windows, in accordance with the ICCCM protocol and subprotocols like those defined by the OPEN LOOK GUI. Some examples of the kinds of information applications communicate through properties are:

Application Preferences—application name and class, icon name, window size and location.

State Information—keyboard focus, window grouping, selection ownership.

Subprotocol Capability—ability to save state, manage input focus among its subwindows, or delete its top-level window.

Service Requests—ask another client to execute a file or perform other file operations.

Arbitrary Data Transfer—cooperating clients can dynamically exchange data in any format (i.e., data is not restricted to text).

Every window can have properties, but as a general rule, properties are placed only on top-level windows and the root window. Service-oriented clients (such as the OPEN LOOK File Manager and Workspace Manager) often use the root window to store queues and other public properties so they can be easily found by other clients. In this way, the root window's properties are similar to the UNIX shell's environment space.

6.2.1.1 Atoms

In the name of speed and efficiency, X uses integer IDs called *atoms* to identify property name and type strings. Property users obtain atoms by registering, or *interning*, a property string with the server. If the string has already been interned, its atom is returned. Otherwise, the server interns the string and returns a newly generated atom.

For example, a client wanting to communicate with the OPEN LOOK File Manager needs to use the properties _OL_FM_QUEUE and _OL_FM_REPLY. To obtain the atoms for these properties, the client would use the Xlib function XInternAtom

```
Atom   XInternAtom(
       Display      *display,
       char         *atom_name,
       Bool         only_if_exists
);
```

to intern the strings "_OL_FM_QUEUE" and "_OL_FM_REPLY":

```
Display      *display;
Atom         _OL_FM_QUEUE, _OL_FM_REPLY;

...
```

306

```
display = XtDisplay(w_top-level);
_OL_FM_QUEUE = XInternAtom(display, "_OL_FM_QUEUE", FALSE);
_OL_FM_REPLY = XInternAtom(display, "_OL_FM_REPLY", FALSE);
```

If the third parameter to XInternAtom is FALSE, the server creates the atom if it doesn't already exist. If our client didn't want to create the atoms but only get them if they were already defined, only_if_exists would have been specified as TRUE. The existence of these atoms does not guarantee that the File Manager is running, however; the atoms could have been interned by another client, or the File Manager could have been running at one time and then exited. Remember that atoms exist until the server is reset or is terminated.

The set of standard X property names and types are automatically interned, so clients can use their predefined atoms without having to call XInternAtom with their string values. These atoms are defined in <X11/Xatom.h> and share the prefix XA_. Unfortunately, the corresponding strings do not have the XA_ prefix, such that

```
XGetAtomName(display, XA_WM_NAME);
```

yields the string "WM_NAME."

As shown in the above OPEN LOOK example, vendor- or organization-specific name and type strings begin with an underscore and an identifying prefix. All OPEN LOOK property strings begin with "_OL_." Of course, you can use whatever variable names you wish for the corresponding atoms, but using the exact spelling as the string is unambiguous and stylistically conveys that their values are constant for any given server execution.

Although the X protocol supports both upper- and lowercase property names and types, using all uppercase ensures compatibility with clients written in case-insensitive languages such as Lisp. For this reason, all of the standard X property strings and OPEN LOOK property strings use uppercase, exclusively.

6.2.2 The Inter-Client Communication Conventions Manual

From its inception, the goal of X Window System has been to provide functionality, not set policy. In practice, it has proved necessary to set at least some policy for clients and window managers to cooperate in the window system.

The *Inter-Client Communications Conventions Manual* (ICCCM), while not endorsing or enforcing any particular user interface for X, standardizes parts of the run-time application environment for X clients and window managers. Specifically, it defines the semantics of standard properties and the etiquette for their use in client communication with window managers and session managers, and in transferring data between clients through selections. Version 1.0 has been adopted by the X Consortium and is part of the standard for the X Window System, Version 11, Release 4 (X11R4).

The ICCCM is certain to undergo changes in the future. The guidelines presented in version 1.0 of the specification represent a minimum set of conventions needed to fill interoperability holes in the X Protocol.

Under most circumstances, ICCCM-conformance is provided transparently through the use of ICCCM-conforming toolkits and user-interface managers, which provide reasonable defaults for information not provided by the client. However, while the defaults may be valid and reasonable, they cannot take full advantage of the ICCCM or the OPEN LOOK GUI.

The next sections show how, with a little extra effort, clients using the OPEN LOOK Intrinsic Toolkit and the Xtutil utility library can set preferences with the Window Manager, execute programs using the Workspace Manager, browse files with the File Manager, and exchange arbitrary data with other clients.

6.2.3 The Window Manager and Session Manager

Most of the standard X window properties are for communicating with the Window Manager and Session Manager. An X Window Manager handles the layout and decorations of client windows, including their icons, while the Session Manager governs the system-level issues, such as mouse and keyboard mapping, screen background, and starting/stopping clients. Their properties and discussion are grouped here, since to a client, the two are virtually indistinguishable, and may even be the same program.[7]

Before the ICCCM standard, window managers and clients either defined their own uses for the standard properties or, more often than not, chose not to use them. Hence, clients often behaved differently with different window managers, working correctly with one particular window manager, or perhaps, with no window manager at all.

Now, by adhering to the ICCCM conventions, a client need not know or care which window manager is running, as long as the window manager also conforms to the conventions. Clients may, of course, exploit the features and characteristics of any window manager, but complete dependence on a particular window manager may render the client useless without it.

The Window Manager reads the property list of a client's top-level window when the window is mapped. The Window Manager also watches for future modifications to the property list by requesting PropertyNotify events on the window, which are sent by the server when it changes the property list of a window.

---

[7]The OPEN LOOK Workspace Manager performs the duties of the Session Manager as defined by the ICCCM, as well as additional OPEN LOOK GUI functionality that we will discuss in the next section. In this text, references to a "Session Manager" means any ICCCM session manager, while "Workspace Manager" denotes the OPEN LOOK Workspace Manager, *olwsm*.

For example, during initialization, a text-editor may set the WM_NAME property on its top-level window to a string indicating the name of the application and name of the file being edited. When the window is mapped, the Window Manager reads this property and displays this string in the window's title bar. If the user opens a different file, the editor changes the WM_NAME property to reflect the name of that file. The Window Manager notices that the property has been changed, and changes the title bar accordingly.

The following table lists the ICCCM-defined Window Manager and Session Manager properties, giving the string name of the property, the property's function, and how a client (or the Toolkit) sets the property.[8] Clients write these properties on their toplevel window, intending them to be read by the Window or Session Manager. The properties WM_STATE and WM_ICON_SIZE are exceptions, since they are written by the Window Manager for the client's benefit.

WM_NAME—title bar string; set with the XtNtitle shell widget resource. Defaults to the filename part of argv[0].

WM_ICON_NAME—icon name string; set using the XtNiconName shell widget resource. Defaults to the filename part of argv[0].

WM_NORMAL_HINTS—client size hints; set using XtNminWidth, XtNminHeight, XtNmaxWidth, XtNmaxHeight, XtNwidthInc, XtNheightInc, XtNminAspectX, XtNminAspectY shell widget resources.

WM_HINTS—additional window-management information; set with XtNinput, XtNinitialState, XtNiconPixmap, XtNiconWindow, XtNx, XtNy, XtNiconMask, XtNwindowGroup shell widget resources.

---

[8]There are actually several ways to set most any property; column three presents the way most consistent with the Toolkit.

310

WM_CLASS—application instance and class names for obtaining resources; instance name is the filename component of argv[0]; class name is the second parameter to OlInitialize.

WM_TRANSIENT_FOR—used by pop-up windows to point to the application's base window; set by the Toolkit for windows created with XtCreatePopupShell.

WM_PROTOCOLS—(including WM_SAVE_YOURSELF, WM_DELETE_WINDOW, and WM_TAKE_FOCUS)—MIT-extensible list of atoms indicating support for optional ICCCM communication protocols (see "WM_PROTOCOLS" below).

WM_COLORMAP_WINDOWS—list of subwindows that use a colormap different than the top-level window; set, if required, with XChangeProperty.

WM_STATE—state-management property used to communicate between the Window Manager and Session Manager; not used by applications.

WM_ICON_SIZE—icon dimensions recommended by the Window Manager clients can read this property with XGetWindowProperty.

WM_COMMAND—shell command string to restart client; set by the client using XSetCommand in response to a WM_SAVE_YOURSELF client message (see "WM_PROTOCOLS" below).

WM_CLIENT_MACHINE—network node name of the machine running the client set automatically by the Toolkit.

6.2.3.1 WM_PROTOCOLS

The WM_PROTOCOLS property is a list of atoms on the client's top-level window indicating which, if any, optional Window Manager or Session Manager protocols the client would like to participate in.

If the client elects to participate, it will be sent a synthetic-event message (with the protocol atom as the message data) from the Window Manager or Session Manager at the proper time, initiating the protocol.

<u>Optional Protocol—Client Action</u>

WM_TAKE_FOCUS—This is a protocol wart to allow support of a variety of input models[9] without changing the X Protocol. It is handled automatically by the OPEN LOOK Toolkit.

WM_SAVE_YOURSELF—Client should save state and set the WM_COMMAND property on its top-level window to a string that can be used to restart the client. This is not a shutdown message. The client should not prompt the user during this operation.

WM_DELETE_WINDOW—User requested the deletion of a top-level window. Client may interact with the user to confirm the delete or get other information, such as a filename for saving changes. Client is not required to terminate, but if it doesn't, it must unmap or destroy the window.

This list is extensible and is, in fact, quite likely to grow in future revisions of the ICCCM.

6.2.3.1.1 Xtutil Support for WM_PROTOCOLS

To make it easy for clients to participate in these protocols, Xtutil provides a callback interface similar to the one you're familiar with for widgets. To use this interface, clients register callbacks to be invoked when Xtutil receives the appropriate message from the

---

[9]The OPEN LOOK GUI uses the *globally active* input model. The other three models are *no input, passive,* and *locally active.*

Window Manager or Session Manager. Callbacks are added with the function AddWMCallbacks:

```
void AddWMCallbacks(va_alist);
```

where the argument list is:

```
Widget          w_top-level,
WMProtocol      protocol_1,
void            (*protocolCallback_1)(),
caddr_t         protocolData_1,      /* client_data */
...
WMProtocol      protocol_N,
void            (*protocolCallback_N)(),
caddr_t         protocolData_N,      /* client_data */
0                                    /* terminate list */
```

The first parameter to AddWMCallbacks is a top-level widget. Following this is variable-length array of triplets:

- an integer identifying the protocol
- a pointer to the callback function
- a possibly NULL value to be passed as the client_data parameter to the callback

A zero terminates the list.

Xtutil invokes the callbacks with parameters similar to widget callbacks, but without the widget:

```
void Callback(
   caddr_t    client_data,  /* registered w/callback */
   caddr_t    call_data     /* NULL for WM callbacks */
);
```

This code fragment would register the function DeleteWindow to be called with the parameter saveInfo as client_data whenever the application was sent the WM_DELETE_WINDOW message:

```
#include <xtutil.h>

void    WMDeleteWindow();

AddWMCallbacks(
        w_toplevel,
        CB_WM_DELETE_WINDOW, WMDeleteWindow, &saveInfo,
        0
);
```

The following example program, wmproto.c, creates a Text widget and elects to participate in the WM_SAVE_YOURSELF and/or WM_DELETE_WINDOW protocols as controlled by the command-line options -saveYourself and -deleteWindow, respectively.

```
/*
 * Demonstrate handling the WM_PROTOCOLS with the Xtutil API.
 * @(#) sccs/s.wmproto.c 1.10 last delta 3/11/90 19:10:26
 *
 * Command-line options:
 *   -saveYourself : participate in WM_SAVE_YOURSELF protocol
 *   -deleteWindow : participate in WM_DELETE_WINDOW protocol
 */
#include <X11/Intrinsic.h>
#include <X11/StringDefs.h>
#include <X11/Shell.h>
#include <X11/Xatom.h>         /* XA_ pre-defined atoms */
#include <Xol/OpenLook.h>
#include <Xol/OlClients.h>     /* OPEN LOOK atoms and properties */
#include <Xol/Text.h>
#include <stdio.h>
#include "xtutil.h"

typedef struct _ArgcArgv {
    int argc;
    char    **argv;
} ArgcArgv;

/*
 * application resource list
 */
Boolean saveYourself, deleteWindow;
```

```
static XtResource    resources[] = {
    {
        "saveYourself",              /* resource name */
        "WMProto",                   /* resource class */
        XtRBoolean,                  /* resource type */
        sizeof(Boolean),             /* resource size */
        (Cardinal) &saveYourself,    /* resource offset */
        XtRImmediate,                /* default type */
        (caddr_t) FALSE              /* default */
    },
    {
        "deleteWindow",              /* resource name */
        "WMProto",                   /* resource class */
        XtRBoolean,                  /* resource type */
        sizeof(Boolean),             /* resource size */
        (Cardinal) &deleteWindow,    /* resource offset */
        XtRImmediate,                /* default type */
        (caddr_t) FALSE              /* default */
    },
};

/*
 * command line option table
 */
static XrmOptionDescRec options[] = {
    {
        "-saveYourself",        /* argv */
        ".saveYourself",        /* resource */
        XrmoptionNoArg,         /* option type */
        (caddr_t) "true"        /* value, if NoArg */
    },
    {
        "-deleteWindow",        /* argv */
        ".deleteWindow",        /* resource */
        XrmoptionNoArg,         /* option type */
        (caddr_t) "true"        /* value, if NoArg */
    },
};

/*
 * These globals are useful throughout the program
 */
Widget  w_toplevel;        /* top level widget in the tree */
Window  toplevelWindow;    /* window of toplevel widget */
Display *ourDisplay;       /* server display we are using */
Screen  *ourScreen;        /* screen we are using */
Window  rootWindow;        /* root window of ourScreen*/

void main(argc, argv)
    unsigned int argc;
    char *argv[];
```

315

```
{
    Widget      CreateInitialWidgets();
    void        WMSaveYourself();
    void        WMDeleteWindow();
    ArgcArgv    saveArgcArgv;

    saveArgcArgv.argc = argc;        /* save for SAVE_YOURSELF */
    saveArgcArgv.argv = argv;

    w_toplevel = OlInitialize(
        NULL,                 /* app name - NOT USED */
        "OlExample",          /* app class */
        options,              /* option table */
        XtNumber(options),    /* nr options in table */
        &argc,                /* addr of main argc */
        argv                  /* main argv */
    );

    /*
     * Use XtGetApplicationResources to process
     * our resource list against the resource database
     * Xrm created from resource files and command line options.
     */
    XtGetApplicationResources(
        w_toplevel,               /* toplevel widget */
        NULL,                     /* resource data offset */
        resources,                /* resource list */
        XtNumber(resources),      /* # of resources */
        NULL,                     /* overriding ArgList */
        0                         /* # of overriding Arg's */
    );

    (void) CreateInitialWidgets(w_toplevel);
    (void) XtRealizeWidget(w_toplevel);

    /*
     * initialize misc global variables
     */
    toplevelWindow = XtWindow(w_toplevel);
    ourDisplay = XtDisplay(w_toplevel);
    ourScreen = XtScreen(w_toplevel);
    rootWindow = XDefaultRootWindow(ourDisplay);

    /*
     * Use the libxtutil.a functions to handle Window Manager
     * events.  We'll handle the application-specific stuff
     * with callbacks.
     */
    if (saveYourself) {
        AddWMCallbacks(
            w_toplevel,
```

```
                    CB_WM_SAVE_YOURSELF, WMSaveYourself, &saveArgcArgv,
                    0
            );
    }

    if (deleteWindow) {
        AddWMCallbacks(
            w_toplevel,
            CB_WM_DELETE_WINDOW, WMDeleteWindow, NULL,
            0
        );
    }

    (void) XtMainLoop();
}


Widget CreateInitialWidgets(w_parent)
    Widget   w_parent;
{

    Widget   w_text;

    w_text =
        XtCreateManagedWidget(
            "Pane",
            textWidgetClass,
            w_parent,
            NULL,
            0
        );

    return(w_text);
}

void WMSaveYourself(client_data, call_data)
    caddr_t client_data;
    caddr_t *call_data; /* not used */
{

    ArgcArgv    *saved = (ArgcArgv *) client_data;

    dbg("WMSaveYourself() got called\n");
    /*
     * Add code to checkpoint state.  This is
     * the time to flush buffers, etc., but NOT
     * the time to prompt user.
     */

    /*
     * MUST set the WM_COMMAND property!!
     */
    XSetCommand(
```

317

```
        ourDisplay,
        toplevelWindow,
        saved->argv,
        saved->argc
    );

    return;
}

void WMDeleteWindow(client_data, call_data)
    caddr_t client_data;
    caddr_t *call_data; /* not used */
{
    dbg("WMDeleteWindow() got called\n");
    /*
     * It is okay to prompt the user for
     * quit/delete confirmation here.
     *
     * Also, it is not neccessary to exit.
     * Instead, we could unmap the window
     * and remain running in the background.
     */
    exit(0);    /* terminate */
}
```

When started with the command line

```
wmproto -deleteWindow
```

the callback WMDeleteWindow is called when the user kills the client using the Window Manager or Session Manager (for example, when the user selects the Quit item in the Window menu).

Similarly, the WMSaveYourself callback is called if the program is started with

```
wmproto -saveYourself
```

Although the WM_SAVE_YOURSELF protocol is a checkpoint facility and not a shutdown facility, the Window Manager or Session Manager may send this message as a shutdown warning if the client did not elect to participate in the WM_DELETE_WINDOW protocol.

The most important thing to note here is that clients participating in WM_SAVE_YOURSELF must write the WM_COMMAND property on receipt of this message. As the example shows, this is easily accomplished using Xlib's XSetCommand.

As an aside, note that both the -deleteWindow and -saveYourself options are triggered with the command line:

```
wmproto -xrm '*WMProto:TRUE'
```

since we gave the resources saveYourself and deleteWindow the same class: WMProto.

To remove callbacks defined with AddWMCallbacks, use DeleteWMCallbacks:

```
void DeleteWMCallbacks(va_alist);
```

where the argument list is:

```
Widget          w_top-level,
WMProtocol      protocol_1,
...
WMProtocol      protocol_N,
0
```

6.2.4 The Workspace Manager

Using properties, clients can request the OPEN LOOK Workspace Manager to:

- execute programs on the machine where the Workspace Manager is running.
- add or delete resources from the .Xdefaults file and the RESOURCE_MANAGER property on the root window.

As with the WM_PROTOCOLS described above, Xtutil provides an easy-to-use interface to these functions.

6.2.4.1 Executing Another Program

To execute another program from within an application, call AskWSMExecute:

```
void AskWSMExecute(
     Widget       wid,
     WsmExecute   *request
);
```

where WsmExecute is a structure defined in xtutil.h:

```
typedef struct _WsmExecute {
   String        command;    /* command to execute */
} WsmExecute;
```

Upon completion of the request, the Workspace Manager sends a message containing the completion status:[10]

WSM_SUCCESS—The command execution was successful.

---

[10]Currently, the request will fail only if the *fork* or *exec* of */bin/sh* fails.

WSM_FORK_FAILURE—The command execution failed during the UNIX fork call.

WSM_EXEC_FAILURE—The command execution failed during the UNIX exec call.

The client can receive this message by registering a callback using the Xtutil function AddWSMCallback, which has a calling sequence and callback synopsis similar to AddWMCallback above:

```
void AddWSMCallbacks(va_alist);
```

where the argument list is:

```
Widget          w_top-level,
WSMProtocol     protocol_1,
void            (*protocolCallback_1)(),
caddr_t         protocolData_1,      /* client_data */
...
WSMProtocol     protocol_N,
void            (*protocolCallback_N)(),
caddr_t         protocolData_N,      /* client_data */
0                                    /* terminate list */
```

The calling sequence of the callbacks is:

```
void Callback(
    caddr_t     client_data,    /* registered w/callback */
    caddr_t     call_data
);
```

Currently, the only valid protocol is CB_WSM_REPLY, which returns the structure WsmReply as the call_data for the callback:

```
typedef struct _WsmReply {
        int     status;
        int     errno_pid;
} WsmReply;
```

The member status is one of WSM_SUCCESS, WSM_FORK_FAILURE, or WSM_EXEC_FAILURE, and errno_pid contains a process ID if status is WSM_SUCCESS and the UNIX error number (defined in /usr/include/sys/errno.h) otherwise.

Workspace Manager callbacks are removed with DeleteWSMCallbacks:

```
void DeleteWSMCallbacks(va_alist);
```

where the argument list is:

```
        Widget          w_top-level,
        WMProtocol      protocol_1,
        ...
        WMProtocol      protocol_N,
        0
```

An example program that demonstrates the use of AddWSMCallbacks is presented at the end of the next section.

6.2.4.2 Adding or Deleting Resources

Upon starting, the OPEN LOOK Workspace Manager writes the RESOURCE_MANAGER root window property with the contents of the user's $HOME/.Xdefaults resource file. The Workspace Manager updates the contents of this property (and the user's .Xdefaults file) when the user modifies settings in any of the Workspace Properties windows. Clients can ask the Workspace Manager to also maintain their properties, with the Xtutil function AskWSMResourceRequest.

```
void AskWSMResourceRequest(
        Widget              wid,
        WsmResourceRequest  *request
);
```

The WsmResourceRequest structure contains a list of resource expression:value strings and specifies whether the resources are to be merged (added) or deleted:

```
typedef struct _WsmResourceRequest {
    int type;   /* WSM_[MERGE,DELETE]_RESOURCES */
    String    *resourceList;
    int resourceCount;
} WsmResourceRequest;
```

The following program communicates to the OPEN LOOK Workspace Manager using the Xtutil functions above. The pane contains a single Text Field for entering a string. The Control Area has a button labeled Execute to execute the string in the Text Field, and a Menu Button labeled Resources that has two button items, one to merge and one to delete the string from the resource database and .Xdefaults file.

```
/*
 * Demonstrate how to communicate with the
 * OPEN LOOK Workspace Manager
 * @(#) sccs/s.wsmproto.c 1.9 last delta 3/11/90 18:51:38
 */
#include <X11/Intrinsic.h>
#include <X11/StringDefs.h>
#include <X11/Shell.h>
#include <X11/Xatom.h>        /* XA_ pre-defined atoms */
#include <Xol/OpenLook.h>
#include <Xol/ButtonStac.h>
#include <Xol/OlClients.h>  /* OPEN LOOK atoms and properties */
#include <Xol/ControlAre.h>
#include <Xol/OblongButt.h>
#include <Xol/TextField.h>
#include <stdio.h>
#include "xtutil.h"

/*
 * These globals are useful throughout the program
 */
Widget  w_toplevel;      /* top level widget in the tree */
Window  toplevelWindow; /* window of toplevel widget */
Display *ourDisplay;     /* server display we are using */
Screen  *ourScreen;      /* screen we are using */
Window  rootWindow;      /* root window of ourScreen */
```

```
void main(argc, argv)
    unsigned int argc;
    char *argv[];
{
    Widget          CreateInitialWidgets();
    void            WSMReply();

    w_toplevel = OlInitialize(
        NULL,                   /* app name */
        "OlExample",            /* app class */
        NULL,                   /* option table */
        0,                      /* nr options in table */
        &argc,                  /* addr of main argc */
        argv                    /* main argv */
    );

    (void) CreateInitialWidgets(w_toplevel);
    (void) XtRealizeWidget(w_toplevel);

    /*
     * initialize misc global variables
     */
    toplevelWindow = XtWindow(w_toplevel);
    ourDisplay = XtDisplay(w_toplevel);
    ourScreen = XtScreen(w_toplevel);
    rootWindow = XDefaultRootWindow(ourDisplay);

    /*
     * Use the libxtutil.a functions to handle the
     * low-level protocol associated with Workspace Manager
     * events; we just provide callbacks.
     */
    AddWSMCallbacks(
        w_toplevel,
        CB_WSM_REPLY,   WSMReply,    NULL,
        0
    );

    (void) XtMainLoop();
}


Widget CreateInitialWidgets(w_parent)
    Widget  w_parent;
{
    Widget          w_frame, w_control, w_button;
    static Widget   w_textField;
    Widget          CreateControl();
    void            ExecuteCommand();
    void            MergeResources(), DeleteResources();
```

```
    /*
     * Create a control area to hold the text field and the
     * action buttons
     */
    w_frame =
        XtCreateWidget(
            "frame",
            controlAreaWidgetClass,
            w_parent,
            tmpArg,
            TmpArgList(
                XtNlayoutType,   OL_FIXEDCOLS,
                XtNmeasure,      1,
                XtNborderWidth, 1,
                0
            )
        );

    /*
     * create the control area to hold the buttons
     */
    w_control = CreateControl(w_frame, &w_textField);

    /*
     * This text field is used for user input of
     * commands and resources
     */
    w_textField =
        XtCreateManagedWidget(
            "textField",
            textFieldWidgetClass,
            w_frame,
            tmpArg,
            TmpArgList(
                XtNwidth,    300,
                0
            )
        );

    XtManageChild(w_control);
    XtManageChild(w_frame);
    return(w_control);
}


/*
 * WSMReply() - the user requested that the
 * Workspace Manager execute a command and it has
 * responded with either the process id of the exec'd
 * processes or the errno if the exec or fork failed
 * for some reason.
```

```
 *
 * NOTE that WSM only reports back on WSM_EXECUTE requests
 * and not resource merge/delete requests.
 */
void WSMReply(client_data, call_data)
    caddr_t client_data;
    caddr_t call_data;
{
    WsmReply        *reply = (WsmReply *) call_data;
    register int    index;
    extern          errno;  /* part of the UNIX C runtime */

    switch (reply->status) {
    case WSM_SUCCESS:
        dbg("WSM_EXECUTE succeeded: pid=%d\n", reply->errno_pid);
        break;
    case WSM_FORK_FAILURE:
        errno = reply->errno_pid;   /* ensure errno is correct */
        perror("WSM_EXECUTE fork() failed");
        break;
    case WSM_EXEC_FAILURE:
        errno = reply->errno_pid;   /* ensure errno is correct */
        perror("WSM_EXECUTE exec() failed");
        break;
    default:
        dbg("WSMReply() - Unknown status: %d\n", reply->status);
        break;
    }

    return;
}


/*
 * ExecuteCommand() - queue an execute request with
 * the Workspace Manager
 */
void ExecuteCommand(wid, client_data, call_data)
    Widget  wid;
    caddr_t client_data;
    caddr_t call_data;
{
    WsmExecute  request;
    Widget      w_textField = *((Widget *) client_data);

    /*
     * Read the current string from the textField widget
     */
    request.command = (String) GetValue(w_textField, XtNstring);
```

```
    /*
     * and send it off to the Workspace Manager via the libxtutil
     * routine.
     */
    AskWSMExecute(wid, &request);    /* Xtutil does the work */

    XFree(request.command);
    return;
}
/*
 * MergeResources() - ask the Workspace Manager to
 * add to .Xdefaults
 */
void MergeResources(wid, client_data, call_data)
    Widget  wid;
    caddr_t client_data;
    caddr_t call_data;
{
    WsmResourceRequest  request;
    Widget          w_textField = *((Widget *) client_data);
    String          resourceList[1];

    /*
     * Read the current string value from the textField
     * widget and use it as the basis for a WSM resource
     * request packet that we ship off to libxtutil.
     * Notice that we could send a list of such resources
     * to be added to the .Xdefaults file.
     */
    request.type = WSM_MERGE_RESOURCES;
    request.resourceList = resourceList;
    request.resourceList[0] =
        (String) GetValue(w_textField, XtNstring);
    request.resourceCount = 1;

    AskWSMResourceRequest(wid, &request);  /* make the request */

    XFree(request.resourceList[0]);
    return;
}

/*
 * DeleteResources() - ask the Workspace Manager to
 * delete from .Xdefaults
 */
void DeleteResources(wid, client_data, call_data)
    Widget  wid;
    caddr_t client_data;
    caddr_t call_data;
{
    WsmResourceRequest  request;
```

327

```
    Widget          w_textField = *((Widget *) client_data);
    String          resourceList[1];

    /*
     * same as above for MergeResources
     */
    request.type = WSM_DELETE_RESOURCES;
    request.resourceList = resourceList;
    request.resourceList[0] =
        (String) GetValue(w_textField, XtNstring);
    request.resourceCount = 1;

    AskWSMResourceRequest(wid, &request);  /* make the request */

    XFree(request.resourceList[0]);
    return;
}


/*
 * CreateControl() - create an application control area
 */
Widget CreateControl(w_parent, pTextField)
    Widget  w_parent, *pTextField;
{
    Widget  w_control, w_button;
    Widget  w_resourceControl, w_resourceMenu;

    /*
     * Create the main control area as a child of the
     * parent parameter
     */
    w_control =
        XtCreateWidget(
            "control",
            controlAreaWidgetClass,
            w_parent,
            tmpArg,
            TmpArgList(
                XtNlayoutType,  OL_FIXEDROWS,
                XtNmeasure, 1,
                XtNborderWidth, 1,
                0
            )
        );

    /*
     * "Execute the string" button is a child of the
     * main control area.
     */
    w_button =
```

```
        XtCreateManagedWidget(
            "executeButton",
            oblongButtonWidgetClass,
            w_control,
            tmpArg,
            TmpArgList(
                XtNlabel, "Execute",
                0
            )
        );
XtAddCallback(
    w_button, XtNselect, ExecuteCommand, pTextField);

/*
 * use a button stack (as a child of the main control area)
 * to hold the resource buttons.
 */
w_resourceMenu =
    XtCreateWidget(
        "resourceMenu",
        buttonStackWidgetClass,
        w_control,
        tmpArg,
        TmpArgList(
            XtNlabel,    "Resources",
            XtNpushpin, OL_NONE,
            0
        )
    );
w_resourceControl =
    (Widget) GetValue(w_resourceMenu, XtNmenuPane);

/*
 * "Add this resource to the .Xdefaults file" button is
 * a child of the resource menu pane.
 */
w_button =
    XtCreateManagedWidget(
        "mergeButton",
        oblongButtonWidgetClass,
        w_resourceControl,
        tmpArg,
        TmpArgList(
            XtNlabel,    "Merge Resources",
            XtNdefault, TRUE,
            0
        )
    );
XtAddCallback(
    w_button, XtNselect, MergeResources, pTextField);
```

329

```
/*
 * "Remove this resource from the .Xdefaults file"
 * button is also a child of the resource menu pane.
 */
w_button =
    XtCreateManagedWidget(
        "deleteButton",
        oblongButtonWidgetClass,
        w_resourceControl,
        tmpArg,
        TmpArgList(
            XtNlabel,    "Delete Resources",
            0
        )
    );
XtAddCallback(
    w_button, XtNselect, DeleteResources, pTextField);

XtManageChild(w_resourceMenu);
XtManageChild(w_control);

return(w_control);
}
```

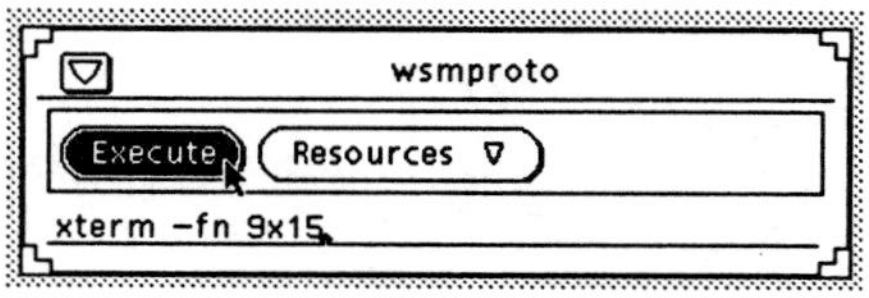

Figure 6.1 Using wsmproto to execute a program

Figure 6.2 Using wsmproto to add resources

6.2.5 The File Manager

Clients can communicate with the OPEN LOOK File Manager to provide users with direct file manipulation, similar to that used on Macintosh computers.

Each icon in the path pane of a File Manager window (and there can be multiple File Manager windows on the screen simultaneously) has a default binding to an action, which is invoked when the icon is double-clicked or dragged onto the workspace. If the icon is dragged on top of another window, the File Manager writes a property containing the dragged file's name on the receiving window. This is known as *drag-and-drop*. In drag-and-drop operations, the File Manager leaves the action binding up to the receiving application. Of course, if the application does not understand File Manager properties, nothing happens, but applications that recognize these properties are free to perform whatever action they deem appropriate. For example, a text editor client could edit the file as text, while a PostScript client could attempt to interpret the file as PostScript code, rendering the output in a window.

An application can also invoke a private File Manager window by writing a request to the File Manager's input queue.[11] In this browse configuration, the File Manager window acts like a command window of the client:

- The title bar of File Manager window reflects the name of the application.
- All actions are bound by the initiating application. Double-clicking an icon causes the File Manager to merely write a property containing the name of the selected file(s) on the initiating window.

---

[11]The File Manager's queue is a property on the root window.

- The File menu button in the File Manager's window contains two button items: Cancel and one with a label specified by the application. Selecting this item is the same as double-clicking an icon.

Clients instantiate a File Manager browse window with a call to AskFMBrowse:

```
#include <xtutil.h>

void AskFMBrowse(
        Widget          wid,
        FmBrowse        *browse
)
```

The FmBrowse structure specifies the initial directory and pattern match string, and the label for the first button item in the File menu Button:

```
typedef struct _FmBrowse {
        String label;
        String directory;
        String pattern;
} FmBrowse;
```

File Manager replies (properties written to client windows) are essentially the same whether or not the client initiated the transaction. Therefore, Xtutil groups them into a single callback, which can differentiate them with a simple switch statement.

To register the File Manager callback, use AddFMCallbacks:

```
void AddFMCallbacks(va_alist);
```

where the argument list is:

```
Widget          w_top-level,
WSMProtocol     protocol_1,
void            (*protocolCallback_1)(),
caddr_t         protocolData_1,       /* client_data */
```

```
...
WSMProtocol     protocol_N,
void            (*protocolCallback_N)(),
caddr_t         protocolData_N,        /* client_data */
0                                      /* terminate list */
```

The calling sequence of the callbacks is the same as the others:

```
void Callback(
   caddr_t     client_data,  /* registered w/callback */
   caddr_t     call_data
);
```

The callback for CB_FM_REPLY receives the FmReply structure in call_data:

```
typedef struct _FmReply {
      int            action;
      String message;
      String directory;
      int            fileCount;
      String *fileList;
} FmReply;
```

where action is one of the following:

FM_COPY, FM_MOVE—One or more files were dropped on your application and directory, fileCount, and fileList detail the filenames.

FM_ACCEPT—A browse operation completed successfully and directory, fileCount, and fileList detail the filenames.

FM_CANCEL—The browse was canceled by the user. The message field may contain an error message.

FM_INVALID—The browse request was invalid. The message field may contain an error message or the directory string (specified in the browse request) that caused the error.

File Manager callbacks are removed with DeleteFMCallbacks:

```
void DeleteFMCallbacks(va_alist);
```

where the argument list is:

```
Widget          w_top-level,
WMProtocol      protocol_1,
...
WMProtocol      protocol_N,
0
```

The following program, fmproto.c, demonstrates communication with the File Manager using the Xtutil interface. The base window it creates is very simple, consisting of only a single button, labeled "Browse...," which, when pressed, requests a File Manager browse window. More importantly, fmproto registers the callback FMReply to handle communication back from the File Manager, including drag-and-drop replies the client does not initiate.

```
/*
 * Demonstrate communication with the OPEN LOOK File Manager
 * @(#) sccs/s.fmproto.c 1.8 last delta 3/11/90 18:51:27
 */
#include <X11/Intrinsic.h>
#include <X11/StringDefs.h>
#include <X11/Shell.h>
#include <X11/Xatom.h>          /* XA_ pre-defined atoms */
#include <Xol/OpenLook.h>
#include <Xol/OlClients.h>      /* OPEN LOOK atoms and properties */
#include <Xol/OblongButt.h>
#include <stdio.h>
#include "xtutil.h"

typedef struct _ArgcArgv {
    int argc;
    char    **argv;
} ArgcArgv;

/*
 * These globals are useful throughout the program
 */
Widget  w_toplevel;     /* top level widget in the tree */
Window  toplevelWindow; /* window of toplevel widget */
Display *ourDisplay;    /* server display we are using */
```

```
Screen  *ourScreen;      /* screen we are using */
Window  rootWindow;      /* Root Window of the screen we are using */

void main(argc, argv)
    unsigned int argc;
    char *argv[];
{
    Widget      wid, CreateInitialWidgets();
    void        PostRealizeHook();

    w_toplevel = OlInitialize(
        NULL,           /* app name */
        "OlExample",    /* app class */
        NULL,           /* option table */
        0,              /* nr options in table */
        &argc,          /* addr of main argc */
        argv            /* main argv */
    );

    wid = CreateInitialWidgets(w_toplevel);

    (void) XtRealizeWidget(w_toplevel);

    /*
     * initialize misc global variables
     */
    toplevelWindow = XtWindow(w_toplevel);
    ourDisplay = XtDisplay(w_toplevel);
    ourScreen = XtScreen(w_toplevel);
    rootWindow = XDefaultRootWindow(ourDisplay);

    PostRealizeHook(wid);       /* complete Application init */

    (void) XtMainLoop();
}


/*
 * CreateInitialWidgets() - application initialization
 * before realizing the widget tree.
 */
Widget CreateInitialWidgets(w_parent)
    Widget  w_parent;
{
    Widget      w_button;
    static FmBrowse browse;

    w_button =
        XtCreateManagedWidget(
            "browse",
            oblongButtonWidgetClass,
```

335

```
                w_parent,
                tmpArg,
                TmpArgList(
                    XtNlabel,           "Browse",
                    XtNlabelType,       OL_POPUP,
                    XtNrecomputeSize,   FALSE,
                    0
                )
        );

    /*
     * Use the libxtutil.a function AskFmBrowse() to queue
     * the browse request with the File Manager when the
     * user SELECT's this button.  Notification of browse
     * completion will come through the callback
     * registered above with AddFMCallbacks().
     */
    browse.label = "Compile";   /* label of button in File */
    browse.directory = ".";      /* directory to browse */
    browse.pattern = "*.c";      /* file pattern */

    XtAddCallback(w_button, XtNselect, AskFMBrowse, &browse);

    return(w_button);
}


/*
 * PostRealizeHook() - complete application initialization
 * after the widget tree is realized
 */
void PostRealizeHook(wid)
    Widget  wid;
{
    void    FMReply();

    /*
     * Set up our File Manager Drag/Drop and Browse callback.
     * FMReply gets called whenever receive a message on
     * our _OL_FM_REPLY property.
     */
    AddFMCallbacks(
        wid,
        CB_FM_REPLY,    FMReply,    NULL,
        0
    );

    return;
}
```

```
/*
 * FMReply() - the user has asked the File Manager to send
 * us a file or files, either in response to our FM_BROWSE
 * request, or by drag and drop from any FM instance.
 */
void FMReply(client_data, call_data)
    caddr_t client_data;
    caddr_t call_data;
{
    FmReply         *reply = (FmReply *) call_data;
    register int    index;

    switch (reply->action) {
    case FM_COPY:
    case FM_MOVE:
    case FM_ACCEPT:
        dbg(
            "FMReply got files. dir = %s, fileCount = %d\n",
            reply->directory,
            reply->fileCount
        );
        for (index = 0; index < reply->fileCount; index++) {
            dbg(
                "\tfileList[%d] = %s\n",
                index,
                reply->fileList[index]
            );
        }

        break;
    case FM_CANCEL:
        dbg("Browse was canceled: message=%s\n", reply->message);
        break;
    case FM_INVALID:
        dbg("Browse invalid: message=%s\n", reply->message);
        break;
    default:
        dbg("FMReply() - Unknown action: %d\n", reply->action);
        break;
    }

    return;
}
```

337

Figure 6.3 fmproto with a File Manager browse window

Figure 6.4 fmproto's button item in the File menu

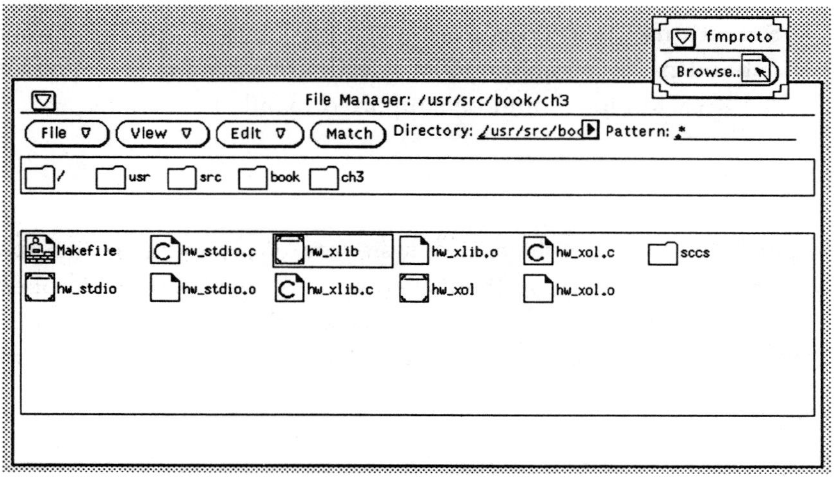

Figure 6.5 Dragging a file onto fmproto[12]

6.2.6 Other Clients

Inter-client communication is not restricted to the OPEN LOOK Window Manager , Workspace Manager, and File Manager. By using one or both of the following techniques, clients can communicate with any other client in the window system:

Properties—As shown above with the OPEN LOOK File Manager and Workspace Manager, window properties are an effective form of inter-client communication between cooperating

---

[12]Note that this picture shows a normal File Manager window (invoked from the Workspace Manager) rather than a browse window. At this writing, browse windows cannot perform drag-and-drop.

applications. Developers are free to design new property protocols and document them for use by other applications.

Selections—Selections are an updated version of the familiar
cut-and-paste metaphor. The selection mechanism is defined by
the ICCCM and should be supported by all applications.

6.2.6.1 Properties

Cooperating clients, perhaps in a suite, can easily exchange information through properties on their windows. A client writes a property
on another client's window, and the target client reads the property
in response to the PropertyNotify event it received as a result of this
write.

Here again, Xtutil provides a callback interface to handle
PropertyNotify events and dispatch to callbacks registered for the
modified property. Using this interface, an application can register a
different callback for each property it expects to see, or it can register
a single callback to handle all properties. Further, Xtutil differenti-
ates between properties being written and deleted, and each property
can have multiple callbacks for each of these actions.

Clients add property callbacks with AddPropertyCallbacks, whose
calling sequence is similar to that of AddWMCallbacks,
AddWSMCallbacks, and AddFMCallbacks, but also has, as an
additional parameter per callback record, the property name to
watch:

```
void AddPropertyCallbacks(va_alist);
```

where the argument list is:

```
Widget              w_top-level,
PropertyProtocol    protocol_1,
Atom                atom_1,                 /* property name */
void                (*protocolCallback_1)(),
```

```
caddr_t                 protocolData_1,      /* client_data */
...
PropertyProtocol        protocol_N,
Atom                    atom_N,              /* property name */
void                    (*protocolCallback_N)(),
caddr_t                 protocolData_N,      /* client_data */
0                                            /* terminate list */
```

The calling sequence of the callbacks is the same as before:

```
void Callback(
    caddr_t    client_data,   /* registered w/callback */
    caddr_t    call_data
);
```

The call_data is a PropertyReply structure:

```
typedef _PropertyReply {
    Boolean    sendEvent;     /* from another client? */
    Window     window;        /* window ID of property */
    Atom       atom;          /* property name */
    Time       time;          /* time property was changed */
    int state; /* new value or deleted */
} PropertyReply;
```

In most cases, the only field a callback needs is window, which is used as input to the Xlib function XGetWindowProperty.

Since Xtutil allows multiple callbacks to be registered per property, the DeletePropertyCallbacks routine requires the exact same parameters given to AddPropertyCallbacks to identify the callback to be removed:

```
void DeletePropertyCallbacks(va_alist);
```

where the argument list is:

```
Widget                  w_top-level,
PropertyProtocol        protocol_1,
Atom                    atom_1,              /* property name */
void                    (*protocolCallback_1)(),
```

```
caddr_t                 protocolData_1,      /* client_data */
...
PropertyProtocol        protocol_N,
Atom                    atom_N,              /* property name */
void                    (*protocolCallback_N)(),
caddr_t                 protocolData_N,      /* client_data */
0                                            /* terminate list */
```

To demonstrate this mechanism, we'll need to take a look at two separate client programs:

> **logger**—Displays text written to the LOG property on its top-level window. This window ID is advertised in the property LOGGER, written on the root window.

> **loguser**—Reads the LOGGER root window property to get the window ID of the logger client. Writes log text to the LOG property on this window.

First, let's look at logger.c:

```
/*
 * Demonstrate how to use properties to communicate
 * between clients.
 *
 * @(#) sccs/s.logger.c 1.8 last delta 3/11/90 18:51:31
 */
#include <X11/Intrinsic.h>
#include <X11/StringDefs.h>
#include <X11/Shell.h>
#include <X11/Xatom.h>        /* XA_ pre-defined atoms */
#include <Xol/OpenLook.h>
#include <Xol/OlClients.h>   /* OPEN LOOK atoms and properties */
#include <Xol/Text.h>
#include <stdio.h>
#include "xtutil.h"

/*
 * These globals are useful throughout the program
 */
Widget  w_toplevel;       /* top level widget in the tree */
Window  toplevelWindow;   /* window of toplevel widget */
Display *ourDisplay;      /* server display we are using */
Screen  *ourScreen;       /* screen we are using */
```

```
Window   rootWindow;      /* root window of ourScreen */

Atom    LOG, LOGGER;     /* atoms used by this program */

void main(argc, argv)
    unsigned int argc;
    char *argv[];
{
    Widget        CreateInitialWidgets(), wid;
    void          PostRealizeHook();

    w_toplevel = OlInitialize(
        NULL,                   /* app name */
        "OlExample",            /* app class */
        NULL,                   /* option table */
        0,                      /* nr options in table */
        &argc,                  /* addr of main argc */
        argv                    /* main argv */
    );

    wid = CreateInitialWidgets(w_toplevel);

    (void) XtRealizeWidget(w_toplevel);

    /*
     * initialize misc global variables
     */
    toplevelWindow = XtWindow(w_toplevel);
    ourDisplay = XtDisplay(w_toplevel);
    ourScreen = XtScreen(w_toplevel);
    rootWindow = XDefaultRootWindow(ourDisplay);

    PostRealizeHook(wid);

    (void) XtMainLoop();
}

/*
 * CreateInitialWidgets() - main application hook,
 * before XtRealizeWidget.
 */
Widget CreateInitialWidgets(w_parent)
    Widget  w_parent;
{
    Widget        w_text;

    w_text =
        XtCreateManagedWidget(
            "text",
            textWidgetClass,
            w_parent,
```

```
            tmpArg,
            TmpArgList(
                XtNverticalSB,        TRUE,
                XtNsourceType,        OL_STRING_SOURCE,
                0
            )
        );

    return(w_text);
}


/*
 * PostRealizeHook() - application's chance to set
 * stuff up AFTER the toplevel widget has been realized.
 * This is important, since before it is realized, none of the
 * window are valid, so things like properties need to
 * happen here.
 */
void PostRealizeHook(wid)
    Widget  wid;          /* widget from CreateInitialWidgets() */
{
    void    Log(), Cleanup();

    LOG = XInternAtom(ourDisplay, "LOG", FALSE);
    LOGGER = XInternAtom(ourDisplay, "LOGGER", FALSE);

    /*
     * Use the libxtutil.a functions to handle the event
     * dispatching for communication using properties.
     * Specifically, we want to know when the LOG property
     * has been written so we can get the text data to put
     * in the log window.
     */
    AddPropertyCallbacks(
        w_toplevel,
        CB_NEW,      /* libxtutil property protocol */
        LOG,         /* atom to watch */
        Log,         /* callback */
        wid,         /* client_data for callback */
        0            /* zero-terminated list */
    );

    /*
     * Write the LOGGER property on the root window with our
     * toplevel window ID.  Clients that wish to log messages
     * can then write text in the LOG property on our window.
     */
    XChangeProperty(
        ourDisplay,                        /* display */
        rootWindow,                        /* window to write on */
```

```
        LOGGER,                              /* property name */
        XA_WINDOW,                           /* property type */
        32,                                  /* format */
        PropModeReplace,                     /* mode to write */
        (unsigned char *) &toplevelWindow,   /* data */
        1                                    /* nelements */
    );

    /*
     * Before we exit, we need to remove the
     * advertise property LOGGER from the root window
     */
    AddWMCallbacks(
        w_toplevel,
        CB_WM_DELETE_WINDOW,    Cleanup,    NULL,
        0
    );

    return;
}


/*
 * Log() - callback for the LOG property.
 */
void Log(client_data, call_data)
    caddr_t client_data;
    caddr_t call_data;
{
    Widget          w_text = (Widget) client_data;
    PropertyReply   *reply = (PropertyReply *) call_data;
    FUNC            textInsert =
                        (FUNC) GetValue(w_text, XtNtextInsert);
    Atom            actual_type;
    int             actual_format;
    unsigned long   nitems;
    unsigned long   bytes_after;
    String          string;


    /*
     * read the text to log from the LOG property
     */
    XGetWindowProperty(
        ourDisplay,      /* display */
        reply->window,   /* window */
        LOG,             /* property name */
        0,               /* offset */
        BUFSIZ,          /* length */
        TRUE,            /* delete? */
        XA_STRING,       /* requested type */
```

```
            &actual_type,
            &actual_format,
            &nitems,
            &bytes_after,
            &string
    );

    if (actual_type != XA_STRING) {
        String  str = XGetAtomName(ourDisplay, actual_type);
        Warning("Log() - got wrong type: %s\n", str);
        XFree(str);
        return;
    }

    if (actual_format != 8) {
        Warning(
            "Log() - expected format 8, got %d\n",
            actual_format
        );
        return;
    }

    if (bytes_after != 0) {
        Warning(
            "Log() - leaving %d bytes_after, max=%d\n",
            bytes_after,
            BUFSIZ
        );
    }

    /*
     * write the text to the widget
     */
    (*textInsert)(w_text, string);
    (*textInsert)(w_text, "\n");

    XFree(string);
    return;
}

/*
 * Cleanup() - wrap up any loose end.
 */
void Cleanup(client_data, call_data)
    caddr_t client_data;
    caddr_t call_data;
{
    XDeleteProperty(ourDisplay, rootWindow, LOGGER);
    XSync(ourDisplay, FALSE);        /* wait for all to finish */
    exit(0);
}
```

In the routine PostRealizeHook, the LOG and LOGGER atoms are interned. Next, we add the Log callback for the LOG property on our top-level window. By using CB_NEW as the PropertyProtocol, we are assured that the callback only gets called when the value is changed, but not when the property is deleted, which happens during the callback.

Still in PostRealizeHook, we advertise our service by writing our window ID as the LOGGER property on the root window. Rather than having this extra level of indirection, we could have had clients simply write the LOG property on the root window, similar to the OPEN LOOK File Manager and Workspace Manager queues, but our method is more efficient, since there are bound to be fewer clients requesting PropertyNotify events on Logger's window than on the root window. Finally, we register the Shutdown callback to delete the LOGGER property from the root window on exit.

The Log callback is quite straightforward: read the string out of the LOG property (deleting its contents), and write the string to the Text widget.

The loguser client is basically the reverse of logger, except that it has a bit more user-interface code to create the Text Field widget for text input and a button to send it:

```
/*
 * Demonstrate how to read properties using Xtutil.
 * @(#) sccs/s.loguser.c 1.8 last delta 3/11/90 18:51:32
 */
#include <X11/Intrinsic.h>
#include <X11/StringDefs.h>
#include <X11/Shell.h>
#include <X11/Xatom.h>       /* XA_ pre-defined atoms */
#include <Xol/OpenLook.h>
#include <Xol/OlClients.h>   /* OPEN LOOK atoms and properties */
#include <Xol/ControlAre.h>
#include <Xol/OblongButt.h>
#include <Xol/TextField.h>
#include <stdio.h>
#include "xtutil.h"
```

```
/*
 * These globals are useful throughout the program
 */
Widget  w_toplevel;      /* top level widget in the tree */
Window  toplevelWindow;  /* window of toplevel widget */
Display *ourDisplay;     /* server display we are using */
Screen  *ourScreen;      /* screen we are using */
Window  rootWindow;      /* root window or ourScreen */

Atom    LOG, LOGGER;
Window  logWindow;       /* window to write LOG property on */

void main(argc, argv)
    unsigned int argc;
    char *argv[];
{
    Widget      CreateInitialWidgets(), wid;
    void        WSMReply();
    void        PostRealizeHook();

    w_toplevel = OlInitialize(
        NULL,                /* app name */
        "OlExample",         /* app class */
        NULL,                /* option table */
        0,                   /* nr options in table */
        &argc,               /* addr of main argc */
        argv                 /* main argv */
    );

    wid = CreateInitialWidgets(w_toplevel);

    (void) XtRealizeWidget(w_toplevel);

    /*
     * initialize misc global variables
     */
    toplevelWindow = XtWindow(w_toplevel);
    ourDisplay = XtDisplay(w_toplevel);
    ourScreen = XtScreen(w_toplevel);
    rootWindow = XDefaultRootWindow(ourDisplay);

    PostRealizeHook(wid);

    (void) XtMainLoop();
}


Widget CreateInitialWidgets(w_parent)
    Widget  w_parent;
{
    Widget          w_frame;
```

```
        static Widget   w_textField;
        Widget          CreateControl();

        /*
         * Create a control area to hold the text field and the
         * action buttons
         */
        w_frame =
            XtCreateWidget(
                "frame",
                controlAreaWidgetClass,
                w_parent,
                tmpArg,
                TmpArgList(
                    XtNlayoutType,  OL_FIXEDCOLS,
                    XtNmeasure,     1,
                    0
                )
            );

        /*
         * Create the control area and associated buttons
         */
        (void) CreateControl(w_frame, &w_textField);

        /*
         * The work pane is so simple we'll just create it here
         */
        w_textField =
            XtCreateManagedWidget(
                "textField",
                textFieldWidgetClass,
                w_frame,
                tmpArg,
                TmpArgList(
                    XtNwidth,   300,
                    0
                )
            );

    XtManageChild(w_frame);
    return(w_frame);
}

/*
 * CreateControl() - create an application control area
 */
Widget CreateControl(w_parent, pTextField)
    Widget  w_parent, *pTextField;
{
    Widget  w_control, w_button;
```

```
    void    LogMessage();

    /*
     * Create the main control area as a child
     * of the parent parameter
     */
    w_control =
        XtCreateWidget(
            "control",
            controlAreaWidgetClass,
            w_parent,
            tmpArg,
            TmpArgList(
                XtNlayoutType,  OL_FIXEDROWS,
                XtNmeasure,     1,
                0
            )
        );

    /*
     * "Log the message" button is a child of the
     * main control area.
     */
    w_button =
        XtCreateManagedWidget(
            "logButton",
            oblongButtonWidgetClass,
            w_control,
            tmpArg,
            TmpArgList(
                XtNlabel, "Log",
                0
            )
        );
    XtAddCallback(w_button, XtNselect, LogMessage, pTextField);

    XtManageChild(w_control);
    return(w_control);
}


/*
 * PostRealizeHook() - setup properties after windows
 * are realized
 */
void PostRealizeHook(wid)
    Widget  wid;
{
    int             rc;
    Atom            actual_type;
    int             actual_format;
```

```
        unsigned long    nitems;
        unsigned long    bytes_after;
        Window           *pWindow;

        LOG = XInternAtom(ourDisplay, "LOG", FALSE);
        LOGGER = XInternAtom(ourDisplay, "LOGGER", FALSE);

retry:
    /*
     * Get the window id to write the LOG property
     */
    rc = XGetWindowProperty(
        ourDisplay,      /* display */
        rootWindow,      /* window to read from */
        LOGGER,          /* property name */
        0,               /* offset */
        sizeof(Window),  /* length */
        FALSE,           /* delete? */
        XA_WINDOW,       /* req_type */
        &actual_type,
        &actual_format,
        &nitems,
        &bytes_after,
        (unsigned char **) &pWindow
    );

    if ((actual_type == None) || (actual_format == 0)) {
        caddr_t Notice();
        int rc;
        enum {
            retryVal,
            exitVal,
        };

        rc = (int)
            Notice(
                wid,
                "LOGGER property non-existent on root window",
                "Retry", retryVal,
                "Exit", exitVal,
                0
            );

        switch (rc) {
        default:
            dbg("unknown return from Notice: %d\n", rc);
        case exitVal:
            exit(-1);
        case retryVal:
            goto retry;
        }
```

```
    }

    logWindow = *pWindow;         /* place to write property */
    XFree(pWindow);

    return;
}


/*
 * LogMessage() - send some text to the message logger
 */
void LogMessage(wid, client_data, call_data)
    Widget  wid;
    caddr_t client_data;
    caddr_t call_data;
{
    Widget      w_textField = *((Widget *) client_data);
    String      string;

    /*
     * Read the current string from the textField widget
     */
    string = (String) GetValue(w_textField, XtNstring);

    /*
     * Write the text to the message logger
     */
    XChangeProperty(
        ourDisplay,             /* display */
        logWindow,              /* window to write on */
        LOG,                    /* property name */
        XA_STRING,              /* property type */
        8,                      /* format */
        PropModeAppend,         /* writing mode */
        string,                 /* data */
        strlen(string)          /* data length in bytes */
    );

    XFree(string);
    return;
}
```

If the LOGGER property is not found on the root window, loguser pops up a Notify box to ask if the user wants to quit or try to read the property again.

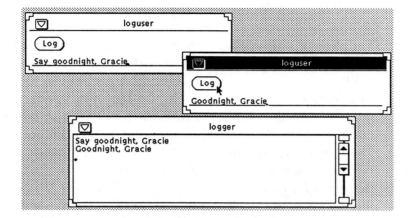

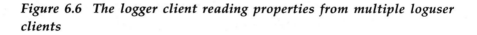

Figure 6.6 The logger client reading properties from multiple loguser clients

6.2.6.2 Selections

Cut buffers are properties used for traditional text cut-and-paste operations between peer clients. They are a holdover from older versions of X, and their functionality has been completely superseded by the *selection* mechanism.

With cut buffers, cut-and-paste was a static operation: the cutting client copied its data (almost always text) into one of the cut buffer properties on the root window, and the pasting client read this data back out. Since there was no direct communication between the exchanging clients, the format of the data had to be defined beforehand, hence the conventional restriction to text.

The selection mechanism is an interactive protocol between exchanging clients, allowing them to exchange arbitrary data by agreeing on the data's content and format at run-time:

- The cutting client asks the server to make it the selection owner,[13] advertising the fact that it has data available to read.
- The pasting client becomes a selection requestor when it asks the server for the contents of the current selection. In this request, the requestor specifies a desired data type and format.
- The server forwards the request to the selection owner, who is responsible for converting the selection data into the requested format. The selection owner can choose to convert the data into the requested format, convert the data into an alternate format, or return a failure status.
- Finally, the selection requestor receives the data (not necessarily in the requested format) or a failure status.

The ICCCM lists the target formats and types valid for selection requests. As of ICCCM Version 1.0, this list included:

```
TARGETS, TIMESTAMP, STRING, PIXMAP, DRAWABLE, BITMAP,
FOREGROUND, BACKGROUND, COLORMAP, ODIF, OWNER_OS, FILE_NAME,
HOST_NAME, CHARACTER_POSITION, LINE_NUMBER, COLUMN_NUMBER,
LENGTH, USER, PROCEDURE, MODULE, PROCESS, TASK, CLASS, NAME,
CLIENT_WINDOW, DELETE, INSERT_SELECTION, INSERT_PROPERTY.
```

This list will grow. The special target TARGET requests the list of target atoms that the selection owner will honor for the currently selected data. Notice that there are several other targets, such as HOST_NAME, USER, PROCESS_ID, and OWNER_OS, that have little or nothing to do with the selection data, but pertain more to the selection owner itself.

---

[13]More precisely, *a* selection owner, since the conventions allow for ownership of any number of selections, with each named by an atom such as PRIMARY, SECONDARY, and CLIPBOARD.

Of course, not all targets are appropriate for all data. A graphics editor would not be expected to convert a selected image into a string, for example. When conversion requests are inappropriate, the selection owner can either refuse the request or provide the data in an alternate format. The latter is preferred, since it may avoid the "go fish" dialog that could otherwise transpire.

6.2.6.2.1 Owning a Selection

All "real" applications are expected to conform to the ICCCM, including selections. Fortunately, the Xt Intrinsics provide a reasonable interface to make managing selections a simple matter of defining a few callbacks. To become a selection owner, use XtOwnSelection:

```
Boolean XtOwnSelection(
        Widget                  widget,
        Atom                    selection,
        Time                    time,
        XtConvertSelectionProc  convert,
        XtLoseSelectionProc     lose,
        XtSelectionDoneProc     done
);
```

The following example, ownselct, demonstrates the use of XtOwnSelection to assert selection ownership of the PRIMARY selection. The ICCCM defines the PRIMARY, SECONDARY, and CLIPBOARD selections for the following purposes:

PRIMARY—Principle means of communication between clients using the selection mechanism

SECONDARY—"Spare" selection atom for requests that require two active selections

CLIPBOARD—Cut-and-paste selection

In reality, clients can use any of these selection atoms arbitrarily and can even define their own. Of course, the point to any protocol standard is to facilitate communication; applications that use nonstandard protocols don't communicate very well with ones that do. Since there is currently no mechanism for determining which selection atoms are recognized in the system, atoms other than those listed above are probably not useful as selections. The examples presented here use the PRIMARY selection.

The timestamp value for any of the selection calls is obtained through the Xtutil function, GetTimestamp. The ICCCM forbids the use of the constant CurrentTime for this value, since it is important for a client to know the exact time it gained ownership. Unfortunately, when using the Toolkit, procuring the real current time is not trivial, since the event dispatching is done by the Toolkit, and callbacks aren't given this information. GetTimestamp does the work for you, so use it anywhere you need the real server time.

Finally, when a conversion request is received from a selection requestor, the Toolkit calls the *convert* callback given in the call to XtOwnSelection. In ownselct, this callback, CBConvertSelection, dispatches to individual conversion routines that do the real work. The advantage to this approach is that the conversion routines can be shared among other convert callbacks for selections of different data types. For example, a graphics editor can use a different convert callback depending on whether text or graphics are selected. The individual conversion routines for common conversion targets such as FILE_NAME, HOST_NAME, and PROCESS can be shared.

```
/*
 * Demonstrate Selection ownership using the OPEN LOOK X Toolkit.
 * @(#) sccs/s.ownselct.c 1.1 last delta 3/11/90 18:52:05
 */
#include <X11/Intrinsic.h>
#include <X11/StringDefs.h>
#include <X11/Shell.h>
#include <X11/Xatom.h>
#include <Xol/OpenLook.h>
#include <Xol/Caption.h>
#include <Xol/ControlAre.h>
#include <Xol/Exclusives.h>
#include <Xol/OblongButt.h>
```

```
#include <Xol/RectButton.h>
#include <Xol/StaticText.h>
#include <stdio.h>
#include "xtutil.h"

Widget  w_toplevel;      /* top level widget in the tree */
Window  toplevelWindow;  /* window of toplevel widget */
char    *ProgramName;    /* printable name of our application */
Display *ourDisplay;     /* server display we are using */
Screen  *ourScreen;      /* screen we are using */
Window  rootWindow;      /* rootWindow of ourScreen */

static Widget   currentButton;  /* currently selected button */
static Time ownTimestamp;    /* timestamp to aquire selection */
static String   appClass = "OlExample";

void main(argc, argv)
    unsigned int argc;
    char *argv[];
{
    Widget  CreateInitialWidgets();

    w_toplevel = OlInitialize(
        NULL,               /* app name - filled by Xt */
        appClass,           /* app class */
        NULL,               /* option list */
        0,                  /* # of options */
        &argc,              /* addr of main argc */
        argv                /* main argv */
    );

    ourDisplay = XtDisplay(w_toplevel);
    ourScreen = XtScreen(w_toplevel);

    (void) CreateInitialWidgets(w_toplevel);

    (void) XtRealizeWidget(w_toplevel);

    toplevelWindow = XtWindow(w_toplevel);
    rootWindow = XDefaultRootWindow(ourDisplay);

    (void) XtMainLoop();
}


Widget CreateInitialWidgets(w_parent)
    Widget  w_parent;
{
    Widget      w_frame;
    Widget      CreateControl(), CreateColorGrid();
```

```
    w_frame =
        XtCreateWidget(
            "frame",
            controlAreaWidgetClass,
            w_parent,
            tmpArg,
            TmpArgList(
                XtNlayoutType,       OL_FIXEDCOLS,
                XtNmeasure,          1,
                XtNalignCaptions,    TRUE,
                0
            )
        );

    (void) CreateControl(w_frame);
    (void) CreateColorGrid(w_frame);

    XtManageChild(w_frame);
    return(w_frame);
}

/******************** Control Area ********************/

static Widget   w_own, w_disown;

/*
 * CreateControl() - create an application control area
 */
Widget CreateControl(w_parent)
    Widget   w_parent;
{
    Widget   w_caption, w_control;
    void     CBOwnSelection(), CBDisownSelection();


    w_caption =  XtCreateManagedWidget(
        "buttonCaption",
        captionWidgetClass,
        w_parent,
        tmpArg,
        TmpArgList(
            XtNlabel,        "PRIMARY Selection:",
            0
        )
    );

    w_control =
        XtCreateWidget(
            "control",
            controlAreaWidgetClass,
            w_caption,
```

```
                tmpArg,
                TmpArgList(
                    XtNlayoutType,   OL_FIXEDROWS,
                    XtNmeasure, 1,
                    0
                )
            );

    /*
     * "Own Selection" button is a child of the control area.
     */
    w_own =
        XtCreateManagedWidget(
            "ownButton",
            oblongButtonWidgetClass,
            w_control,
            tmpArg,
            TmpArgList(
                XtNlabel, "Own",
                0
            )
        );
    XtAddCallback(w_own, XtNselect, CBOwnSelection, NULL);

    /*
     * "Release Selection" button is a child of the control area.
     */
    w_disown =
        XtCreateManagedWidget(
            "disownButton",
            oblongButtonWidgetClass,
            w_control,
            tmpArg,
            TmpArgList(
                XtNlabel,    "Disown",
                XtNbusy,     TRUE,
                0
            )
        );
    XtAddCallback(w_disown, XtNselect, CBDisownSelection, NULL);

    XtManageChild(w_control);
    return(w_control);
}


/*
 * CBOwnSelection() - request selection ownership.  Note that,
 * to support the ICCCM, the constant CurrentTime is not
 * an appropriate time value to XtOwnSelection.
 */
```

```
void CBOwnSelection(wid, client_data, call_data)
    Widget  wid;
    caddr_t client_data;
    caddr_t call_data;
{
    Boolean     ownIt;
    Boolean     CBConvertSelection();
    void        CBLostSelection();
    extern Time ownTimestamp;    /* remember for convert req */


    ownTimestamp = GetTimestamp(wid);
    ownIt =
        XtOwnSelection(
            w_toplevel,
            XA_PRIMARY,             /* typical */
            ownTimestamp,
            CBConvertSelection, /* convert callback */
            CBLostSelection,    /* lose_selection callback */
            NULL                /* done callback */
        );

    if (ownIt == TRUE) {
        SetValue(w_own, XtNbusy, TRUE);
        SetValue(w_disown, XtNbusy, FALSE);
    }
    return;
}

/*
 * CBDisownSelection() - tell the toolkit that we are
 * voluntarily giving up the selection ownership.
 *
 * Note that the widget and selection MUST be the same as in the
 * XtOwnSelection call and the timestamp must be >= the time used
 * in that call.
 */
void CBDisownSelection(wid, client_data, call_data)
    Widget  wid;
    caddr_t client_data;
    caddr_t call_data;
{
    XtDisownSelection(w_toplevel, XA_PRIMARY, GetTimestamp(wid));
    return;
}

typedef struct _SelectionConverter {
    String      atomName;
    Atom        atom;
    Boolean     (*convertProc)();
} SelectionConverter;
```

```
/*
 * CBConvertSelection - called by the toolkit to convert
 * our selection into another format, which we handle
 * through a table of conversion routines.  Note that a
 * complete application may need a CBConvertSelection
 * callback equivalent per type of selection it supports,
 * since some conversions are not appropriate for all
 * selection types.  By using conversion routines as we
 * have done here, the common conversions can be referenced
 * from any CBConvertSelection equivalent.
 */
Boolean CBConvertSelection(
    wid, pSelection, pTarget, pType, pValue, pLength, pFormat
)
    Widget          wid;
    Atom            *pSelection;
    Atom            *pTarget;
    Atom            *pType;          /* return */
    caddr_t         *pValue;         /* return */
    unsigned long   *pLength;        /* return */
    int             *pFormat;        /* return */
{
    Boolean ConvertToTarget(), ConvertToTimestamp(),
        ConvertToPixmap(), ConvertToDrawable(),
        ConvertToPixel(), ConvertToColormap(),
        ConvertToOwnerOS(), ConvertToHostname(), ConvertToUser(),
        ConvertToProcess(), ConvertToClass(), ConvertToName(),
        ConvertToClientWindow();

    static SelectionConverter   converters[] = {
        { "TIMESTAMP",      NULL,   ConvertToTimestamp },
        { "DRAWABLE",       NULL,   ConvertToDrawable },
        { "FOREGROUND",     NULL,   ConvertToPixel },
        { "BACKGROUND",     NULL,   ConvertToPixel },
        { "COLORMAP",       NULL,   ConvertToColormap },
        { "OWNER_OS",       NULL,   ConvertToOwnerOS },
        { "HOST_NAME",      NULL,   ConvertToHostname },
        { "USER",           NULL,   ConvertToUser },
        { "PROCESS",        NULL,   ConvertToProcess },
        { "CLASS",          NULL,   ConvertToClass },
        { "NAME",           NULL,   ConvertToName },
        { "CLIENT_WINDOW",  NULL,   ConvertToClientWindow },
    };
#define NR_CONVERTERS   \
    (sizeof(converters) / sizeof(converters[0]))

    static Atom     TARGETS;            /* conversions we do here */
    static Boolean  inited = FALSE;
    register unsigned int       count;
    register SelectionConverter *pConvert;
```

```
    if (inited == FALSE) {
        for (
            pConvert = converters,
            count = NR_CONVERTERS;

            count--;

            pConvert++
        ) {
            pConvert->atom =
                XInternAtom(ourDisplay, pConvert->atomName);
        }

        TARGETS = XInternAtom(ourDisplay, "TARGETS");

        inited = TRUE;
    }

    /*
     * TARGETS is a special request to return the list of
     * selection conversions that we support.
     */
    if (*pTarget == TARGETS) {
        register Atom          *pAtom;

        *pValue = XtMalloc(NR_CONVERTERS * sizeof(Atom));
        for (
            pAtom = (Atom *) *pValue,
            pConvert = converters,
            count = NR_CONVERTERS;

            count--;

            pAtom++,
            pConvert++
        ) {
            *pAtom = pConvert->atom;
        }
        *pType = XA_ATOM;
        *pLength = NR_CONVERTERS;
        *pFormat = 32;

        return(TRUE);
    }

    /*
     * Dispatch on the requested target
     */
    for (
```

```
            pConvert = converters,
            count = NR_CONVERTERS;

            count--;

            pConvert++
    ) {
        if (pConvert->atom == *pTarget) {
            return(
                (*pConvert->convertProc)(
                    wid,
                    pSelection,
                    pTarget,
                    pType,
                    pValue,
                    pLength,
                    pFormat
                )
            );
        }
    }
    return(FALSE);              /* don't have a converter */
}


/*
 * CBLostSelection() - selection ownership has been usurped by
 * some other client.
 */
void CBLostSelection(wid, selection)
    Widget  wid;
    Atom    selection;
{
    extern Widget   w_own, w_disown;

    SetValue(w_own, XtNbusy, FALSE);
    SetValue(w_disown, XtNbusy, TRUE);
}

/******************** Converters ************************/

Boolean ConvertToTimestamp(
    wid, pSel, pTarget, pType, pVal, pLen, pFormat
)
    Widget          wid;
    Atom            *pSel;
    Atom            *pTarget;
    Atom            *pType;          /* return */
    caddr_t         *pVal;           /* return */
    unsigned long   *pLen;           /* return */
    int             *pFormat;        /* return */
```

```
{
    extern Time ownTimestamp;
                        /* set in the own selection routine */

    *pType = XA_INTEGER;
    *pVal = (caddr_t) XtMalloc(sizeof(ownTimestamp));
    *((Time *) *pVal) = ownTimestamp;
    *pLen = 1;
    *pFormat = 32;
    return(TRUE);
}

Boolean ConvertToDrawable(
    wid, pSel, pTarget, pType, pVal, pLen, pFormat
)
    Widget          wid;
    Atom            *pSel;
    Atom            *pTarget;
    Atom            *pType;      /* return */
    caddr_t         *pVal;       /* return */
    unsigned long   *pLen;       /* return */
    int             *pFormat;    /* return */
{
    extern Widget   currrentButton;    /* set in CBColorSelect */

    *pType = XA_DRAWABLE;
    *pVal = (caddr_t) XtMalloc(sizeof(Drawable));
    *((Drawable *) *pVal) = XtWindow(currentButton);
    *pLen = 1;
    *pFormat = 32;
    return(TRUE);
}

Boolean ConvertToPixel(
    wid, pSel, pTarget, pType, pVal, pLen, pFormat
)
    Widget          wid;
    Atom            *pSel;
    Atom            *pTarget;
    Atom            *pType;      /* return */
    caddr_t         *pVal;       /* return */
    unsigned long   *pLen;       /* return */
    int             *pFormat;    /* return */
{
    extern Widget   currrentButton;    /* set in CBColorSelect */
    static Atom FOREGROUND=None, PIXEL=None;


    if (FOREGROUND == None) {
        FOREGROUND =
            XInternAtom(ourDisplay, "FOREGROUND", FALSE);
```

```
        PIXEL = XInternAtom(ourDisplay, "PIXEL", FALSE);
    }

    *pType = PIXEL;
    *pVal = (caddr_t) XtMalloc(sizeof(Pixel));
    if (*pTarget == FOREGROUND) {
        *((Pixel *) *pVal) =
            GetValue(currentButton, XtNforeground);
    } else {
        *((Pixel *) *pVal) =
            GetValue(currentButton, XtNbackground);
    }
    *pLen = 1;
    *pFormat = 32;
    return(TRUE);
}

Boolean ConvertToColormap(
    wid, pSel, pTarget, pType, pVal, pLen, pFormat
)
    Widget          wid;
    Atom            *pSel;
    Atom            *pTarget;
    Atom            *pType;          /* return */
    caddr_t         *pVal;           /* return */
    unsigned long   *pLen;           /* return */
    int             *pFormat;        /* return */
{
    extern Widget       currrentButton;
    Window              win;
    XWindowAttributes   xwa;

    win = XtWindow(currentButton);
    if (XGetWindowAttributes(ourDisplay, win, &xwa) == 0) {
        Warning(
            "ConvertToColormap() - couldn't get window info\n"
        );
        return(FALSE);
    }
    *pType = XA_COLORMAP;
    *pVal = (caddr_t) XtMalloc(sizeof(Colormap));
    *((Colormap *) *pVal) = xwa.colormap;
    *pLen = 1;
    *pFormat = 32;
    return(TRUE);
}

Boolean ConvertToOwnerOS(
    wid, pSel, pTarget, pType, pVal, pLen, pFormat
)
    Widget          wid;
```

```
    Atom            *pSel;
    Atom            *pTarget;
    Atom            *pType;          /* return */
    caddr_t         *pVal;           /* return */
    unsigned long   *pLen;           /* return */
    int             *pFormat;        /* return */
{
    static String   str = "Unix";

    *pType = XA_STRING;
    *pVal = (caddr_t) XtMalloc(strlen(str) + 1);
    strcpy(*pVal, str);
    *pLen = strlen(str);
    *pFormat = 8;
    return(TRUE);
}

#include <sys/utsname.h>            /* System V dependent */

Boolean ConvertToHostname(
    wid, pSel, pTarget, pType, pVal, pLen, pFormat
)
    Widget          wid;
    Atom            *pSel;
    Atom            *pTarget;
    Atom            *pType;          /* return */
    caddr_t         *pVal;           /* return */
    unsigned long   *pLen;           /* return */
    int             *pFormat;        /* return */
{
    struct utsname  name;

    if (uname(&name) < 0) {
        perror("ConvertToHostname(): uname failed\n");
        return(FALSE);
    }
    *pType = XA_STRING;
    *pVal = (caddr_t) XtMalloc(strlen(name.nodename) + 1);
    strcpy(*pVal, name.nodename);
    *pLen = strlen(name.nodename);
    *pFormat = 8;
    return(TRUE);
}

#include <pwd.h>                    /* System V dependent */

Boolean ConvertToUser(
    wid, pSel, pTarget, pType, pVal, pLen, pFormat
)
    Widget          wid;
    Atom            *pSel;
```

```
    Atom            *pTarget;
    Atom            *pType;         /* return */
    caddr_t         *pVal;          /* return */
    unsigned long   *pLen;          /* return */
    int             *pFormat;       /* return */
{
    struct passwd   *getpwuid();
    String          *name;
    struct passwd   *pw;

    pw = getpwuid(getuid());
    if (pw == NULL) {
        Warning("ConvertToUser: getpwuid failed\n");
        return(FALSE);
    }
    *pType = XA_STRING;
    *pVal = (caddr_t) XtMalloc(strlen(pw->pw_name) + 1);
    strcpy(*pVal, pw->pw_name);
    *pLen = strlen(pw->pw_name);
    *pFormat = 8;
    return(TRUE);
}

Boolean ConvertToProcess(
    wid, pSel, pTarget, pType, pVal, pLen, pFormat
)
    Widget          wid;
    Atom            *pSel;
    Atom            *pTarget;
    Atom            *pType;         /* return */
    caddr_t         *pVal;          /* return */
    unsigned long   *pLen;          /* return */
    int             *pFormat;       /* return */
{
    *pType = XA_INTEGER;
    *pVal = (caddr_t) XtMalloc(sizeof(int));
    *((int *) *pVal) = getpid();
    *pLen = 1;
    *pFormat = 32;
    return(TRUE);
}

Boolean ConvertToClass(
    wid, pSel, pTarget, pType, pVal, pLen, pFormat
)
    Widget          wid;
    Atom            *pSel;
    Atom            *pTarget;
    Atom            *pType;         /* return */
    caddr_t         *pVal;          /* return */
    unsigned long   *pLen;          /* return */
```

```
    int             *pFormat;        /* return */
{
    extern String   appClass;

    *pType = XA_STRING;
    *pVal = (caddr_t) XtMalloc(strlen(appClass) + 1);
    strcpy(*pVal, appClass);
    *pLen = strlen(appClass);
    *pFormat = 8;
    return(TRUE);
}

Boolean ConvertToName(
    wid, pSel, pTarget, pType, pVal, pLen, pFormat
)
    Widget          wid;
    Atom            *pSel;
    Atom            *pTarget;
    Atom            *pType;          /* return */
    caddr_t         *pVal;           /* return */
    unsigned long   *pLen;           /* return */
    int             *pFormat;        /* return */
{
    String  wname;

    XFetchName(ourDisplay, toplevelWindow, &wname);
    *pType = XA_STRING;
    *pVal = (caddr_t) XtMalloc(strlen(wname) + 1);
    strcpy(*pVal, wname);
    *pLen = strlen(wname);
    *pFormat = 8;
    return(TRUE);
}

Boolean ConvertToClientWindow(
    wid, pSel, pTarget, pType, pVal, pLen, pFormat
)
    Widget          wid;
    Atom            *pSel;
    Atom            *pTarget;
    Atom            *pType;          /* return */
    caddr_t         *pVal;           /* return */
    unsigned long   *pLen;           /* return */
    int             *pFormat;        /* return */
{
    extern Widget   currrentButton;     /* set in CBColorSelect */

    *pType = XA_WINDOW;
    *pVal = (caddr_t) XtMalloc(sizeof(Window));
    *((Window *) *pVal) = toplevelWindow;
    *pLen = 1;
```

```
    *pFormat = 32;
    return(TRUE);
}

/*********************** Color Grid ************************/

Widget CreateColorGrid(w_parent)
    Widget  w_parent;
{
    register int    nCells, index;
    Widget        w_caption, w_colors, w_button, AddRectButton();

    /*
     * Create a caption to label the color grid
     */
    w_caption =
        XtCreateWidget(
            "colorCaption",
            captionWidgetClass,
            w_parent,
            tmpArg,
            TmpArgList(
                XtNlabel,    "Color:",
                0
            )
        );

    /*
     * Try and determine the number of cells in the colormap.
     * The best we can do is determine the number in the
     * default colormap.
     */
    nCells =
        XDisplayCells(ourDisplay, XDefaultScreen(ourDisplay));

    /*
     * Create the exclusive container - but don't manage it until
     * we have added the rectangular buttons.
     */
    w_colors =
        XtCreateWidget(
            "colorPane",                /* instance name */
            exclusivesWidgetClass,      /* class name */
            w_caption,                  /* parent widget */
            tmpArg,                     /* arg list */
            TmpArgList(
                XtNlayoutType,       OL_FIXEDCOLS,
                XtNmeasure,          SquareRoot(nCells),
                0
            )
        );
```

369

```
    /*
     * Add buttons as children of the Exclusive widget
     */
    for (index = 0; index < nCells; index++) {
        w_button = AddRectButton(w_colors, (Pixel) index);
        if (index == 0)
            currentButton = w_button;
    }

    XtManageChild(w_colors);
    XtManageChild(w_caption);
    return(w_caption);
}

/*
 * SquareRoot() - quick and dirty integer square-root, used to
 * compute the size of a display matrix.
 */
SquareRoot(i)
    register unsigned i;
{
    register unsigned j=1;

    while (i > (1 << ++j))
        ;

    return(j);
}


Widget AddRectButton(w_parent, pixel)
    Widget  w_parent;
    Pixel   pixel;
{
    Widget      w_button;
    void        CBColorSelect();


    w_button =
        XtCreateManagedWidget(
            "colorButton",          /* instance name */
            rectButtonWidgetClass,  /* widget class */
            w_parent,               /* parent widget */
            tmpArg,                 /* arg list */
            TmpArgList(
                XtNbackground,      pixel,
                XtNlabel,           "   ",
                0
            )
        );
```

```
    XtAddCallback(w_button, XtNselect, CBColorSelect, w_button);
    return(w_button);
}


static void CBColorSelect(wid, client_data, call_data)
    Widget  wid;
    caddr_t client_data;
    caddr_t call_data;
{
    extern Widget   currentButton;

    currentButton = (Widget) client_data;
    return;
}
```

Note that the convert callback is given a doubly indirect pointer to the data: the callback writes the address of the data to the address in the pointer passed into the callback. The callback must allocate space for the data, which will be freed by the Toolkit, unless the client specified a *done* callback in the call to XtOwnSelection.

6.2.6.2.2 Requesting a Selection

Obtaining the value of the current selection is also a two-part procedure. First, the client requests the selection:

```
void XtGetSelectionValue(
      Widget                  widget,
      Atom                    selection,
      Atom                    target,
      XtSelectionCallbackProc callback,
      caddr_t                 client_data,
      Time                    time
);
```

Not surprisingly, the parameters are similar to XtOwnSelection. The callback routine receives data typical of properties, including type, value, length, and format information.

371

The example program getselct demonstrates how to get selection values with the Toolkit:

```
/*
 * Demonstrate how to get selection values
 * @(#) sccs/s.getselct.c 1.7 last delta 3/11/90 18:51:28
 */
#include <X11/Intrinsic.h>
#include <X11/Selection.h>
#include <X11/StringDefs.h>
#include <X11/Shell.h>
#include <X11/Xatom.h>
#include <Xol/OpenLook.h>
#include <Xol/AbbrevStac.h>
#include <Xol/Caption.h>
#include <Xol/ControlAre.h>
#include <Xol/FExclusive.h>
#include <Xol/RectButton.h>
#include <Xol/OblongButt.h>
#include <Xol/StaticText.h>
#include <stdio.h>
#include "xtutil.h"

Widget  w_toplevel;      /* top level widget in the tree */
Window  toplevelWindow;  /* window of toplevel widget */
char    *ProgramName;    /* printable name of our application */
Display *ourDisplay;     /* server display we are using */
Screen  *ourScreen;      /* screen we are using */
Window  rootWindow;      /* root window of ourScreen */

static Widget  w_current;
static Atom currentAtom;

typedef struct _Item {
    String      label;   /* label and atom name */
    Atom        atom;    /* atom */
} Item;

/*
 * we are using XtNclientData to hold the interned
 * atoms of the names/labels
 */
static String itemFields[] = {
    XtNlabel, XtNclientData
};
#define NR_ITEM_FIELDS \
    (sizeof(itemFields) / sizeof(itemFields[0]))
```

```
/*
 * This list is per the Inter-Client Communications
 * Conventions Manual, Ver 1.0
 */
static Item items[] = {
    { "BACKGROUND",         None,   },
    { "BITMAP",             None,   },
    { "CHARACTER_POSITION", None,   },
    { "CLASS",              None,   },
    { "CLIENT_WINDOW",      None,   },
    { "COLORMAP",           None,   },
    { "COLUMN_NUMBER",      None,   },
    { "DELETE",             None,   },
    { "DRAWABLE",           None,   },
    { "FILE_NAME",          None,   },
    { "FOREGROUND",         None,   },
    { "HOST_NAME",          None,   },
    { "INSERT_PROPERTY",    None,   },
    { "INSERT_SELECTION",   None,   },
    { "LENGTH",             None,   },
    { "LINE_NUMBER",        None,   },
    { "LIST_LENGTH",        None,   },
    { "MODULE",             None,   },
    { "NAME",               None,   },
    { "ODIF",               None,   },
    { "OWNER_OS",           None,   },
    { "PIXMAP",             None,   },
    { "PROCEDURE",          None,   },
    { "PROCESS",            None,   },
    { "STRING",             None,   },
    { "TARGETS",            None,   },
    { "TASK",               None,   },
    { "TIMESTAMP",          None,   },
    { "USER",               None,   },
};
#define NR_ITEMS        (sizeof(items) / sizeof(items[0]))
#define DEFAULT_ITEM    0

#ifndef XA_PIXEL
Atom    XA_PIXEL;       /* if not in Xatom.h, fake it */
#endif
#ifndef XA_SPAN
Atom    XA_SPAN;        /* if not in Xatom.h, fake it */
#endif


void main(argc, argv)
    unsigned int argc;
    char *argv[];
{
    Widget  CreateInitialWidgets();
```

```
    w_toplevel = OlInitialize(
        NULL,                    /* app name - filled by Xt */
        "OlExample",             /* app class */
        NULL,                    /* option list */
        0,                       /* # of options */
        &argc,                   /* addr of main argc */
        argv                     /* main argv */
    );


    ourDisplay = XtDisplay(w_toplevel);
    ourScreen = XtScreen(w_toplevel);

    (void) CreateInitialWidgets(w_toplevel);

    (void) XtRealizeWidget(w_toplevel);

    /*
     * initialize misc global variables
     */
    toplevelWindow = XtWindow(w_toplevel);
    rootWindow = XDefaultRootWindow(ourDisplay);

    (void) XtMainLoop();
}


Widget CreateInitialWidgets(w_parent)
    Widget   w_parent;
{
    Widget   w_frame, w_button, CreateControl(), CreatePane();

    w_frame =
        XtCreateWidget(
            "frame",                   /* instance name */
            controlAreaWidgetClass,    /* widget class */
            w_parent,                  /* parent widget */
            tmpArg,                    /* arg list */
            TmpArgList(
                XtNlayoutType,     OL_FIXEDCOLS,
                XtNmeasure,        1,
                0
            )
        );

    (void) CreateControl(w_frame);    /* Top Control Area */
    (void) CreatePane(w_frame);       /* Work Pane */

    XtManageChild(w_frame);
    return(w_frame);
```

374

```
}

/******************* Control Area setup *********************/

Widget CreateControl(w_parent)
    Widget  w_parent;
{
    Widget  w_control, w_stack, w_button;
    Widget  AddAbbrevStack();
    void    GetSelection();

    /*
     * Create the application control area, consisting of
     * an abbrev stack (plus label and preview window)
     * to select the conversion target and an action
     * button below it.
     */
    w_control =
        XtCreateWidget(
            "control",                  /* instance name */
            controlAreaWidgetClass,     /* widget class */
            w_parent,                   /* parent widget */
            tmpArg,                     /* arg list */
            TmpArgList(
                XtNlayoutType,      OL_FIXEDCOLS,
                XtNmeasure,         1,
                XtNrecomputeSize,   FALSE,
                0
            )
        );

    w_stack = AddAbbrevStack(w_control);

    /*
     * Add a button to retrieve the current selection contents
     */
    w_button =
        XtCreateManagedWidget(          /* action button */
            "getButton",
            oblongButtonWidgetClass,
            w_control,
            tmpArg,
            TmpArgList(
                XtNlabel,           "Get PRIMARY Selection",
                XtNrecomputeSize,   TRUE,
                0
            )
        );
    XtAddCallback(w_button, XtNselect, GetSelection, NULL);
```

```
    XtManageChild(w_control);
    return(w_control);
}


/*
 * GetSelection() - ask the toolkit for the current
 * selection value
 */
void GetSelection(wid, client_data, call_data)
    Widget   wid;
    caddr_t  client_data;
    caddr_t  call_data;
{
    void        CBSelection();
    extern Time GetTimestamp();
    Time        currentTime;

    currentTime = GetTimestamp(wid);
    XtGetSelectionValue(
        wid,              /* widget requesting the selection */
        XA_PRIMARY,       /* selection */
        currentAtom,      /* target */
        CBSelection,      /* callback */
        currentTime,      /* client_data for above callback */
        currentTime       /* time of request */
    );
    return;
}

/*
 * AddAbbrevStack() - add an abbreviated button stack
 * and attach a menu
 */
Widget AddAbbrevStack(w_parent)
    Widget   w_parent;
{
    Widget  w_control, w_stack, w_menuPane;
    String  AddTargetMenu(), defaultString;

    /*
     * For abbreviated stacks, the application is
     * responsible for providing a "current selection"
     * window, which we do here using a static text widget.
     * We have also chosen to provide a label for the
     * abbrev stack using another static text widget.
     */
    w_control =
        XtCreateWidget(
            "control",                /* instance name */
            controlAreaWidgetClass,   /* widget class */
```

```
            w_parent,                  /* parent widget */
            tmpArg,                    /* arg list */
            TmpArgList(
                XtNlayoutType,      OL_FIXEDROWS,
                XtNmeasure,         1,
                XtNrecomputeSize,   FALSE,
                0
            )
        );

    (void) XtCreateManagedWidget(
        "label",                   /* instance name */
        staticTextWidgetClass,     /* widget class */
        w_control,                 /* parent widget */
        tmpArg,
        TmpArgList(
            XtNstring,             "Convert to:",
            XtNborderWidth,        0,
            0
        )
    );

    /*
     * Create an abbreviated button stack and its menu
     */
    w_stack =
        XtCreateWidget(
            "fontFamily",              /* instance name */
            abbrevStackWidgetClass,    /* widget class */
            w_control,                 /* parent widget */
            tmpArg,                    /* arglist */
            TmpArgList(
                XtNtitle,              "Conversion Target",
                XtNpushpin,            OL_OUT,
                0
            )
        );
    w_menuPane = (Widget) GetValue(w_stack, XtNmenuPane);
    defaultString = AddTargetMenu(w_menuPane);
    XtManageChild(w_stack);

    /*
     * Add the preview-window widget to display the currently selected
     * menu item.
     */
    w_current =
        XtCreateManagedWidget(
            "current",                 /* instance name */
            staticTextWidgetClass,     /* widget class */
            w_control,                 /* parent widget */
            tmpArg,
```

```
                TmpArgList(
                    XtNwidth,              150,
                    XtNrecomputeSize,      FALSE,
                    XtNgravity,            NorthWestGravity,
                    XtNstring,             defaultString,
                    0
                )
            );
    SetValue(w_stack, XtNpreviewWidget, w_current);

    XtManageChild(w_control);
    return(w_control);
}

/*
 * AddTargetMenu() - create the menu for the
 * selection targets and return the string describing
 * the default item.
 */
String AddTargetMenu(w_parent)
    Widget  w_parent;
{
    extern Atom      currentAtom;
    extern Item      items[];
    extern String    itemFields[];
    register Item    *pItem;
    register int     count;
    Widget           w_choice;
    void             CBSelectItem();

    /*
     * Intern the atoms that match the atom names in each Item
     */
    for (
        pItem = items,
        count = NR_ITEMS;

        count--;

        pItem++
    ) {
        pItem->atom =
            XInternAtom(ourDisplay, pItem->label, FALSE);
    }
    currentAtom = items[DEFAULT_ITEM].atom;

#ifndef XA_PIXEL
    XA_PIXEL =
        XInternAtom(ourDisplay, "PIXEL", FALSE);      /* fake */
#endif
#ifndef XA_SPAN
```

```
        XA_SPAN =
            XInternAtom(ourDisplay, "SPAN", FALSE);        /* fake */
#endif

    /*
     * Use a flat widget for the menu panel
     */
    w_choice =
        XtCreateManagedWidget(
            "choice",
            flatExclusivesWidgetClass,
            w_parent,
            tmpArg,
            TmpArgList(
                XtNlayoutType,       OL_FIXEDROWS,
                XtNmeasure,          10,
                XtNitems,            items,
                XtNnumItems,         NR_ITEMS,
                XtNitemFields,       itemFields,
                XtNnumItemFields,    NR_ITEM_FIELDS,
                XtNlabelJustify,     OL_LEFT,
                XtNselectProc,       CBSelectItem,
                XtNsameWidth,        OL_ALL,
                XtNsameHeight,       OL_ALL,
                0
            )
        );

    OlFlatSetValues(
        w_choice,
        DEFAULT_ITEM,               /* sub-object to modify */
        tmpArg,
        TmpArgList(
            XtNdefault,             TRUE,
            0
        )
    );

    return(items[DEFAULT_ITEM].label);
}

void CBSelectItem(wid, client_data, call_data)
    Widget  wid;
    caddr_t client_data;
    caddr_t call_data;
{
    extern Widget    w_current;
    extern Atom      currentAtom;
    OlFlatCallData   *ol_flat_call_data =
                            (OlFlatCallData *) call_data;
    Item             *itemHead =
```

```
                                (Item *) ol_flat_call_data->items;

    SetValue(
        w_current,
        XtNstring,
        itemHead[ol_flat_call_data->item_index].label
    );
    currentAtom = itemHead[ol_flat_call_data->item_index].atom;

    return;
}

/********************** Work Pane ***********************/
static Widget   w_wid, w_selection, w_timestamp, w_type,
        w_value, w_length, w_format;

Widget CreatePane(w_parent)
    Widget w_parent;
{
    Widget  w_control, CreateCaptionedStaticText();

    /*
     * We use the pane to display the value of the
     * PRIMARY selection, as returned by the toolkit in
     * CBSelection.  Here, we just create the widgets and
     * let CBSelection fill in contents when they are valid.
     */
    w_control =
        XtCreateWidget(
            "workPane",
            controlAreaWidgetClass,
            w_parent,
            tmpArg,
            TmpArgList(
                XtNlayoutType,      OL_FIXEDCOLS,
                XtNmeasure,      1,
                XtNalignCaptions,   TRUE,
                0
            )
        );

    w_wid = CreateCaptionedStaticText(w_control, "Widget:");
    w_selection =
        CreateCaptionedStaticText(w_control, "Selection:");
    w_timestamp =
        CreateCaptionedStaticText(w_control, "Time requested:");
    w_type = CreateCaptionedStaticText(w_control, "Type:");
    w_length = CreateCaptionedStaticText(w_control, "Length:");
    w_format = CreateCaptionedStaticText(w_control, "Format:");
    w_value = CreateCaptionedStaticText(w_control, "Value:");
```

```
    XtManageChild(w_control);
    return(w_control);
}

/*
 * CreateCaptionedStaticText() - convenience routine to
 * create caption widgets with static text children.
 * Note that, unlike most of our CreateXX() routines,
 * this one returns a child, rather than the highest-level
 * widget created here.
 */
Widget CreateCaptionedStaticText(w_parent, label)
    Widget   w_parent;
    String   label;
{
    Widget   w_caption, w_statText;

    w_caption =
        XtCreateWidget(
            "caption",
            captionWidgetClass,
            w_parent,
            tmpArg,
            TmpArgList(
                XtNlabel,          label,
                0
            )
        );

    w_statText =
        XtCreateManagedWidget(
            "text",
            staticTextWidgetClass,
            w_caption,
            tmpArg,
            TmpArgList(
                XtNborderWidth,      0,
                XtNrecomputeSize,    TRUE,
                XtNwrap,             TRUE,
                0
            )
        );

    XtManageChild(w_caption);
    return(w_statText);
}
```

```
/*
 * CBSelection() - called by the toolkit with a selection value
 */
void CBSelection(
    wid, client_data, pSelection, pType, value, pLength, pFormat)

    Widget          wid;
    caddr_t         client_data;
    Atom            *pSelection;
    Atom            *pType;
    caddr_t         value;
    unsigned long   *pLength;
    int             *pFormat;
{
    Widget      w_popup;
    String      str;
    char        buf[BUFSIZ];
    static char widgetBuf[16], timestampBuf[16], formatBuf[16],
            lengthBuf[16], valueBuf[BUFSIZ];

    sprintf(widgetBuf, "0x%x", wid);                /* widget */
    SetValue(w_wid, XtNstring, widgetBuf);

    sprintf(timestampBuf, "%u", client_data);   /* timestamp */
    SetValue(w_timestamp, XtNstring, timestampBuf);

    if (*pType == None) {
        SetValue(w_type, XtNstring, "None");
        SetValue(w_selection, XtNstring, "");
        SetValue(w_length, XtNstring, "");
        SetValue(w_format, XtNstring, "");
        SetValue(w_value, XtNstring, "");
    } else if (*pType == XT_CONVERT_FAIL) {
        SetValue(w_type, XtNstring, "XT_CONVERT_FAIL");
        SetValue(w_selection, XtNstring, "");
        SetValue(w_length, XtNstring, "");
        SetValue(w_format, XtNstring, "");
        SetValue(w_value, XtNstring, "");
    } else {
        str = XGetAtomName(ourDisplay, *pType);     /* type */
        SetValue(w_type, XtNstring, str);
        XFree(str);

        str = XGetAtomName(ourDisplay, *pSelection);
                                            /* selection */
        SetValue(w_selection, XtNstring, str);
        XFree(str);

        sprintf(lengthBuf, "%d", *pLength);     /* length */
        SetValue(w_length, XtNstring, lengthBuf);
```

```
sprintf(formatBuf, "%d", *pFormat);      /* format */
SetValue(w_format, XtNstring, formatBuf);

if (*pType == XA_STRING) {
    SetValue(w_value, XtNstring, (String) value);
} else if (*pType == XA_ATOM) {
    register        count;
    register Atom   *pAtom;

    valueBuf[0] = 0;     /* so strcat works */
    for (
        pAtom = (Atom *) value,
        count = *pLength;

        count--;

        pAtom++
    ) {
        str = XGetAtomName(ourDisplay, *pAtom);
        strcat(valueBuf, str);
        XFree(str);
        if (count)
            strcat(valueBuf, ", ");
    }
    SetValue(w_value, XtNstring, valueBuf);
} else {
    register char   *pByte;
    register short  *pWord;
    register long   *pLong;
    register        count;
    char            tmpBuf[16];
    String          convertString;

    if ((*pType == XA_INTEGER)) {
        convertString = "%d";
    } else if (
        (*pType == XA_CARDINAL) ||
        (*pType == XA_PIXEL) ||
        (*pType == XA_SPAN)
    ) {
        convertString = "%u";
    } else {
        convertString = "0x%x";
    }

    valueBuf[0] = 0;     /* so strcat works */

    switch (*pFormat) {
    case 32:
        for (
            pLong = (long *) value,
```

```
                            count = *pLength;

                            count--;

                            pLong++
                    ) {
                        sprintf(tmpBuf, convertString, *pLong);
                        strcat(valueBuf, tmpBuf);
                        if (count)
                            strcat(valueBuf, ", ");
                    }
                    break;
                case 16:
                    for (
                        pWord = (short *) value,
                        count = *pLength;

                        count--;

                        pWord++
                    ) {
                        sprintf(tmpBuf, convertString, *pWord);
                        strcat(valueBuf, tmpBuf);
                        if (count)
                            strcat(valueBuf, ", ");
                    }
                    break;
                case 8:
                    for (
                        pByte = (char *) value,
                        count = *pLength;

                        count--;

                        pByte++
                    ) {
                        sprintf(tmpBuf, convertString, *pByte);
                        strcat(valueBuf, tmpBuf);
                        if (count)
                            strcat(valueBuf, ", ");
                    }
                    break;
                default:
                    sprintf(valueBuf,
                            "invalid format: %d", *pFormat);
                }
                SetValue(w_value, XtNstring, valueBuf);
            }
        }

    return;
}
```

Note the two special case values of *pType in CBSelection:

None—The selection owner could not honor the request.

XT_CONVERT_FAIL—The selection owner did not complete the conversion in the time allowed by the Toolkit, usually indicating that the selection owner crashed or that selection ownership is otherwise invalid.

The following frames illustrate ownselct and getselct communicating with selections.

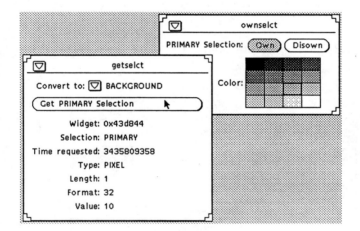

Figure 6.7 Getting the primary selection value of type PIXEL

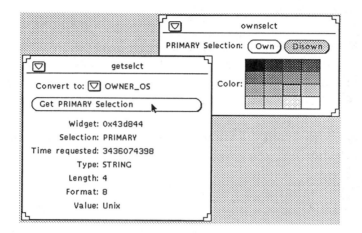

Figure 6.8 Obtaining information about the selection owner

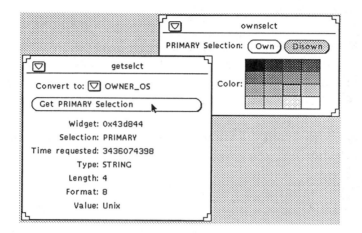

Figure 6.9 Conversion requests supported by getselct

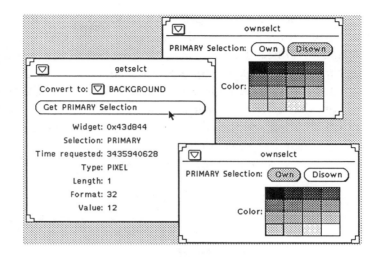

Figure 6.10   Multiple selection owners

The OPEN LOOK Intrinsic Toolkit automatically implements STRING selections for any text it displays. To see how this works, sweep out some text using the SELECT mouse button. The widget has just become the PRIMARY selection owner. Use getselct to read the selection, with STRING as the target.

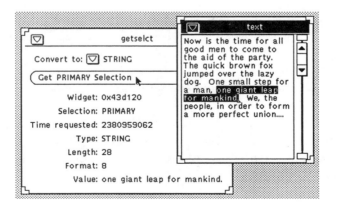

Figure 6.11   Automatic OPEN LOOK selections

The Scrolling List widget supports selections, too, but only if enabled by the application. Recompile scrlist.c from Chapter 5 with XtNselectable defined TRUE. Now, clicking SELECT on an item to make it current also makes it an active selection in the ICCCM sense. Use the ADJUST button to add a few more items to the selection, and then become the selection owner by pressing the COPY key (<Ctrl-c>, by default),[14] Read the the selection as before with getselct. In Figure 6.12 we read the selection with getselct after selecting Alaska, California, Hawaii, Oregon, and Washington.

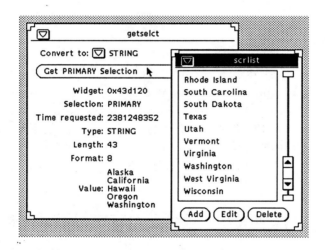

Figure 6.12 Selections using the Scrolling List widget

Users may cut also cut items from the Scrolling List with the CUT key, by default <Ctrl-x>. The XtNuserDeleteItems callback, CBDeleteItems, actually implements the delete, since the application controls the list data.

---

[14]Note that the text becomes highlighted.

6.3 Additional Functionality

6.3.1 Icons

Graphical user interfaces are inherently visually oriented. Therefore, it make sense to provide graphic icons for your applications to visually identify them when they are iconified by the Window Manager. The OPEN LOOK File Manager also uses icons to identify applications and their data files in path panes.

To see how this works, we'll create some icon bitmaps and associate them with a sample program.

6.3.1.1 Window Managers

Window managers are responsible for displaying some representation of an application when that application is iconified. The actual representation is left up to the designer of the window manager, but application developers are able to provide hints to the window manager as to their icon's appearance. Like the rest of X, icons are an exercise in communication and cooperation.

Although some window managers allow full-depth pixmaps or even tiny windows to be used as icons, the only safe bet for interoperability between window managers is reasonably sized (say, 32x32 pixels) bitmaps. Some window managers also allow irregularly shaped icons by using a second bitmap as an icon mask, but don't rely on this.

Caveats aside, adding a simple bitmap icon to an application is a near-trivial task. First, create the bitmap with the x bitmap editor. The bitmap should be some graphic representation of the application but not include its name, since the Window Manager is required to display the application's name with the icon, anyway.

For our example program, let's create a 32x32 bitmap and write it to the file midiicon.xbm:[15]

```
$ bitmap midiicon.xbm 32x32 &
```

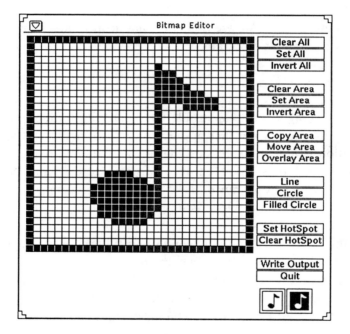

Figure 6.13 Using the x bitmap editor to create an icon

---

[15]The xbm suffix denotes an X *bitm*ap. This is purely a convention of this book.

Files created with bitmap are ASCII text, suitable for including in C code:

```
#define midiicon_width 32
#define midiicon_height 32
static char midiicon_bits[] = {
    0xff, 0xff, 0xff, 0xff, 0x01, 0x00, 0x00, 0x80,
    0x01, 0x00, 0x00, 0x80, 0x01, 0x00, 0x00, 0x80,
    0x01, 0x00, 0x04, 0x80, 0x01, 0x00, 0x1c, 0x80,
    0x01, 0x00, 0x3c, 0x80, 0x01, 0x00, 0x7c, 0x80,
    0x01, 0x00, 0xfc, 0x81, 0x01, 0x00, 0xfc, 0x87,
    0x01, 0x00, 0xc4, 0x87, 0x01, 0x00, 0x04, 0x80,
    0x01, 0x00, 0x04, 0x80, 0x01, 0x00, 0x04, 0x80,
    0x01, 0x00, 0x04, 0x80, 0x01, 0x00, 0x04, 0x80,
    0x01, 0x00, 0x04, 0x80, 0x01, 0x00, 0x04, 0x80,
    0x01, 0x78, 0x04, 0x80, 0x01, 0xfc, 0x05, 0x80,
    0x01, 0xfe, 0x07, 0x80, 0x01, 0xfe, 0x07, 0x80,
    0x01, 0xfe, 0x07, 0x80, 0x01, 0xfc, 0x07, 0x80,
    0x01, 0xfc, 0x03, 0x80, 0x01, 0xf0, 0x01, 0x80,
    0x01, 0x00, 0x00, 0x80, 0x01, 0x00, 0x00, 0x80,
    0x01, 0x00, 0x00, 0x80, 0xff, 0xff, 0xff, 0xff};
```

Xlib supports this format directly, with subroutines such as XCreateBitmapFromData and XReadBitmapFile. Using these two routines, our example code allows icon bitmap data to be read at run-time out of a file or compiled into the program.

```
/*
 * Demonstrate how to attach a window manager icon
 * to an application.
 * @(#) sccs/s.midi.c 1.5 last delta 3/11/90 18:51:33
 */
#include <X11/Intrinsic.h>
#include <X11/StringDefs.h>
#include <X11/Shell.h>
#include <X11/Xatom.h>
#include <Xol/OpenLook.h>
#include <Xol/StaticText.h>
#include <stdio.h>
#include <xtutil.h>      /* libxutil.a include file */

Widget  w_toplevel;      /* top level widget in the tree */
Window  toplevelWindow;  /* window of toplevel widget */
Display *ourDisplay;     /* server display we are using */
Screen  *ourScreen;      /* screen we are using */
Window  rootWindow;      /* rootWindow of ourScreen */
```

```
void main(argc, argv)
    unsigned int argc;
    char *argv[];
{
    void    CreateIcon();

    w_toplevel = OlInitialize(
        NULL,                   /* app name - filled by Xt */
        "OlExample",            /* app class */
        NULL,                   /* option list */
        0,                      /* # of options */
        &argc,                  /* addr of main argc */
        argv                    /* main argv */
    );

    (void) XtCreateManagedWidget(
        "frame",
        staticTextWidgetClass,
        w_toplevel,
        tmpArg,
        TmpArgList(
            XtNstring,   "Iconize me!",
            0
        )
    );

    (void) XtRealizeWidget(w_toplevel);

    toplevelWindow = XtWindow(w_toplevel);
    ourDisplay = XtDisplay(w_toplevel);
    ourScreen = XtScreen(w_toplevel);
    rootWindow = XDefaultRootWindow(ourDisplay);

    CreateIcon();               /* attach the icon */

    (void) XtMainLoop();
}


#define COMPILE_ICON

#ifdef COMPILE_ICON
#include "midiicon.xbm"     /* icon bitmap */
#else
#define ICON_FILE           "midiicon.xbm"
#endif

/*
 * CreateIcon() - associate an icon with our application.
 * The pixmap data was created using the X bitmap editor,
```

```
 * "bitmap."
 */
void CreateIcon()
{
    Pixmap          iconPixmap, iconMask;
    int             rc;
    unsigned int    width, height;
    int             xHot, yHot;
    Boolean         SizeOkay();

#ifdef COMPILE_ICON
    iconPixmap =
        XCreateBitmapFromData(
            ourDisplay,            /* X display */
            rootWindow,            /* window */
            midiicon_bits,         /* pixmap data */
            midiicon_width,        /* width */
            midiicon_height        /* height */
        );

    if (SizeOkay(midiicon_width, midiicon_height) != TRUE)
        Warning("icon pixmap may not be displayed\n");

    SetValue(w_toplevel, XtNiconPixmap, iconPixmap);

#else                          /* read at runtime */
    rc =
        XReadBitmapFile(
            ourDisplay,        /* X display */
            rootWindow,        /* window */
            ICON_FILE,
            &width,
            &height,
            &iconPixmap,
            &xHot,
            &yHot
        );
    switch (rc) {
        default:
            Warning(
                "unknown status of XReadBitmapFile: %d\n", rc);
            return;
        case BitmapOpenFailed:
            Warning(
                "could not open bitmap file %s\n", ICON_FILE);
            return;
        case BitmapFileInvalid:
            Warning(
                "file %s not valid bitmap data\n", ICON_FILE);
            return;
        case BitmapNoMemory:
```

393

```
                Warning(
                    "server out of memory loading icon pixmap\n");
                return;
            case BitmapSuccess:
                if (SizeOkay(width, height) != TRUE)
                    Warning("icon pixmap may not be displayed\n");
                SetValue(w_toplevel, XtNiconPixmap, iconPixmap);
                break;
    }
#endif
    return;
}


/*
 * SizeOkay() - ensure that our icon size is kosher with
 * the window manager.
 */
Boolean SizeOkay(width, height)
{
    XIconSize       *iconSize;
    register XIconSize  *pSize;
    int         count;

    /*
     * check to see if the window manager
     * has icon size preferences
     */
    if (
        XGetIconSizes(
            ourDisplay,
            toplevelWindow,
            &iconSize,
            &count
        ) == 0
    ) {
        return(TRUE);           /* window manager doesn't care */
    }

    for (pSize = iconSize; count--; pSize++) {
        if (
            (width >= pSize->min_width) &&
            (width <= pSize->max_width) &&
            (height >= pSize->min_height) &&
            (height >= pSize->max_height)
        ) {
            XFree(iconSize);
            return(TRUE);
        }
    }
```

```
    XFree(iconSize);
    return(FALSE);
}
```

We arbitrarily chose 32x32 as the icon bitmap dimensions; this is a "reasonable" size and should be acceptable to any window manager. The example code checks this size against the range of sizes that the Window Manager advertises in the WM_ICON_SIZE property on the root window. Although we can't easily resize the bitmap if it is out of range, a "real" application might provide several icon bitmaps and select one at run-time, based on the Window Manager preferences and screen pixel resolution.

This screen image shows several iconified applications, including midi, running under the OPEN LOOK Window Manager:

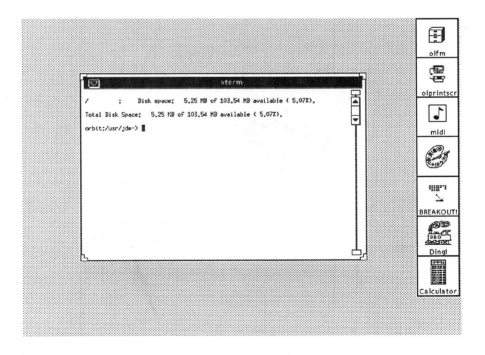

Figure 6.14   Examples of icons using the OPEN LOOK Window Manager

6.3.1.2 The File Manager

The OPEN LOOK File Manager graphically represents files as icons, using pattern-matching rules to bind icons and actions to these files. These rules and their syntax are documented in Appendix E of *The OPEN LOOK Graphical User Interface User's Guide.*

Applications that use application-specific data files will want to provide two icon bitmaps: one for the application's executable file and one for the data files. The data-file icon should be a smaller graphic, framed by a rectangle with one corner folded over to look like a document. All File Manager icons should be 24x24 pixels.

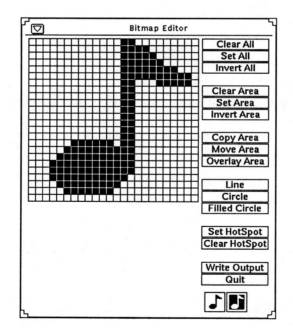

Figure 6.15   Creating the program icon

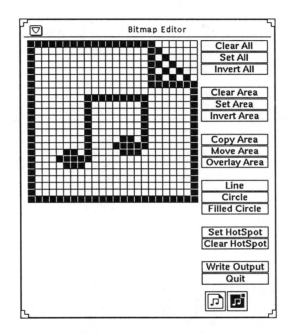

Figure 6.16 Creating the data-file icon

The file midiprog.xbm now contains:

```
#define midiprog_width 24
#define midiprog_height 24
static char midiprog_bits[] = {
    0x00, 0x60, 0x00, 0x00, 0xe0, 0x01, 0x00, 0xe0,
    0x03, 0x00, 0xe0, 0x07, 0x00, 0xe0, 0x1f, 0x00,
    0xe0, 0x7f, 0x00, 0x60, 0x7c, 0x00, 0x60, 0x00,
    0x00, 0x60, 0x00, 0x00, 0x60, 0x00, 0x00, 0x60,
    0x00, 0x00, 0x60, 0x00, 0x00, 0x60, 0x00, 0x00,
    0x60, 0x00, 0x00, 0x60, 0x00, 0xc0, 0x6f, 0x00,
    0xe0, 0x7f, 0x00, 0xf0, 0x7f, 0x00, 0xf8, 0x7f,
    0x00, 0xf8, 0x7f, 0x00, 0xf8, 0x3f, 0x00, 0xf0,
    0x1f, 0x00, 0xe0, 0x0f, 0x00, 0x00, 0x00, 0x00};
```

and mididata.xbm contains

```
#define mididata_width 24
#define mididata_height 24
static char mididata_bits[] = {
    0xff, 0xff, 0x03, 0x01, 0x00, 0x06, 0x01, 0x00,
    0x0a, 0x01, 0x00, 0x16, 0x01, 0x00, 0x2a, 0x01,
    0x00, 0x56, 0x01, 0x00, 0xfe, 0x01, 0x00, 0x80,
    0x01, 0xff, 0x81, 0x01, 0x01, 0x81, 0x01, 0x01,
    0x81, 0x01, 0x01, 0x81, 0x01, 0x01, 0x81, 0x01,
    0x01, 0x81, 0x01, 0x61, 0x81, 0x01, 0xf1, 0x81,
    0x61, 0xe1, 0x80, 0xf1, 0x01, 0x80, 0xe1, 0x00,
    0x80, 0x01, 0x00, 0x80, 0x01, 0x00, 0x80, 0x01,
    0x00, 0x80, 0x01, 0x00, 0x80, 0xff, 0xff, 0xff};
```

While we're at it, let's create an icon file for help text and call it helpdata.xbm:

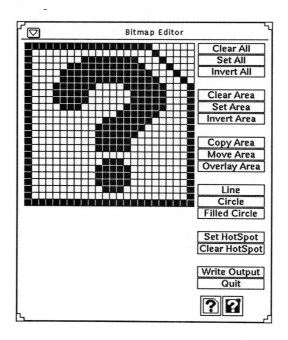

Figure 6.17 Creating the help data icon

Its contents should look something like this:

```
#define helpdata_width 24
#define helpdata_height 24
static char helpdata_bits[] = {
    0xff, 0xff, 0x03, 0x01, 0x00, 0x04, 0x01, 0xff,
    0x08, 0xc1, 0xff, 0x11, 0xe1, 0xff, 0x23, 0xe1,
    0xff, 0x47, 0xf1, 0xc3, 0x8f, 0xf1, 0x81, 0x8f,
    0xf1, 0x81, 0x8f, 0xe1, 0xc0, 0x8f, 0x01, 0xe0,
    0x87, 0x01, 0xf8, 0x83, 0x01, 0xfc, 0x81, 0x01,
    0xfc, 0x80, 0x01, 0x7c, 0x80, 0x01, 0x7c, 0x80,
    0x01, 0x00, 0x80, 0x01, 0x38, 0x80, 0x01, 0x7c,
    0x80, 0x01, 0x7c, 0x80, 0x01, 0x7c, 0x80, 0x01,
    0x38, 0x80, 0x01, 0x00, 0x80, 0xff, 0xff, 0xff};
```

To register the icons with the File Manager, the icon bitmaps must be placed in the icon search path, and the appropriate pattern-matching rules must be added to the binding file.

The search path is specified by the environment variable OLFMICONPATH, which has the same format as the shell PATH variable: directory names separated by a colon. The directory /usr/X/clients/olfm/bitmaps is implicitly appended to this path.

The binding-rules file defaults to /usr/X/clients/olfm/.olfmrc, but this file is not read if the file .olfmrc is in the user's home directory. It would have been nice if the user's .olfmrc simply overrode any rules from the default file, rather than preventing its use. As it stands, users will have to update their .olfmrc file when new applications are installed.

6.3.1.2.1 Installing the Icons

First, shut down the File Manager daemon (italic text will be different on your system):

```
$ ps -e | fgrep olfm
591 ptmx        1:27 olfm
$ kill 591
```

Install the icon files in the default directory:

```
$ cp helpdata.xbm /usr/X/clients/olfm/bitmaps
$ cp mididata.xbm /usr/X/clients/olfm/bitmaps
$ cp midiprog.xbm /usr/X/clients/olfm/bitmaps
```

or set OLFMICONPATH to the current directory:

```
$ OLFMICONPATH=$PWD; export OLFMICONPATH
```

Edit either /usr/X/clients/olfm/.olfmrc or $HOME/.olfmrc to contain:

```
menu cprog 'C Program Source'
    'Compile'
    'exec xterm -e /bin/sh -c "cc -c %s 2>&1 | /usr/bin/pg"';

on 'core',
   '*.bak'    -  'exec xterm -e ${EDITOR:-vi} %s'  junk.icon
                 '(cat %s | lp -c)';

on '*.c',
   '*.h'
        cprog  'exec xterm -e ${EDITOR:-vi} %s'  Csource.icon
                 '(cat %s | lp -c)';

on 'makefile',
   'Makefile',
   'S.makefile',
   'S.Makefile',
   '*.mk'
            -  'exec xterm -e ${EDITOR:-vi} %s'  make.icon
                 '(cat %s | lp -c)';

on '*.icon',
   '*.icn',
```

```
     '*.xbm' -  'exec bitmap %s'                 icon.icon
                '(cat %s | lp -c)';

on 'midi'   -  'exec %s'                         midiprog.xbm ;

on '*.mid'  -  'exec midi %s'                    mididata.xbm ;

on '*.help',
   '*.hlp'  -  'exec xterm -e ${EDITOR:-vi} %s'  helpdata.xbm
                '(cat %s | lp -c)';
```

The last three rules are additions to the standard .olfmrc, and the fourth-to-the-last entry adds the suffix patterns .icn and .xbm to the rule for .icon files. The rules that we added

- associate the midiprog.xbm icon with the midi program.
- associate the mididata.xbm icon with files that have the .mid suffix.
- associate the helpdata.xbm icon with files with the suffix .help or .hlp.

Create some dummy midi data files so you can see the data-file binding:

```
$ touch demo1.mid demo2.mid midisong.mid
```

Now compile midi.c and copy or link the executable to a directory explicitly named in your login PATH. (The File Manager executes bound actions from the user's HOME directory, rather than from the current directory.)

Start the File Manager daemon:

```
$ olfm &
```

and instantiate a browse window using the Workspace Manager Utilities menu.

Using the File Manager, change directories back to where you have
the source examples for this chapter. If you have been following
along with the chapter examples, the File Manager pane should look
something like this:

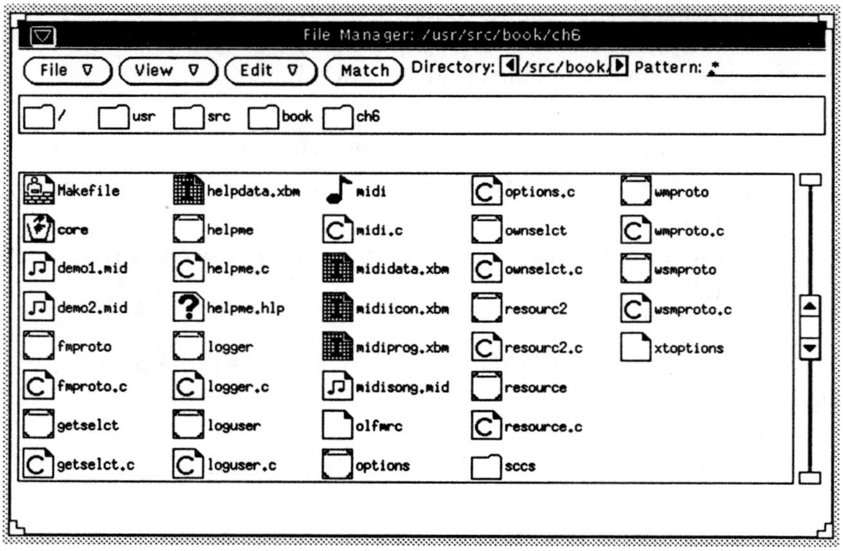

Figure 6.18 File Manager icon binding

All of the *.mid files have the mididata.xbm icon, midi has the
midiprog.xbm icon, *.hlp files have the helpdata.xbm icon, and *.xbm
files have the File Manager bitmap icon, icon.icon. Furthermore, if
you double-click on midi or on one of the *.mid files, the midi program
is executed.

6.3.2 On-Line Help

The *OPEN LOOK Level 1 Trademark Guide* stipulates that all OPEN LOOK applications operating in the OPEN LOOK GUI environment[16] must provide on-screen help for selectable objects in that application, such as buttons and sliders. Well-designed applications will have more extensive help available, including help for input fields, control areas, and for the application in general.

Happily, the OPEN LOOK Intrinsic Toolkit provides flexible and convenient Help registration routines that make conforming to this part of the specification quite painless: In most cases, a single call after creating the widget is all that is required.

Applications can attach Help to widgets, classes, windows, gadgets, and flat widgets. Source for Help can be a string, a file, or indirect through a function call.[17]

The following program demonstrates how to incorporate the OPEN LOOK Help facilities into an application:

```
/*
 * Demonstrate how to provide various flavors of Help.
 * sccs/s.helpme.c 1.9 last delta 3/11/90 18:51:30
 */
#include <X11/Intrinsic.h>
#include <X11/StringDefs.h>
#include <X11/Shell.h>
#include <X11/Xatom.h>        /* XA_ pre-defined atoms */
#include <Xol/OpenLook.h>
#include <Xol/OlClients.h>    /* OPEN LOOK atoms and properties */
#include <Xol/ControlAre.h>
```

[16]The HELP facility is part of the complete OPEN LOOK GUI environment and may not be supported when components of that environment (notably *olwm*) are not available.

[17]Applications can also intercept the Help machinery to handle the Help event completely.

```
#include <Xol/StaticText.h>
#include <Xol/TextField.h>
#include <Xol/Text.h>
#include <stdio.h>
#include "xtutil.h"

/*
 * These globals are useful throughout the program
 */
Widget  w_toplevel;       /* top level widget in the tree */
Window  toplevelWindow;   /* window of toplevel widget */
Display *ourDisplay;      /* server display we are using */
Screen  *ourScreen;       /* screen we are using */
Window  rootWindow;       /* Root Window of the screen we are using */

void main(argc, argv)
    unsigned int argc;
    char *argv[];
{
    Widget      wid, CreateInitialWidgets();
    void        PostRealizeHook();

    w_toplevel = OlInitialize(
        NULL,               /* app name */
        "OlExample",        /* app class */
        NULL,               /* option table */
        0,                  /* nr options in table */
        &argc,              /* addr of main argc */
        argv                /* main argv */
    );

    wid = CreateInitialWidgets(w_toplevel);

    (void) XtRealizeWidget(w_toplevel);

    /*
     * initialize misc global variables
     */
    toplevelWindow = XtWindow(w_toplevel);
    ourDisplay = XtDisplay(w_toplevel);
    ourScreen = XtScreen(w_toplevel);
    rootWindow = XDefaultRootWindow(ourDisplay);

    PostRealizeHook(wid);                   /* complete initialization */

    (void) XtMainLoop();
}


Widget CreateInitialWidgets(w_parent)
    Widget  w_parent;
```

```
{
    Widget  w_control;
    Widget  DemoNoHelp(), DemoStringHelp(), DemoDiskHelp();
    Widget  DemoIndirectHelp(), DemoFlatHelp(), DemoClassHelp();

    w_control =
        XtCreateWidget(
            "control",
            controlAreaWidgetClass,
            w_parent,
            tmpArg,
            TmpArgList(
                XtNlayoutType,  OL_FIXEDCOLS,
                XtNmeasure,      1,
                0
            )
        );

    (void) DemoNoHelp(w_control);
    (void) DemoStringHelp(w_control);
    (void) DemoDiskHelp(w_control);
    (void) DemoIndirectHelp(w_control);
    (void) DemoClassHelp(w_control);
    (void) DemoFlatHelp(w_control);

    XtManageChild(w_control);
    return(w_control);
}

void PostRealizeHook(wid)
    Widget  wid;
{
    /*
     * Provide general help for this application.
     */
    OlRegisterHelp(
        OL_WINDOW_HELP,      /* id_type */
        toplevelWindow,      /* id */
        "Application",       /* tag */
        OL_STRING_SOURCE,    /* source_type */
"This application demonstrates techniques for providing help."
    );

    return;
}


/*
 * DemoNoHelp() - don't associate any help
 */
Widget DemoNoHelp(w_parent)
```

```
        Widget  w_parent;
{
        Widget  w_text;

        w_text =
            XtCreateManagedWidget(
                "noHelpDemo",
                textFieldWidgetClass,
                w_parent,
                tmpArg,
                TmpArgList(
                    XtNstring,  "No help attached to this widget",
                    XtNgravity, WestGravity,
                    XtNborderWidth, 1,
                    0
                )
            );

        return(w_text);
}

/*
 * DemoStringHelp() - demonstrate the simplest
 * method to provide help text.
 */
Widget DemoStringHelp(w_parent)
        Widget  w_parent;
{
        Widget  w_text;

        w_text =
            XtCreateManagedWidget(
                "stringHelpDemo",
                staticTextWidgetClass,
                w_parent,
                tmpArg,
                TmpArgList(
                    XtNstring,      "Uses OL_STRING_SOURCE help",
                    XtNgravity,     WestGravity,
                    XtNborderWidth, 1,
                    0
                )
            );

        /*
         * Add help using a static string
         */
        OlRegisterHelp(
            OL_WIDGET_HELP,     /* id_type */
            w_text,             /* id */
            "String",           /* tag */
```

```
            OL_STRING_SOURCE,    /* source_type */
            "This help text is a string in the application."
        );

        return(w_text);
    }



/*
 * DemoDiskHelp() - demonstrate how to provide and access
 * help disk using a file on disk.  The OPEN LOOK
 * help machinery reads and displays this text when the
 * user requests help on this object.
 */
Widget DemoDiskHelp(w_parent)
    Widget  w_parent;
{
    static String   helpFilename = "helpme.hlp";
    Widget  w_text;

    w_text =
        XtCreateManagedWidget(
            "diskHelpDemo",
            staticTextWidgetClass,
            w_parent,
            tmpArg,
            TmpArgList(
                XtNstring,      "Uses OL_DISK_SOURCE help",
                XtNgravity,     WestGravity,
                XtNborderWidth, 1,
                0
            )
        );

    /*
     * Add the help using the name of a file with help text
     */
    OlRegisterHelp(
        OL_WIDGET_HELP,     /* id_type */
        w_text,             /* id */
        "Disk",             /* tag */
        OL_DISK_SOURCE,     /* source_type */
        helpFilename        /* source */
    );

    return(w_text);
}


/*
 * DemoIndirectHelp() - provide help text at run time
```

```
 * by providing access to it indirectly via a function call.
 */
Widget DemoIndirectHelp(w_parent)
    Widget   w_parent;
{
    static void HelpFunc();
    Widget   w_text;

    w_text =
        XtCreateManagedWidget(
            "indirectHelpDemo",
            staticTextWidgetClass,
            w_parent,
            tmpArg,
            TmpArgList(
                XtNstring,      "Uses OL_INDIRECT_SOURCE help",
                XtNgravity,     WestGravity,
                XtNborderWidth, 1,
                0
            )
        );

    /*
     * Add help by specifying a routine to be called
     * to provide the help text.
     */
    OlRegisterHelp(
        OL_WIDGET_HELP,      /* id_type */
        w_text,              /* id */
        "Indirect",          /* tag */
        OL_INDIRECT_SOURCE,  /* source_type */
        HelpFunc             /* source */
    );

    return(w_text);
}

/*
 * HelpFunc() - generate and provide help text
 * at the time the help is requested.
 */
void HelpFunc(idType, id, srcX, srcY, sourceType, source)
    OlDefine   idType;      /* type of object */
    XtPointer  id;          /* object identifier */
    Position   srcX, srcY;  /* pointer pos when HELP pressed */
    OlDefine   *sourceType; /* return */
    XtPointer  *source;     /* return */
{
    static char help[BUFSIZ];
    static int  count=1;
```

```
    *sourceType = OL_STRING_SOURCE;
    *source = (XtPointer) help; /* point at our buffer */

    strcpy(help,
        "This is an example of dynamically created help text:");

    sprintf(
        &help[strlen(help)],            /* concatentate */
        "\n\txy=[%d, %d]\n\tcount=%d\n", srcX, srcY, count++
    );

    return;
}

/*
 * DemoClassHelp() - demonstrate how help text can be
 * applied across all instances of a class.
 */
Widget DemoClassHelp(w_parent)
    Widget  w_parent;
{
    static void HelpFunc();
    Widget  w_text;

    w_text =
        XtCreateManagedWidget(
            "classHelpDemo",
            staticTextWidgetClass,
            w_parent,
            tmpArg,
            TmpArgList(
                XtNstring, "Uses OL_CLASS_HELP",
                XtNgravity, WestGravity,
                XtNborderWidth, 1,
                0
            )
        );

    w_text =
        XtCreateManagedWidget(
            "classHelpDemo",
            staticTextWidgetClass,
            w_parent,
            tmpArg,
            TmpArgList(
                XtNstring, "Uses the same OL_CLASS_HELP",
                XtNgravity, WestGravity,
                XtNborderWidth, 1,
                0
            )
        );
```

```
    /*
     * Attach help text to the class, which will be
     * picked up by all widgets of this class that
     * do not already have help associated
     * with them.
     */
    OlRegisterHelp(
        OL_CLASS_HELP,              /* id_type */
        staticTextWidgetClass,      /* id */
        "Class",                    /* tag */
        OL_STRING_SOURCE,           /* source_type */
        "This line of help is attached to the Static Text class."
    );

    return(w_text);
}

/*
 * DemoFlatHelp (and supporting data structures) -
 * demonstrate one method of providing help text for
 * flat widgets
 */

#include <Xol/FCheckBox.h>

typedef struct _Item {
    String      label;
} Item;

static String   itemFields[] = {
    XtNlabel,
};
#define NR_ITEM_FIELDS  \
    (sizeof(itemFields) / sizeof(itemFields[0]))

static Item items[] = {
    /* XtNlabel,    */
    { "Flat Widget #1",},
    { "Flat Widget #2",},
    { "Flat Widget #3",},
    { "Flat Widget #4",},

};
#define NR_ITEMS    (sizeof(items) / sizeof(items[0]))

static char *FlatItemHelpText[] = {
    "This is some help for flat widget item #1.",
    "This is some help for flat widget item #2.",
    "This is some help for flat widget item #3.",
    "This is some help for flat widget item #4.",
```

```
};

Widget DemoFlatHelp(w_parent)
    Widget   w_parent;
{
    Widget          w_flat;
    OlFlatHelpId    flatHelpId;
    int             count;

    w_flat =
        XtCreateManagedWidget(
            "flatWidget",                  /* instance name */
            flatCheckBoxWidgetClass,       /* widget class */
            w_parent,                      /* parent widget */
            tmpArg,                        /* arg list */
            TmpArgList(
                XtNitems,           items,
                XtNnumItems,        NR_ITEMS,
                XtNitemFields,      itemFields,
                XtNnumItemFields,   NR_ITEM_FIELDS,
                XtNborderWidth,     1,
                XtNlayoutType,      OL_FIXEDROWS,
                XtNmeasure,         2,
                0
            )
        );

    /*
     * Add help to the container
     */
    OlRegisterHelp(
        OL_WIDGET_HELP,         /* id_type */
        w_flat,                 /* id */
        "FlatWidget",           /* tag */
        OL_STRING_SOURCE,       /* source_type */
        "This help is attached to the Flat container widget."
    );

    /*
     * Add help to each of the sub-items
     */
    flatHelpId.widget = w_flat;
    for (count = 0; count < NR_ITEMS; count++) {
        flatHelpId.item_index = count;
        OlRegisterHelp(
            OL_FLAT_HELP,           /* id_type */
            &flatHelpId,            /* id */
            "FlatItem",             /* tag */
            OL_STRING_SOURCE,       /* source_type */
            FlatItemHelpText[count]
        );
```

```
    }

    return(w_flat);
}
```

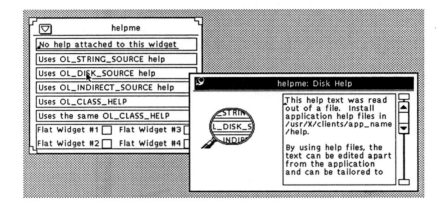

Figure 6.19 Helpme demonstrating OL_DISK_SOURCE Help

The OL_DISK_SOURCE Help reads the text from the file helpme.hlp:

```
This help text was read out of a file.   Install application help
files in /usr/X/clients/app_name/help.

By using help files, the text can be edited apart from the
application and can be tailored to suit different languages or
expertise levels.

Note that embedded newlines are preserved and lines are wrapped
automatically at whitespace.   Therefore, help text files should
only use newlines to separate paragraphs.
```

Applications should install Help text files in the directory /usr/X/clients/app_name/help or /usr/lib/X11/app_name/help, consistent with the rest of the window system installation.

6.4 Going Further

If you've gone through this entire book, you've read hundreds of pages of text and thousands of lines of code, and by now should feel pretty comfortable developing interesting and useful X applications with the OPEN LOOK Intrinsic Toolkit. However, no one book could possibly answer all of your questions or teach you everything there is to know about any subject, let alone ones as rich and complex as the OPEN LOOK GUI and X Window System. Depending on your needs, you may have specific areas you wish to learn more about.

- If you wish to develop graphics applications, you'll want to have a book on Xlib, such as the *Xlib Programming Manual* by Adrian Nye (Volume 1 of the O'Reilly set) or *X Window System* by Scheiffler, Gettys, and Newman. In both cases, use Chapter 2 from this book to direct you to the important graphics issues. Use the OPEN LOOK Stub and Scrolled Window combination shown in Chapter 5 to implement scrollable graphics panes.

- If you need to develop your own user-interface controls, refer to the *OPEN LOOK Graphical User Interface Specification* for stylistic guidelines and to the *AT&T XWIN Programmer's Guide* for the nitty-gritty details of how to use the Xt Intrinsics internals to develop new widgets.

- Finally, if your application requires an extremely complex or reconfigurable user interface, you might want to consider using a user-interface management system (UIMS) such as AT&T OPEN LOOK Express™. OPEN LOOK Express is the OPEN LOOK version of UIMX, a powerful development tool that lets you lay out and prototype the user interface without going through the traditional edit-compile-test cycle. Armed with the knowledge you have acquired from this text, you will have no trouble using OPEN LOOK Express to quickly develop powerful user interfaces for your applications.

Appendix

The Xtutil Utility Library

This appendix contains the source code for the Xtutil utility library used by the program examples in this book.

Makefile—builds the Xtutil utility library, libxtutil.a

```
#
# Makefile for the Appendix of "An OPEN LOOK at UNIX"
# by John David Miller
#
# @(#) sccs/s.Makefile 1.9 last delta 2/19/90 19:51:47
#
# DEBUG = -g
DEBUG = -DDEBUG
STRIP = -s
# OPTIM = -O

# The next two lines are for AT&T XWIN installations
CFLAGS = -I/usr/X/include -I/usr/include $(DEBUG) $(OPTIM)

# MIT-style X Window System installations might use these lines:
# CFLAGS = $(DEBUG) $(OPTIM)

LIB = libxtutil.a
OBJS = arglist.o dbg.o fm.o image.o init.o notice.o \
    property.o timestam.o token.o warning.o wm.o wsm.o

all: $(LIB)

$(LIB) : $(OBJS)
    ar rv $(LIB) $?

clean:
    -rm -f $(LIB) *.o
```

arglist.c—builds variable-length Arg lists

```
/*
 * arglist.c - OPEN LOOK Intrinsic Toolkit utility file
 * to manipulate Arg lists.
 *
 * @(#) sccs/s.arglist.c 1.7 last delta 2/4/90 22:10:08
 */

#include <X11/Intrinsic.h>
#include <stdio.h>
#include <varargs.h>

#define NARGS   20
Arg       tmpArg[NARGS];

/*
 * TmpArgList() - set names and values of Args in a
 * global ArgList.  Passed list of name/value pairs is
 * zero terminated.
 *
 * in:
 *      name1, value1,
 *      name2, value2,
 *      ....
 *      0
 *
 * out:
 *      count of name/value pairs
 *
 * side effects:
 *      name/value pairs are set in the global array, "tmpArg"
 *
 * (See UNIX documentation for varargs details.)
 */

int TmpArgList(va_alist)
    va_dcl                  /* variable arg list declaration */
{
    va_list         ap;     /* vararg list pointer */
    register Arg    *ptr;   /* ptr into global arg array */
    register unsigned  count;  /* count of arg pairs we set */
    String          name;   /* name field of Arg */
    XtArgVal        value;  /* value field of Arg */

    va_start(ap);           /* start variable arg list processing */

    for (
        count = 0,
        ptr = tmpArg;
```

```
            ((name = va_arg(ap, String)) != 0) && (count < NARGS);

            count++,
            ptr++
    ) {
            value = va_arg(ap, XtArgVal);   /* fetch value */
            XtSetArg(*ptr, name, value);     /* NO AUTO-INCREMENT */
                                    /* XtSetArg() is a macro */
    }

    if (name != 0) {
            OlWarning("TmpArgList: had more args than space");
    }

    va_end(ap);      /* end variable arg list processing */

    return(count);       /* return number of arg pairs set */
}

XtArgVal GetValue(wid, resource)
    Widget  wid;
    String  resource;
{
    static XtArgVal value;
    Arg arg[1];

    XtSetArg(arg[0], resource, &value);
    XtGetValues(wid, arg, 1);
    return(value);
}

void SetValue(wid, resource, value)
    Widget      wid;
    String      resource;
    XtArgVal    value;
{
    Arg arg[1];

    XtSetArg(arg[0], resource, value);
    XtSetValues(wid, arg, 1);
    return;
}
```

dbg.c—debugging printf routine

```
/*
 * @(#) sccs/s.dbg.c 1.3 last delta 2/4/90 22:10:10
 */
#include <stdio.h>

int debug = 1;

/*
 * dbg() - hack to control debug printf's.  WARNING: if
 * this doesn't work on your machine, ensure that the
 * type for p0-10 matches your stack type.  That is,
 * if your stack pushes things as longs, change the
 * declaration here.  (On almost all UNIX machines,
 * stack_type == int == long == 32 bits)
 */
dbg(format, p0, p1, p2, p3, p4, p5, p6, p7, p8, p9, p10)
    char    *format;
    int p0, p1, p2, p3, p4, p5, p6, p7, p8, p9, p10;
{
    if (debug)
    fprintf(stderr,
        format, p0, p1, p2, p3, p4, p5, p6, p7, p8, p9, p10);
}
```

fm.c—implements OPEN LOOK File Mana callback interface

```
/*
 * @(#) sccs/s.fm.c 1.8 last delta 2/17/90 13:52:47
 *
 * Handle the OPEN LOOK File Manager protocol
 */
#include <X11/Intrinsic.h>
#include <X11/StringDefs.h>
#include <X11/Xatom.h>
#include <Xol/OlClients.h>
#include <stdio.h>
#include <varargs.h>
#include "xtutilp.h"

extern Atom _OL_FM_QUEUE;   /* interned by OPEN LOOK Toolkit */
extern Atom _OL_FM_REPLY;   /* interned by OPEN LOOK Toolkit */

/*
 * Notice that this is a single callback.  Using a callback
 * list is left as an exercise to the reader.
 */
static CallbackRecord   CBFMreply;
```

418

```
/*
 * AskFMBrowse() - post a request to the OPEN LOOK File Manager
 * to initiate client-service mode.  In other words, use the
 * File Manager as a browser.
 */
void AskFMBrowse(wid, browse)
    Widget      wid;
    FmBrowse    *browse;
{
    String      buffer[BUFSIZ];

    InitXtutil(wid);

    sprintf(
        buffer,
        "%c%d%c%d%c%s%c%s%c%s%c%d%c%d%c%d%c%s%c%s%c%s%c%s%c",
        FM_BROWSE,
        XtWindow(wid),              DELIM,  /* window */
        0,                          DELIM,  /* serial number */
        _xtutilPriv.sysname,        DELIM,  /* sysname */
        _xtutilPriv.nodename,       DELIM,  /* nodename */
        _xtutilPriv.applname,       DELIM,  /* app name */
        _xtutilPriv.uid,            DELIM,  /* uid */
        _xtutilPriv.gid,            DELIM,  /* gid */
        XtWindow(wid),              DELIM,  /* window group */
        browse->directory,         DELIM,  /* directory */
        browse->pattern,           DELIM,  /* pattern */
        browse->label,             DELIM,  /* label */
        "",                         DELIM   /* reserved */
    );

    /*
     * Place the request on the File Manager's queue
     * on the root window
     */
    XChangeProperty(
        _xtutilPriv.ourDisplay, /* display */
        _xtutilPriv.rootWindow, /* window */
        _OL_FM_QUEUE,           /* property name */
        XA_STRING,              /* property type */
        8,                      /* format: 8, 16, or 32 */
        PropModeAppend,         /* prepend, replace, append */
        buffer,                 /* data */
        strlen(buffer)          /* length in bytes */
    );

    return;
}
```

```
/*
 * AddFMCallbacks() - handle low-level communications protocol
 * from the OPEN LOOK File Manager.  Dispatch to
 * application-provided code on events.  This routine uses a
 * variable-length argument list of the following format:

     Widget  wid,
     int protocol_1,
     FUNC    protocolCallback_1,
     caddr_t protocolData_1,
     ...
     int protocol_N,
     FUNC    protocolCallback_N,
     caddr_t protocolData_N,
     0

 * The first parameter is a widget.  Following this is a
 * variable-length array of triplets - the protocol ID, a ptr
 * to the protocol callback function, and a possibly-NULL
 * value that will be passed as a parameter to the protocol
 * callback function.  A zero terminates the list.
 *
 * Synopsis of callbacks:

     void    CallbackFunc(client_data, call_data)
         caddr_t client_data;
         caddr_t call_data;  (specific to the event)
 */
void AddFMCallbacks(va_alist)
    va_dcl              /* variable arg list declaration */
{
    extern void FMEventHandler();
    va_list     ap;     /* vararg list pointer */
    Widget      wid;
    int     protocol;

    va_start(ap);       /* start variable arg list processing */

    wid = va_arg(ap, Widget);   /* get widget */
    InitXtutil(wid);        /* initialize utility toolkit */

    while ((protocol = va_arg(ap, int)) != 0) {
        switch (protocol) {
        case CB_FM_REPLY:
            CBFMreply.func = va_arg(ap, FUNC);
            CBFMreply.data = va_arg(ap, caddr_t);
            /*
             * Tell the Intrinsics to call our event handler
             * when the properties change on this window.
             */
            XtAddEventHandler(
```

```
                wid,
                PropertyChangeMask, /* event mask */
                FALSE,              /* no nonmaskables */
                FMEventHandler,     /* XtEventHandler */
                NULL                /* client_data */
            );

            break;
        default:
            Warning(
                "unknown request in AddFMCallbacks: %d\n",
                protocol
            );
            break;
        }
    }
    va_end(ap);
    return;
}

/*
 * DeleteFMCallbacks() - allow added callbacks to be removed.
 * This routine uses a variable-length argument list of
 * the following format:

    Widget  wid,
    int protocol_1, // 1st callback protocol of disinterest
    ...
    int protocol_N, // last callback protocol of disinterest
    0

 */
void DeleteFMCallbacks(va_alist)
    va_dcl              /* variable arg list declaration */
{
    va_list     ap;     /* vararg list pointer */
    Widget      wid;
    int     protocol;


    va_start(ap);       /* start variable arg list processing */

    wid = va_arg(ap, Widget);   /* get widget */
    InitXtutil(wid);            /* init util stuff */

    while ((protocol = va_arg(ap, int)) != 0) {
        switch (protocol) {
        case CB_FM_REPLY:
            CBFMreply.func = NULL;
            CBFMreply.data = NULL;
            XtRemoveEventHandler(
```

421

```
                wid,
                PropertyChangeMask,  /* event mask */
                FALSE,               /* no nonmaskables */
                FMEventHandler,      /* XtEventHandler */
                NULL                 /* client_data */
            );
            break;
        default:
            Warning(
                "unknown request in DeleteFMCallbacks(): %d\n",
                protocol
            );
            break;
        }
    }
    va_end(ap);
    return;
}

static void FMEventHandler(wid, client_data, event)
    Widget  wid;
    caddr_t client_data;
    XEvent  *event;
{
    Atom          actual_type;
    unsigned long nitems;
    unsigned long bytes_after;
    int           message = event->xproperty.atom;
    int           actual_format;


    if (
        (event->type != PropertyNotify) ||
        (event->xproperty.state != PropertyNewValue)
    ) {
        return;
    }

    if (message == _OL_FM_REPLY) {
        FmReply reply;
        String  sysname, nodename;
        int     serial;
        String  prop;
        String  token;


        XGetWindowProperty(
            _xtutilPriv.ourDisplay,
            XtWindow(wid),
            message,
            0,                  /* offset */
```

```
        BUFSIZ,          /* length */
        TRUE,            /* delete */
        XA_STRING,
        &actual_type,
        &actual_format,
        &nitems,
        &bytes_after,
        &prop
);

/*
 * Parse the property string written by the File Manager.
 * The format of this string was designed for maximum
 * compactness, albeit at the cost of complexity.
 *
 * The first byte is the action with the rest of the
 * string separated into tokens by the delimiter
 * character, 0x1f.  The directory and filename(s)
 * are subtokenized with a space as the delimiter.
 *
 * For more information, see the AT&T OPEN LOOK GUI
 * Programmer's Guide.
 */
reply.action = prop[0];      /* not separated by DELIM */

InitTokenizer(&prop[1]);
serial = atoi(NextToken(DELIM));
sysname = NextToken(DELIM);
nodename = NextToken(DELIM);

switch (reply.action) {
case FM_ACCEPT:
case FM_MOVE:
case FM_COPY:
    /*
     * this token is actually several subtokens
     * separated by spaces:
     *   directory filename1 ... filenameN
     */
    reply.message = NULL;
    reply.directory = NextToken(SPACE);

    reply.fileCount = 1;
    reply.fileList = (String *) malloc(sizeof(String));
    reply.fileList[0] = NextToken(SPACE);

    while ((token = NextToken(SPACE)) != NULL) {
        reply.fileList =
            (String *) realloc(
                reply.fileList,
                ++reply.fileCount *
```

```
                            sizeof(String)
                    );
                reply.fileList[reply.fileCount - 1] = token;
            }
            break;

        case FM_CANCEL:
        case FM_INVALID:
            reply.message = NextToken();
            reply.directory = NULL;
            reply.fileCount = 0;
            reply.fileList = NULL;
            break;
        default:
            Warning(
                "FMEventHandler: unknown action: %d\n",
                reply.action
            );
            return;        /* not much we can do */
        }

        /*
         * invoke application-supplied callback
         */
        if (CBFMreply.func != NULL) {
            (*CBFMreply.func)(CBFMreply.data, &reply);
        }

        XFree(prop);
    }
    return;
}
```

image.c—builds an Xlib Image struct from bitmap data

```
/*
 * image.c - OPEN LOOK Intrinsic Toolkit utility file to
 * manipulate images
 *
 * @(#) sccs/s.image.c 1.3 last delta 2/4/90 22:10:14
 */

#include <X11/Intrinsic.h>
#include <stdio.h>

/*
 * XYBitmapImageFromData() - build an Image structure out
 * of bitmap data generated from the bitmap(1) program.
 * Xlib provides a similar function, XCreateBitmapFromData()
```

```
 * for building pixmaps, but not one for Images.
 */
XImage  *XYBitmapImageFromData(wid, pBits, width, height)
    Widget      wid;
    char        *pBits;       /* bits from bitmap(1) or equiv. */
    Dimension   width, height;
{
    Display             *display;
    Window              window;
    XImage              *image, *XCreateImage();
    XWindowAttributes   winAttr;
    Visual              *visual;

    display = XtDisplay(wid);

    /*
     * We need to come up with a Visual struct to use.
     * Preferably, we can get the visual associated with the
     * widget's window.  If the widget does not have a valid
     * window (usually because it hasn't been initialized or
     * the widget is actually a gadget) then we use the
     * default visual.
     */
    window = XtWindow(wid);
    if (window == 0) {
#ifdef notdef
        OlWarning(
          "XtWindow() returned zero in XYBitmapImageFromData()\n"
        );
#endif
        visual =
            XDefaultVisual(display, XDefaultScreen(display));
    } else {
        XGetWindowAttributes(display, window, &winAttr);
        visual = winAttr.visual;
    }

    /*
     * Create an Image structure/object.  Xlib uses the Image
     * structure as a specification for writing/reading
     * pixmap data to/from the server.
     *
     * Note that we have to make some adjustments to the
     * structure after it is created, since XCreateImage()
     * sets up the structure to match your machine's native
     * bit and byte order.  However, we know that the data
     * from bitmap(1) is in a particular format, regardless
     * of what machine it is on.
     *
     *  It is assumed that pBits is in the following format:
     *      format=XYPixmap
```

```
 *          bit_order=LSBFirst
 *          byte_order=LSBFirst
 *          bitmap_unit=8
 *          bitmap_pad=8
 *          xoffset=0
 *          no extra bytes per scan line
 */
image =
    XCreateImage(
        display,
        visual,
        1,                      /* depth */
        XYBitmap,               /* format */
        0,                      /* offset */
        pBits,                  /* bitmap data */
        width,
        height,
        8,                      /* bitmap_pad */
        (width + 7) >> 3    /* bytes_per_line */
    );

image->bitmap_bit_order = LSBFirst;
image->byte_order = LSBFirst;

return(image);
}
```

init.c—internal initialization

```
/*
 * @(#) sccs/s.init.c 1.3 last delta 2/4/90 22:10:15
 */
#include <X11/Intrinsic.h>
#include <X11/StringDefs.h>
#include <X11/Xatom.h>
#include <Xol/OlClients.h>
#include <sys/utsname.h>
#include <varargs.h>
#include <stdio.h>
#include "xtutilp.h"

_XtutilPriv _xtutilPriv;

void InitXtutil(wid)
    Widget  wid;        /* toplevel widget, presumably */
{
    struct utsname  unameBuf;
```

```
#ifndef notdef
    /*
     * Warning: this is an undocumented OPEN LOOK Toolkit
     * call and may go away.  In that case, use the code below
     */
    _xtutilPriv.applname = (String) _OlGetApplicationTitle();
#else
    XFetchName(
        XtDisplay(wid),
        XtWindow(wid),
        &_xtutilPriv.applname
    );
#endif

    if (_xtutilPriv.inited == TRUE)
        return;

#ifndef notdef
    /*
     * Warning: this is an undocumented libXol.a function.
     * It may go away in a future release.  The routine
     * merely ensures that wid is a toplevel shell widget.
     */
    wid = (Widget) _OlGetShellOfWidget(wid);
#endif
    _xtutilPriv.toplevelWidget = wid;
    _xtutilPriv.toplevelWindow = XtWindow(wid);
    _xtutilPriv.ourDisplay = XtDisplay(wid);
    _xtutilPriv.ourScreen = XtScreen(wid);
    _xtutilPriv.rootWindow =
XDefaultRootWindow(_xtutilPriv.ourDisplay);


    uname(&unameBuf);
    _xtutilPriv.sysname = unameBuf.sysname;
    _xtutilPriv.nodename = unameBuf.nodename;

    _xtutilPriv.gid = getgid();
    _xtutilPriv.uid = getuid();

    _xtutilPriv.inited = TRUE;
    return;
}
```

427

notice.c—implements application-model OPEN LOOK Notice boxes

```
/*
 * Convenient routine to popup an application-defined NOTICE box
 * @(#) sccs/s.notice.c 1.2 last delta 2/4/90 22:10:17
 */
#include <X11/Intrinsic.h>
#include <X11/StringDefs.h>
#include <Xol/OpenLook.h>
#include <Xol/OblongButt.h>
#include <Xol/Notice.h>
#include <varargs.h>
#include "xtutilp.h"


typedef struct _Choice {
    struct _Choice  *next;
    Widget      wid;
} Choice;

static caddr_t  returnVal;
static Boolean  done;

/*
 * Notice() - application-modal notice box, with
 * caller-defined buttons and return values.
 *
 * Synopsis:
 *
 *   caddr_t Notice(va_alist)
 *   {
 *       Widget  w_parent
 *       String  message
 *       String  buttonLabel_1
 *       caddr_t returnValue_1
 *       ....
 *       String  buttonLabel_N
 *       caddr_t returnValue_N
 *       0
 *   }
 */
caddr_t Notice(va_alist)
    va_dcl
{
    va_list             ap;
    register Choice     *pFirst=NULL, *pLast=NULL, *pChoice;
    Widget              wid, w_notice, w_text, w_control;
    void                NoticeCB(), FreeList();
    String              label;
```

```
va_start(ap);              /* start VARARGS */

wid = va_arg(ap, Widget);
InitXtutil(wid);           /* initialize Utility Library */

/*
 * Create the Notice popup shell widget.  Note that we use
 * XtCreatePopupShell() instead of XtCreateWidget().
 * Note also that the notice widget automatically freezes
 * the rest of the application when it is popped up.
 */
w_notice =
    XtCreatePopupShell(
        "notice",          /* instance name */
        noticeShellWidgetClass, /* widget class */
        wid,               /* parent widget */
        tmpArg,            /* arg list */
        TmpArgList(
            XtNemanateWidget,   wid,
            0
        )
    );

/*
 * Read back the widget IDs of the textArea and
 * controlArea widgets, implicitly created with the
 * popup shell.
 */
XtGetValues(
    w_notice,              /* widget ID */
    tmpArg,                /* arg list */
    TmpArgList(
        XtNtextArea,     &w_text,    /* read textArea ID */
        XtNcontrolArea, &w_control, /* get controlArea ID */
        0
    )
);

/*
 * Display a message in the text area
 */
SetValue(w_text, XtNstring, va_arg(ap, String));

/*
 * Create choice buttons, as per the passed list of
 * button labels and return values.  Choice buttons
 * are children of the notice widget's control area.
 */
while((label = va_arg(ap, String)) != 0) {
```

429

```
    pChoice = (Choice *) malloc(sizeof(Choice));
    if (pChoice == NULL) {
        Error(
            "couldn't alloc %d bytes in Notice()\n",
            sizeof(Choice)
        );
    }

    pChoice->next = NULL;
    pChoice->wid =
        XtCreateManagedWidget(
            label,
            oblongButtonWidgetClass,
            w_control,
            tmpArg,
            TmpArgList(
                XtNlabel,    label,
                0
            )
        );

    XtAddCallback(
        pChoice->wid,
        XtNselect,
        NoticeCB,
        va_arg(ap, caddr_t) /* return value */
    );

    /*
     * chain into list
     */
    if (pFirst == NULL) {
        pLast = pFirst = pChoice;
    } else {
        pLast->next = pChoice;
        pLast = pChoice;
    }
}
va_end(ap);          /* end VARARGS */

/*
 * Popup the notice box
 */
XtPopup(w_notice, XtGrabExclusive);

/*
 * Take over event processing until our callback sets
 * the "done" semaphore telling us that the user has
 * made a choice.
 */
for (done = FALSE; done != TRUE;) {
```

```
        XEvent   xevent;

        XtNextEvent(&xevent);
        XtDispatchEvent(&xevent);
    }

    /*
     * destroy widgets used in popup
     */
    FreeList(pFirst);
    XtDestroyWidget(w_notice);

    /*
     * return selected value
     */
    return(returnVal);
}


static void NoticeCB(wid, client_data, call_data)
    Widget   wid;
    caddr_t  client_data;          /* return value */
    caddr_t  call_data;
{
    returnVal = client_data;
    done = TRUE;
    return;
}


/*
 * FreeList() - free the list (from the bottom up).
 */
static void FreeList(list)
    Choice   *list;
{
    if (list->next == NULL) {
        free(list);
        return;
    } else {
        FreeList(list->next);    /* free rest of the list first */
        free(list);              /* then free this one */
    }
}
```

property.c—providack interfasce to inter-client communication with properties

```
/*
 * @(#) sccs/s.property.c 1.3 last delta 2/4/90 22:10:18
 */
#include <X11/Intrinsic.h>
#include <X11/StringDefs.h>
#include <X11/Xatom.h>
#include <Xol/OlClients.h>
#include <stdio.h>
#include <varargs.h>
#include "xtutilp.h"

/*
 * PropertyCallbackRecord: info for an entry in the
 * callback list.  Note that these callbacks are more
 * complex than the simple, single callbacks for WM, WSM,
 * and FM callbacks.  This callback list had to be much more
 * flexible, since the user could specify any arbitrary Atom
 * to use as the main callback key.
 */
typedef struct _PropertyCallbackRecord {
    struct _PropertyCallbackRecord  *next;
    PropertyProtocol        protocol;   /* CB_NEW, CB_DELETE */
    Atom                    atom;       /* atom of interest */
    FUNC                    func;       /* callback function */
    caddr_t                 data;       /* client_data */
} PropertyCallbackRecord;

/*
 * The callback linked-list (done the hard way).
 */
PropertyCallbackRecord  *pFirst=NULL, *pLast=NULL;


/*
 * AddPropertyCallbacks() - register callbacks to be called
 * by activity of properties on our toplevel window.
 * Note that multiple callbacks can be registered for the
 * same property and protocol (New or Delete).
 *
 * This routine uses a variable-length argument list of the
 * following format:

    Widget              w_toplevel,
    PropertyProtocol    protocol_1,         // CB_NEW, CB_DELETE
    Atom                atom_1,             // property ID
    FUNC                protocolCallback_1, // callback
    caddr_t             protocolData_1,     // client_data
```

```
        ...
    PropertyProtocol        protocol_N,
    Atom                    atom_N,
    FUNC                    protocolCallback_N,
    caddr_t                 protocolData_N,
    0

 * The first parameter is a toplevel shell widget.  Following
 * this is a variable-length array of quadruples - the
 * protocol ID, the property to watch, a ptr to the protocol
 * callback function, and a possibly-NULL value that will be
 * passed as a parameter to the protocol callback function.
 * A zero terminates the list.
 *
 * Synopsis of callbacks:

    void    CallbackFunc(client_data, call_data)
        caddr_t client_data;
        caddr_t call_data;

 * where call_data is a pointer to a PropertyReply structure.
 */
void AddPropertyCallbacks(va_alist)
    va_dcl              /* variable arg list declaration */
{
    extern void             PropertyEventHandler();
    va_list                 ap;     /* vararg list pointer */
    Widget                  wid;
    int                     protocol;
    PropertyCallbackRecord  *pRec;

    va_start(ap);           /* start variable arg list processing */

    wid = va_arg(ap, Widget);   /* get toplevel widget */
    InitXtutil(wid);            /* initialize utility toolkit */

    /*
     * Add new callback records to the end of the list
     */
    while ((protocol = va_arg(ap, int)) != 0) {
        pRec = (PropertyCallbackRecord *)
            malloc(sizeof(PropertyCallbackRecord));
        if (!pRec) {
            Warning("AddPropertyCallbacks : malloc failed\n");
            return;
        }
        pRec->next = NULL;
        pRec->protocol = protocol;
        pRec->atom = va_arg(ap, Atom);
        pRec->func = va_arg(ap, FUNC);
        pRec->data = va_arg(ap, caddr_t);
```

433

```
        if (pFirst == NULL) {    /* first ever */
            pFirst = pLast = pRec;
            XtAddEventHandler(
                _xtutilPriv.toplevelWidget,
                PropertyChangeMask,     /* event mask */
                FALSE,                  /* no nonmaskables */
                PropertyEventHandler,   /* XtEventHandler */
                NULL                    /* client_data */
            );
        } else {
            pLast->next = pRec; /* chain in */
            pLast = pRec;       /* point to new last */
        }
    }
    va_end(ap);
    return;
}


/*
 * DeletePropertyCallbacks() - remove callbacks from the list.
 * All fields of the delete request must match the request
 * originally made to AddPropertyCallbacks.
 *
 * This routine uses a variable-length argument list of
 * the following format:

    Widget              w_toplevel,
    PropertyProtocol    protocol_1,
    Atom                atom_1,
    FUNC                protocolCallback_1,
    caddr_t             protocolData_1,
    ...
    PropertyProtocol    protocol_N,
    Atom                atom_N,
    FUNC                protocolCallback_N,
    caddr_t             protocolData_N,
    0

 * The first parameter is a toplevel shell widget.
 * Following this is a variable-length array of quadruples -
 * the protocol ID, the atom to watch, a ptr to the protocol
 * callback function, and a possibly-NULL value that will be
 * passed as a parameter to the protocol callback function.
 * A zero terminates the list.
 */
void DeletePropertyCallbacks(va_alist)
    va_dcl                  /* variable arg list declaration */
{
    extern void             PropertyEventHandler();
```

```
va_list               ap;        /* vararg list pointer */
Widget                wid;
int                   protocol;
PropertyCallbackRecord *pThis, *pPrev, match;

va_start(ap);          /* start variable arg list processing */

wid = va_arg(ap, Widget);    /* get toplevel widget */
InitXtutil(wid);            /* initialize utility toolkit */

while ((protocol = va_arg(ap, int)) != 0) {
    match.protocol = protocol;
    match.atom = va_arg(ap, Atom);
    match.func = va_arg(ap, FUNC);
    match.data = va_arg(ap, caddr_t);

    /*
     * see if it matches any registered callback records
     */
    for (
        pPrev = NULL,
        pThis = pFirst;

        pThis != NULL;
    ) {
        if (
            (pThis->protocol != match.protocol) ||
            (pThis->atom != match.atom) ||
            (pThis->func != match.func) ||
            (pThis->data != match.data)
        ) {
            pPrev = pThis;
            pThis = pThis->next;
            continue;        /* nope */
        }

        /*
         * if the element is the first in the chain,
         * eliminate it by moving the pFirst pointer to
         * the next element.  otherwise, eliminate it by
         * pointing around it.  also ensure that we keep
         * the pointer to the end of the list valid.
         */
        if (pThis == pFirst) {
            if (pFirst == pLast)     /* only one */
                pLast = NULL;
            pFirst = pThis->next;   /* point at 2nd */
            free(pThis);            /* free 1st */
            pThis = pFirst;         /* point at new 1st */

            if (pFirst == NULL) {
```

```
                        XtRemoveEventHandler(
                            _xtutilPriv.toplevelWidget,
                            PropertyChangeMask,
                            FALSE,
                            PropertyEventHandler,
                            NULL
                        );
                    }
            } else {
                pPrev->next = pThis->next; /* point around */
                if (pThis == pLast)
                    pLast = pPrev;
                free(pThis);
                pThis = pPrev->next;
            }
        }

    }
    va_end(ap);
    return;
}

static void PropertyEventHandler(wid, client_data, event)
    Widget  wid;
    caddr_t client_data;
    XEvent  *event;
{
    PropertyProtocol        protocol;
    PropertyReply           reply;
    PropertyCallbackRecord  *pThis;
    XPropertyEvent          xprop;
    Atom                    atom;


    if (event->type != PropertyNotify) {
        return;
    }

    xprop = event->xproperty;
    atom = xprop.atom;

    switch (xprop.state) {
    case PropertyNewValue:
        protocol = CB_NEW;
        break;
    case PropertyDelete:
        protocol = CB_DELETE;
        break;
    default:
        Warning(
            "PropertyEventHandler: unrecognized state: %d\n",
```

```
            xprop.state
        );
        return;
    }

    /*
     * initialize call_data
     */
    reply.sendEvent =   xprop.send_event;
    reply.atom =        atom;
    reply.window =      xprop.window;
    reply.time =        xprop.time;
    reply.state =       xprop.state;

    /*
     * Call callbacks that match the atom and protocol.
     * Note that the atom "None" in the callback list
     * matches all atoms.
     */
    for (
        pThis = pFirst;

        pThis != NULL;

        pThis = pThis->next
    ) {
        if (
            ((pThis->atom == atom) || (pThis->atom == None)) &&
            (pThis->protocol == protocol)
        ) {
            (*pThis->func)(pThis->data, &reply);   /* callback */
        }
    }

    return;
}
```

timestam.c—fetches the current server time with a single call

```
/*
 * @(#) sccs/s.timestam.c 1.4 last delta 2/4/90 22:10:20
 * Get current timestamp.
 */
#include <X11/Intrinsic.h>
#include <X11/StringDefs.h>
#include <X11/Xatom.h>
#include "xtutilp.h"


/*
 * GetTimestamp() - return a Time value suitable for use
 * in ICCCM selection processing.
 */
Time GetTimestamp(wid)
    Widget  wid;
{
    XEvent      xevent;
    Time        time;
    void        DoNothing();
    Bool        GotTime();
    Display     *ourDisplay;
    Widget      toplevelWidget;
    Window      toplevelWindow;


    InitXtutil(wid);

    ourDisplay = _xtutilPriv.ourDisplay;
    toplevelWidget = _xtutilPriv.toplevelWidget;
    toplevelWindow = _xtutilPriv.toplevelWindow;

    /*
     * Add an event handler to ensure that the server
     * is sending us PropertyNotify events
     */
    AddPropertyCallbacks(
        toplevelWidget,     /* wid */
        CB_NEW,             /* property protocol */
        XA_WM_NAME,         /* existing property */
        DoNothing,          /* callback */
        NULL,               /* client-data */
        0                   /* terminate the list */
    );

    /*
     * append zero-length data to a property to generate
     * an event.
```

```
    */
    XChangeProperty(
        ourDisplay,             /* display */
        toplevelWindow,         /* window */
        XA_WM_NAME,             /* property */
        XA_STRING,              /* type */
        8,                      /* format */
        PropModeAppend,         /* mode */
        "",                     /* data */
        0                       /* nelements */
    );

#define APPLICATION_MODAL
#ifdef APPLICATION_MODAL
    /*
     * Application-modal event processing: the next call
     * effectively blocks the execution of the rest of the
     * application until we can satisfy our goal of getting a
     * current timestamp.  This is useful to ensure that
     * the state of our application doesn't change while we
     * are trying to finish this task.  It would be useful if
     * what we are doing required other event processing, such
     * as mouse tracking, since no events get dispatched until
     * our caller returns.
     *
     * XPeekIfEvent calls GotTime with events out of the
     * queue (but does not remove them) until GotTime
     * returns TRUE.  As a side effect, GotTime sets the
     * value of time.
     */
    XPeekIfEvent(ourDisplay, &xevent, GotTime, &time);
#else
    /*
     * Using this code, we take over the event dispatch loop
     * until we get an event with a timestamp.  Note that this
     * type of processing is non-modal: we continue processing
     * events while trying to satisfy our own needs.  This is
     * useful if the action is not state-critical and may
     * take awhile to complete.
     */
    for (
        time = 0;

        time == 0;

        GotTime(ourDisplay, &xevent, &time) /* sets time */
    ) {
        XtNextEvent(&xevent);           /* get an event */
        XtDispatchEvent(&xevent);       /* dispatch it */
    }
#endif
```

```
    /*
     * remove this callback from the chain, since it isn't needed
     * anymore
     */
    DeletePropertyCallbacks(
        toplevelWidget,         /* wid */
        CB_NEW,                 /* property protocol */
        XA_WM_NAME,             /* existing property */
        DoNothing,              /* callback */
        NULL,                   /* client-data */
        0                    /* terminate the list */
    );

    return(time);
}


static Bool GotTime(pDisplay, pEvent, pTime)
    Display *pDisplay;
    XEvent  *pEvent;
    Time    *pTime;
{
    switch(pEvent->type) {
    case ButtonPress:
    case ButtonRelease:
        *pTime = pEvent->xbutton.time;
        return(TRUE);
    case EnterNotify:
    case LeaveNotify:
        *pTime = pEvent->xcrossing.time;
        return(TRUE);
    case KeyPress:
    case KeyRelease:
        *pTime = pEvent->xkey.time;
        return(TRUE);
    case MotionNotify:
        *pTime = pEvent->xmotion.time;
        return(TRUE);
    case PropertyNotify:
        *pTime = pEvent->xproperty.time;
        return(TRUE);
    case SelectionClear:
        *pTime = pEvent->xselectionclear.time;
        return(TRUE);
    case SelectionNotify:
        *pTime = pEvent->xselection.time;
        return(TRUE);
    case SelectionRequest:
        *pTime = pEvent->xselectionrequest.time;
        return(TRUE);
```

440

```
    default:
        return(FALSE);
    }
}


static void DoNothing(client_data, call_data)
    caddr_t client_data, *call_data;
{
    return;
}
```

token.c—internal olfm and olwsm property parsing routines

```
/*
 * @(#) sccs/s.token.c 1.2 last delta 2/4/90 22:10:22
 *
 * File Manager and Workspace Manager communications
 * protocol parsing code
 */
#include <X11/Intrinsic.h>
#include "xtutilp.h"

static String   tail;

/*
 * InitTokenizer() - reset the token finder to the
 * new string to be parsed
 */
void InitTokenizer(str)
    String  str;
{
    tail = str;
}

/*
 * NextToken() - return the next string token, up to the
 * DELIM or NULL character, replacing the DELIM character
 * with a NULL.  Calls to NextToken() after the last
 * token returns NULL.
 */
String NextToken(delim)
    int delim;
{
    String  head = tail;    /* start where we left off */

    if (*tail == '\0')
        return(NULL);
    while ((*tail != '\0') && (*tail != delim)) {
```

```
        ++tail;
    }
    if (*tail != '\0') {
        *tail = '\0';   /* NULL-terminate the token */
        ++tail;         /* point to next char for next time */
    }
    return(head);
}
```

warning.c—printf interfaces to OlWarning and OlError

```
/*
 * @(#) sccs/s.warning.c last delta 2/4/90 22:10:24
 */
#include <stdio.h>

/*
 * Warning() - hack to add printf capability to OlWarning.
 * WARNING: if this doesn't work on your machine, ensure
 * that the type for p0-10 matches your stack type.
 * That is, if your stack pushes things as shorts, change
 * the declaration here.  (On almost all UNIX machines,
 * stack_type == int == long == 32 bits)
 */
Warning(format, p0, p1, p2, p3, p4, p5, p6, p7, p8, p9, p10)
    char    *format;
    int p0, p1, p2, p3, p4, p5, p6, p7, p8, p9, p10;
{
    char    buf[BUFSIZ];

    sprintf(
        buf,
        format,
        p0, p1, p2, p3, p4, p5, p6, p7, p8, p9, p10
    );
    OlWarning(buf);
}

Error(format, p0, p1, p2, p3, p4, p5, p6, p7, p8, p9, p10)
    char    *format;
    int p0, p1, p2, p3, p4, p5, p6, p7, p8, p9, p10;
{
    char    buf[BUFSIZ];

    sprintf(
        buf,
        format,
        p0, p1, p2, p3, p4, p5, p6, p7, p8, p9, p10
    );
```

```
    OlError(buf);
}
```

wm.c—implements OPEN LOOK Window Manager callback interface

```
/*
 * @(#) sccs/s.wm.c 1.9 last delta 2/4/90 22:10:25
 */
#include <X11/Intrinsic.h>
#include <X11/StringDefs.h>
#include <X11/Xatom.h>
#include <Xol/OlClients.h>
#include "xtutilp.h"
#include <stdio.h>
#include <varargs.h>

/*
 * Notice that these are single callbacks per protocols.  Using
 * a callback list is left as an exercise to the reader.
 */
static CallbackRecord    CBsaveYourself=NULL, CBdeleteWindow=NULL;
static Boolean           requestedDeleteWindow = FALSE;
static Boolean           requestedSaveYourself = FALSE;
static Boolean           initedToolkit = FALSE;

/*
 * AddWMCallbacks() - participate in the ICCCM WM_PROTOCOLS
 * conventions.
 *
 * This routine uses a variable-length argument list of
 * the following format:

    Widget  w_toplevel,
    int     protocol_1,         // 1st callback protocol
    FUNC    protocolCallback_1, // pointer to callback routine
       caddr_t protocolData_1,      // client_data to pass to
callback
    ...
    int     protocol_N,         // last callback protocol
    FUNC    protocolCallback_N,
    caddr_t protocolData_N,
    0                           // zero-terminated list

 * The first parameter is a toplevel shell widget.
 * Following this is a variable-length array of triplets -
 * the protocol ID, a ptr to the protocol callback function,
 * and a possibly-NULL value that will be passed as a
 * parameter to the protocol callback function.  A zero
 * terminates the list.
```

```
 *
 * Synopsis of callbacks:

    void    CallbackFunc(client_data, call_data)
        caddr_t client_data;
        caddr_t call_data;  (specific to the event)
 */
void AddWMCallbacks(va_alist)
    va_dcl              /* variable arg list declaration */
{
    extern void WMEventHandler();
    va_list     ap;     /* vararg list pointer */
    Widget      wid;
    int         protocol;

    va_start(ap);       /* start variable arg list processing */

    wid = va_arg(ap, Widget);   /* get toplevel widget */

    InitXtutil(wid);            /* init util stuff */

    while ((protocol = va_arg(ap, int)) != 0) {
        switch (protocol) {
        case CB_WM_DELETE_WINDOW:
            CBdeleteWindow.func = va_arg(ap, FUNC);
            CBdeleteWindow.data = va_arg(ap, caddr_t);
            if (requestedDeleteWindow == FALSE) {
                requestedDeleteWindow = TRUE;
                XChangeProperty(
                    _xtutilPriv.ourDisplay,
                    _xtutilPriv.toplevelWindow,
                    WM_PROTOCOLS,
                    XA_ATOM,
                    32,
                    PropModeAppend,
                    (char *) &WM_DELETE_WINDOW,
                    1
                );
            }
            break;
        case CB_WM_SAVE_YOURSELF:
            CBsaveYourself.func = va_arg(ap, FUNC);
            CBsaveYourself.data = va_arg(ap, caddr_t);
            if (requestedSaveYourself == FALSE) {
                requestedSaveYourself = TRUE;
                XChangeProperty(
                    _xtutilPriv.ourDisplay,
                    _xtutilPriv.toplevelWindow,
                    WM_PROTOCOLS,
                    XA_ATOM,
                    32,
```

```
                      PropModeAppend,
                      (char *) &WM_SAVE_YOURSELF,
                      1
                );
            }
            break;
        default:
            Warning(
                "unknown request in AddWMCallbacks(): %d\n",
                protocol
            );
            break;
        }
    }

    /*
     * Tell the Intrinsics to call our event handler when we get
     * sent a message from another client.  (Actually, since
     * ClientMessage events have no specific event mask,
     * our event handler will get called for all
     * GraphicsExpose, NoExpose, SelectionClear,
     * SelectionRequest, SelectionNotify, ClientMessage,
     * and MappingNotify events.)
     */
    if (initedToolkit == FALSE) {
        initedToolkit = TRUE;
        XtAddEventHandler(
            _xtutilPriv.toplevelWidget,
            NoEventMask,     /* ClientMessages have no mask */
            TRUE,            /* yes, please send nonmaskables */
            WMEventHandler, /* XtEventHandler */
            NULL            /* client_data */
        );
    }

    va_end(ap);

    return;
}


/*
 * DeleteWMCallbacks() - allow added callbacks to be removed.
 * This routine uses a variable-length argument list of
 * the following format:

    Widget  w_toplevel,
    int     protocol_1, // 1st callback protocol of disinterest
    ...
    int     protocol_N, // last callback protocol of disinterest
    0
```

```
*/
void DeleteWMCallbacks(va_alist)
    va_dcl                /* variable arg list declaration */
{
    va_list         ap;        /* vararg list pointer */
    Widget          wid;
    Atom            *protocolList;
    Atom            actual_type;
    int             actual_format;
    unsigned long   nitems;
    unsigned long   bytes_after;
    void            DeleteAtomFromList();
    int             protocol;
    int             rc;


    va_start(ap);        /* start variable arg list processing */

    wid = va_arg(ap, Widget);    /* get toplevel widget */
    InitXtutil(wid);             /* init util stuff */

    /*
     * Fetch the current contents of the WM_PROTOCOLS property
     */
    rc = XGetWindowProperty(
        _xtutilPriv.ourDisplay,
        _xtutilPriv.toplevelWindow,
        WM_PROTOCOLS,
        0,                  /* offset */
        10,                 /* length */
        FALSE,              /* delete == FALSE */
        XA_ATOM,            /* req_type */
        &actual_type,
        &actual_format,
        &nitems,
        &bytes_after,
        (unsigned char *) &protocolList
    );

#ifdef DEBUG
{
    register    i;
    dbg(
        "got WM_PROTOCOLS: nitems=%d, actual_format=%d\n",
        nitems,
        actual_format
    );
    for(i=0;i<nitems;i++) {
        String  str;
```

```
        str =
            XGetAtomName(
                _xtutilPriv.ourDisplay,
                protocolList[i]
            );
        dbg("\t%s\n", str);
        XFree(str);
    }
}
#endif
    if (rc != Success) {
        Warning(
            "DeleteWMCallbacks() get WM_PROTOCOLS failed.\n"
        );
        return;
    }
    if ((nitems == 0) ||
        (actual_format == 0) ||
        (actual_type == None)
    ) {
        Warning("DeleteWMCallbacks() - no WM_PROTOCOL items\n");
        return;
    }
    if (actual_type != XA_ATOM) {
        String  str =
            XGetAtomName(_xtutilPriv.ourDisplay, actual_type);
        Warning(
            "DeleteWMCallbacks() - WM_PROTOCOL is a %s\n", str
        );
        XFree(str);
        return;
    }
    if (bytes_after) {
        Warning(
            "DeleteWMCallbacks() - ignoring bytes_after=%d\n",
            bytes_after
        );
    }

    while ((protocol = va_arg(ap, int)) != 0) {
        switch (protocol) {
        case CB_WM_DELETE_WINDOW:
            if (requestedDeleteWindow == TRUE) {
                requestedDeleteWindow = FALSE;
                CBdeleteWindow.func = NULL;
                CBdeleteWindow.data = NULL;
                DeleteAtomFromList(
                    protocolList,
                    &nitems,
                    WM_DELETE_WINDOW
                );
```

```
                }
                break;
        case CB_WM_SAVE_YOURSELF:
            if (requestedSaveYourself == TRUE) {
                requestedSaveYourself = FALSE;
                CBsaveYourself.func = NULL;
                CBsaveYourself.data = NULL;
                DeleteAtomFromList(
                    protocolList,
                    &nitems,
                    WM_SAVE_YOURSELF
                );
            }
            break;
        default:
            Warning(
                "unknown request in DeleteWMCallbacks(): %d\n",
                protocol
            );
            break;
        }
    }
    va_end(ap);

#ifdef DEBUG
{
    register    i;
    dbg("writing WM_PROTOCOLS: nitems=%d\n", nitems);
    for(i=0;i<nitems;i++) {
        String  str;

        str =
            XGetAtomName(
                _xtutilPriv.ourDisplay,
                protocolList[i]
            );
        dbg("\t%s\n", str);
        XFree(str);
    }
}
#endif

#ifdef notdef
    XtUnmapWidget(_xtutilPriv.toplevelWidget);
#endif

    /*
     * write back the WM_PROTOCOLS property
     */
    XChangeProperty(
        _xtutilPriv.ourDisplay,
```

```
            _xtutilPriv.toplevelWindow,
            WM_PROTOCOLS,
            XA_ATOM,
            32,
            PropModeReplace,
            (unsigned char *) protocolList,
            nitems
        );
        XFree(protocolList);

#ifdef notdef
        XtMapWidget(_xtutilPriv.toplevelWidget);
#endif

        /*
         * remove the event handler from the chain, if it
         * isn't needed.
         */
        if (!(requestedSaveYourself || requestedDeleteWindow)) {
            initedToolkit = FALSE;
            XtRemoveEventHandler(
                _xtutilPriv.toplevelWidget,
                NoEventMask,    /* ClientMessages have no mask */
                TRUE,           /* yes, please send nonmaskables */
                WMEventHandler, /* XtEventHandler */
                NULL            /* client_data */
            );
        }

        return;
}


/*
 * WMEventHandler() - dispatch client-defined callbacks as
 * a result of WM_PROTOCOL messages from the Workspace
 * Manager and/or Window Manager.
 */
static void WMEventHandler(wid, client_data, event)
    Widget  wid;
    caddr_t client_data;
    XEvent  *event;
{
    XClientMessageEvent   *xclient = &event->xclient;
    int                   message = xclient->data.l[0];
    int                   timestamp = xclient->data.l[1];
    extern CallbackRecord CBdeleteWindow, CBsaveYourself;

    if (
        (event->type != ClientMessage) ||
        (xclient->message_type != WM_PROTOCOLS)
```

```
        ) {
            return;
        }

        if (message == WM_DELETE_WINDOW) {

            /*
             * It is okay for the callback to prompt the user for
             * quit/delete confirmation here.
             *
             * Also, it is not neccessary for the callback
             * to ultimately call exit(), although that is
             * the typical action.  Instead, it could unmap
             * the window and remain running in the background.
             */

            if (CBdeleteWindow.func) {
                (*CBdeleteWindow.func)(CBdeleteWindow.data, NULL);
            }

        } else if (message == WM_SAVE_YOURSELF) {

            /*
             * Call callback to checkpoint state.  The callback
             * should flush buffers and save temp files, etc.,
             * but should NOT prompt the user.
             *
             * Callback MUST set the WM_COMMAND property to signal
             * the Workspace Manager and/or Window Manager that
             * it is done.
             */

            if (CBsaveYourself.func) {
                (*CBsaveYourself.func)(CBsaveYourself.data, NULL);
            }
        } else if (message == WM_TAKE_FOCUS) {
            /*
             * do nothing - toolkit handles this automatically
             */
        } else {
            String  tmp =
                XGetAtomName(_xtutilPriv.ourDisplay, message);
            dbg(
                "WMEventHandler: got misc WM_PROTOCOLS message: %s\n",
                tmp
            );
            XFree(tmp);
        }

        return;
}
```

```
/*
 * DeleteAtomFromList() - get rid of an atom in a list of
 * atoms.  Return value is to update *pNitems with the
 * number of remaining atoms in the list.
 */
void DeleteAtomFromList(pAtomList, pNitems, atom)
    Atom        *pAtomList;
    unsigned    *pNitems;
    Atom        atom;
{
    Atom        *pAtom;     /* walking pointer */
    int         nitems;

    for (
        pAtom = pAtomList,
        nitems = *pNitems;

        nitems--;

        pAtom++
    ) {
        if (*pAtom == atom) {
            *pNitems -= 1;  /* decrement the count of the list */
        } else {
            *pAtomList++ = *pAtom;  /* keep this atom */
        }
    }
    return;
}
```

wsm.c—implements OPEN LOOK Workspace Manager callback interface

```
/*
 * @(#) sccs/s.wsm.c 1.5 last delta 2/4/90 22:10:27
 */
#include <X11/Intrinsic.h>
#include <X11/StringDefs.h>
#include <X11/Xatom.h>
#include <Xol/OlClients.h>
#include <stdio.h>
#include <varargs.h>
#include "xtutilp.h"

extern Atom _OL_WSM_QUEUE;  /* interned by OPEN LOOK Toolkit */
extern Atom _OL_WSM_REPLY;  /* interned by OPEN LOOK Toolkit */
```

```
/*
 * Notice that these are single callbacks.  Using a callback
 * list is left as an exercise to the reader.
 */
static CallbackRecord    CBWSMreply;
static Boolean           requestedWSMreply = FALSE;
static Boolean           initedToolkit = FALSE;


/*
 * AskWSMExecute() - post a request to the OPEN LOOK
 * Workspace Manager to execute a command.
 */
void AskWSMExecute(wid, request)
    Widget      wid;
    WsmExecute  *request;
{
    void        _AskWSMCommon();

    _AskWSMCommon(wid, WSM_EXECUTE, request->command);
    return;
}


/*
 * AskWSMResourceRequest() - post a request to the
 * OPEN LOOK Workspace Manager to add or delete resources
 * from the .Xdefaults file.
 */
void AskWSMResourceRequest(wid, request)
    Widget              wid;
    WsmResourceRequest  *request;
{
    void        _AskWSMCommon();
    char        buffer[BUFSIZ];
    register String pBuffer;
    int     count;

    if (
        (request->type != WSM_MERGE_RESOURCES) &&
        (request->type != WSM_DELETE_RESOURCES)
    ) {
        Warning(
            "AskWSMResourceRequest: unrecognized req type %d\n",
            request->type
        );
        return;
    }

    /*
     * Assemble a single resource string out of the individual
     * resources by concatenating the strings and terminating
```

```
     * each resource string with a newline (\n).
     */
    for (
        pBuffer = buffer,
        count = 0;

        count < request->resourceCount;   /* copy all strings */

        ++count
    ) {
        register String pResource;

        /*
         * copy individual resource string
         */
        for (
            pResource = request->resourceList[count];

            *pResource != '\0';

            *pBuffer++ = *pResource++
        );

        *pBuffer++ = '\n';  /* insert newline instead of NULL */
    }
    *pBuffer = '\0';         /* NULL terminate */

    _AskWSMCommon(wid, request->type, buffer);
    return;
}

static void _AskWSMCommon(wid, action, string)
    Widget  wid;
    int action;   /* WSM_EXECUTE, WSM_[MERGE,DELETE]_RESOURCES */
    String  string;     /* command or resource string */
{
    char    buffer[BUFSIZ];

    InitXtutil(wid);

    sprintf(
        buffer,
        "%c%d%c%d%c%s%c%s%c%s%c%d%c%d%c%s%c%s%c",
        action,
        _xtutilPriv.toplevelWindow, DELIM,  /* window */
        0,                          DELIM,  /* serial number */
        _xtutilPriv.sysname,        DELIM,  /* sysname */
        _xtutilPriv.nodename,       DELIM,  /* nodename */
        _xtutilPriv.applname,       DELIM,  /* app name */
        _xtutilPriv.uid,            DELIM,  /* uid */
        _xtutilPriv.gid,            DELIM,  /* gid */
```

```
            string,                  DELIM,   /* cmd/resources */
            "",                      DELIM    /* reserved */
    );

    /*
     * Place the request on the Workspace Manager's queue on
     * the root window
     */
    XChangeProperty(
        _xtutilPriv.ourDisplay,  /* display */
        _xtutilPriv.rootWindow,  /* window */
        _OL_WSM_QUEUE,           /* property name */
        XA_STRING,               /* property type */
        8,                       /* format: 8, 16, or 32 */
        PropModeAppend,          /* prepend, replace, append */
        buffer,                  /* data */
        strlen(buffer)           /* length in bytes */
    );

    return;
}


/*
 * AddWSMCallbacks() - handle low-level communications
 * protocol from the OPEN LOOK Workspace Manager.
 * Dispatch to application-provided code on events.
 *
 * This routine uses a variable-length argument list of
 * the following format:

    Widget  w_toplevel,
    int     protocol_1,
    FUNC    protocolCallback_1,
    caddr_t protocolData_1,
    ...
    int     protocol_N,
    FUNC    protocolCallback_N,
    caddr_t protocolData_N,
    0

 * The first parameter is a toplevel shell widget.
 * Following this is a variable-length array of triplets -
 * the protocol ID, a ptr to the protocol callback function,
 * and a possibly-NULL value that will be passed as a parameter
 * to the protocol callback function.  A zero terminates the
 * list.
 *
 * Synopsis of callbacks:

    void    CallbackFunc(client_data, call_data)
        caddr_t client_data;
```

```
            caddr_t call_data;   (specific to the event)
 */
void AddWSMCallbacks(va_alist)
    va_dcl              /* variable arg list declaration */
{
    extern void WSMEventHandler();
    va_list     ap;     /* vararg list pointer */
    Widget      wid;
    int     protocol;

    va_start(ap);       /* start variable arg list processing */

    wid = va_arg(ap, Widget);   /* get toplevel widget */

    InitXtutil(wid);    /* initialize utility toolkit */

    while ((protocol = va_arg(ap, int)) != 0) {
        switch (protocol) {
        case CB_WSM_REPLY:
            requestedWSMreply = TRUE;
            CBWSMreply.func = va_arg(ap, FUNC);
            CBWSMreply.data = va_arg(ap, caddr_t);
            break;
        default:
            Warning(
                "unknown request in AddWSMCallbacks: %d\n",
                protocol
            );
            break;
        }
    }

    /*
     * Tell the Intrinsics to call our event handler when
     * the properties change on this window.
     */
    if (!initedToolkit && requestedWSMreply) {
        initedToolkit = TRUE;
        XtAddEventHandler(
            _xtutilPriv.toplevelWidget,     /* widget */
            PropertyChangeMask,             /* event mask */
            FALSE,                          /* don't send nonmaskables */
            WSMEventHandler,                /* XtEventHandler */
            NULL                            /* client_data */
        );
    }

    va_end(ap);

    return;
}
```

```
/*
 * DeleteWSMCallbacks() - allow added callbacks to be removed.
 * This routine uses a variable-length argument list of
 * the following format:

    Widget  w_toplevel,
    int     protocol_1, // 1st callback protocol of disinterest
    ...
    int     protocol_N, // last callback protocol of disinterest
    0

 */
void DeleteWSMCallbacks(va_alist)
    va_dcl                  /* variable arg list declaration */
{
    va_list     ap;         /* vararg list pointer */
    Widget      wid;
    int         protocol;


    va_start(ap);           /* start variable arg list processing */

    wid = va_arg(ap, Widget);    /* get toplevel widget */
    InitXtutil(wid);             /* init util stuff */

    while ((protocol = va_arg(ap, int)) != 0) {
        switch (protocol) {
        case CB_WSM_REPLY:
            requestedWSMreply = FALSE;
            CBWSMreply.func = NULL;
            CBWSMreply.data = NULL;
            break;
        default:
            Warning(
                "unknown request in DeleteWSMCallbacks(): %d\n",
                protocol
            );
            break;
        }
    }
    va_end(ap);


    /*
     * remove the event handler from the chain, if it isn't
needed.
     */
    if (initedToolkit && !requestedWSMreply) {
        initedToolkit = FALSE;
```

```
            XtRemoveEventHandler(
                _xtutilPriv.toplevelWidget,        /* widget */
                PropertyChangeMask,                /* event mask */
                FALSE,                      /* don't send nonmaskables */
                WSMEventHandler,                   /* XtEventHandler */
                NULL                               /* client_data */
            );
        }

        return;
    }

    static void WSMEventHandler(wid, client_data, event)
        Widget  wid;
        caddr_t client_data;
        XEvent  *event;
    {
        Atom            actual_type;
        unsigned long   nitems;
        unsigned long   bytes_after;
        int             message = event->xproperty.atom;
        int             actual_format;


        if (
            (event->type != PropertyNotify) ||
            (event->xproperty.state != PropertyNewValue)
        ) {
            return;
        }

        if (message == _OL_WSM_REPLY) {
            WsmReply    reply;
            String      sysname, nodename;
            int         serial;
            String      prop;

            XGetWindowProperty(
                _xtutilPriv.ourDisplay,
                _xtutilPriv.toplevelWindow,
                message,
                0,              /* offset */
                BUFSIZ,         /* length */
                TRUE,           /* delete */
                XA_STRING,
                &actual_type,
                &actual_format,
                &nitems,
                &bytes_after,
                &prop
            );
```

```
        /*
         * Parse the property string written by the
         * Workspace Manager.  The format of this string
         * was designed for maximum compactness, albeit at
         * the cost of complexity.
         *
         * The first byte is the return status, with the rest of
         * the string separated into tokens by the delimiter
         * character, 0x1f.
         *
         * For more information, see the AT&T OPEN LOOK GUI
         * Programmer's Guide.
         */
        reply.status = prop[0];      /* not separated by DELIM */

        InitTokenizer(&prop[1]);
        serial = atoi(NextToken(DELIM));
        sysname = NextToken(DELIM);
        nodename = NextToken(DELIM);
        reply.errno_pid = atoi(NextToken(DELIM));

        /*
         * invoke application-supplied callback
         */
        if (CBWSMreply.func != NULL) {
            (*CBWSMreply.func)(CBWSMreply.data, &reply);
        }

        XFree(prop);

    }
    return;
}
```

xtutil.h—public interface definition file for Xtutil

```
/*
 * xtutil.h - header file for files using libxtutil.a functions
 * @(#) sccs/s.xtutil.h 1.14 last delta 2/19/90 19:51:07
 */

/*
 * Misc. Toolkit support
 */
#define min(a,b)    (((a) < (b)) ? (a) : (b))
#define max(a,b)    (((a) > (b)) ? (a) : (b))

typedef void    (*FUNC)();
```

```
extern Arg  tmpArg[];  /* tmp for building name/value arg list */

extern int  TmpArgList();   /* fills arg with name/value pairs */
extern XtArgVal GetValue(); /* get a single resource value */
extern void SetValue();     /* set a single resource value */
extern XImage  *XYBitmapImageFromData();
                            /* create image from bitmap data */
extern Time GetTimestamp(); /* get current server time */

/*************** Inter-client communications API ***************/
/*
 Synopsis of Add[WM,WSM,FM]Callbacks():

 void Add[WM,WSM,FM]Callbacks(wid, var_list_of_tripples)
       Widget  wid;
       enum    protocolID_1;      // identifies callback list
       void    (*callback_1)();   // callback function
       caddr_t client_data_1;     // client-supplied data
       ....
       enum    protocolID_N;
       void    (*callback_N)();
       caddr_t client_data_N;
       int     0;                 // zero-terminate the list

 Synopsis of application callbacks :

 void Callback(client_data, call_data)
       caddr_t client_data;  // val given to AddXXXCallbacks()
       caddr_t *call_data;   // info from the util event handler

 The call_data is specific to the callback and is
 documented with the declarations below.

 Synopsis of Delete[WM,WSM,FM]Callbacks():

 void Delete[WM,WSM,FM]Callbacks(wid, var_list_of_tripples)
       Widget  wid;
       enum    protocolID_1;      // identifies callback list
       ....
       enum    protocolID_N;      // identifies callback list
       int     0;                 // zero-terminate the list
 */

/*
 * OPEN LOOK Window Manager support:
 *  AddWMCallbacks() - client provides callbacks for WM events
 *  DeleteWMCallbacks() - remove callbacks added
 *       with AddWMCallbacks()
 */
typedef enum _WMProtocol {
```

```
        CB_WM_DELETE_WINDOW = 1,
                    /* quit or otherwise remove toplevel window */
                    /* call_data == NULL */
        CB_WM_SAVE_YOURSELF,
                    /* save state w/o prompting the user */
                    /* call_data == NULL */
        /* CB_WM_TAKE_FOCUS,
                    /* shouldn't be used by applications */
        /* CB_WM_SHUTDOWN,
                    /* proposed shutdown protocol */
} WMProtocol;

extern void AddWMCallbacks();
                        /* hook in client-supplied callbacks */
extern void DeleteWMCallbacks();
                        /* delete hook to callbacks */


/*
 * OPEN LOOK File Manager support:
 *  AddFMCallbacks() - client provides callbacks for FM events
 *  AskFMBrowse() - invoke File Manager in client-service mode
 *  FmBrowse - info struct for client to pass to AskFMBrowse()
 *  FmDrop - passed to drop callback for user-initiated copy/move
 *  FmReply - passed to reply callback for browse-initiated
 *       action.
 */

/* OPEN LOOK File Manager messages */
#define FM_ACTIVATE 1   /* used by WSM to invoke FM session */
#define FM_BROWSE   2   /* used by clients to req service mode */

#define FM_COPY     3   /* user is copying a file to here */
#define FM_MOVE     4   /* user is moving a file to here */

#define FM_CANCEL   9   /* user canceled a FM_BROWSE */
#define FM_ACCEPT  10   /* selected a file during FM_BROWSE */
#define FM_INVALID 11   /* request to FM_BROWSE was invalid */

typedef struct _FmBrowse {
    String  label;  /* action label for button in File menu */
    String  directory;  /* directory to browse */
    String  pattern;    /* file pattern to match */
} FmBrowse;

typedef struct _FmReply {
    int action;     /* FM_[COPY, MOVE, CANCEL, ACCEPT, INVALID] */
    String  message;    /* possible error message */
    String  directory;  /* full or relative pathname */
    int fileCount;      /* number of file names in fileList */
    String  *fileList;  /* one or more file names */
} FmReply;
```

460

```
typedef enum _FMProtocol {
    CB_FM_REPLY = 1,    /* msg from FM_BROWSE, FM_COPY, FM_MOVE */
                        /* call_data == FmReply struct */
} FMProtocol;

extern void AskFMBrowse();/* invokes FM in client-service mode */
extern void AddFMCallbacks();    /* add CB handlers for FM msgs */
extern void DeleteFMCallbacks();          /* remove CB handlers */


/*
 * OPEN LOOK Workspace Manager support
 *  AddWSMCallbacks() - client supplies callbacks for WSM events
 *  AskWSMExecute() - use the Workspace Manager to exec a program
 *  AskWSMResourceRequest() - use WSM to merge/delete resources
 *      from .Xdefaults
 *  WsmExecute - info struct for client to pass to
 *      RequestExecute()
 *  WsmReply - WSM-returned data regarding the status
 *      of WSM_EXECUTE
 *  WsmResourceRequest - client requests merge or delete of
 *      resources
 */

#ifndef WSM_EXECUTE /* OPEN LOOK Workspace Manager messages { */
#define WSM_EXECUTE          1    /* have WSM execute a client */
#define WSM_TERMINATE        2    /* used by Window Manager */
#define WSM_SAVE_TERMINATE   3    /* used by Window Manager */
#define WSM_EXIT             4    /* used by Window Manager */
#define WSM_MERGE_RESOURCES  5    /* write props to .Xdefaults */
#define WSM_DELETE_RESOURCES  6   /* delete propertiess */

#define WSM_SUCCESS          1    /* WSM_EXECUTE succeeded */
#define WSM_FORK_FAILURE     2    /* WSM_EXECUTE fork failed */
#define WSM_EXEC_FAILURE     3    /* WSM_EXECUTE exec failed */
#endif            /* } OPEN LOOK Workspace Manager messages   */

typedef struct _WsmExecute {
    String  command;    /* command string to fork and exec */
} WsmExecute;

typedef struct _WsmReply {
    int status;
            /* WSM_SUCCESS, WSM_FORK_FAILURE, WSM_EXEC_FAILURE */
    int errno_pid;  /* errno if fail, process id if succeeded */
} WsmReply;

typedef struct _WsmResourceRequest {
    int type;                 /* WSM_[MERGE,DELETE]_RESOURCES */
    String *resourceList;
```

```
                    /* list of NULL-terminated resource strings */
    int resourceCount;      /* number of resources in list */
} WsmResourceRequest;

typedef enum _WSMProtocol {
    CB_WSM_REPLY = 1,   /* handle reply from WSM_EXECUTE */
                        /* call_data == WsmReply struct */
} WSMProtocol;

extern void AskWSMExecute();
                    /* handle WSM_EXECUTE protocol */
extern void AskWSMResources();
                    /* handle WSM_XXX_RESOURCES protocol */
extern void AddWSMCallbacks();
                    /* setup _OL_WSM_REPLY handlers */
extern void DeleteWSMCallbacks();
                    /* remove _OL_WSM_REPLY handlers */


/*
 * Property Callback support:
 *  AddPropertyCallbacks() - client supplied callbacks for
 *      properties
 *  DeletePropertyCallbacks() - remove callbacks from the list
 *
 * Synopsis for both AddPropertyCallbacks and
 *      DeletePropertyCallbacks:

    Widget              w_toplevel,
    PropertyProtocol    protocol_1,         // CB_NEW, CB_DELETE
    Atom                atom_1,             // property ID
    FUNC                protocolCallback_1, // callback
    caddr_t             protocolData_1,     // client_data
    ...
    PropertyProtocol    protocol_N,
    Atom                atom_N,
    FUNC                protocolCallback_N,
    caddr_t             protocolData_N,
    0

 * The first parameter is a toplevel shell widget.
 * Following this is a variable-length array of quadruples -
 * the protocol ID, the property to watch, a ptr to the
 * protocol callback function, and a possibly-NULL value
 * that will be passed as a parameter to the protocol
 * callback function.  A zero terminates the list.
 */
typedef struct _PropertyReply {
    Boolean     sendEvent;  /* true if from another client */
    Window      window;     /* window ID to use to GetProp */
    Atom        atom;       /* atom of prop that was touched */
```

```
    Time       time;        /* time the property was changed */
    int        state;  /* PropertyNewValue, PropertyDeleted */
} PropertyReply;

typedef enum _PropertyProtocol {
    CB_NEW = 1,      /* property was written */
                     /* call_data == &PropertyReply struct */
    CB_DELETE,       /* property was deleted */
                     /* call_data == &PropertyReply struct */
} PropertyProtocol;

extern void AddPropertyCallbacks();
extern void DeletePropertyCallbacks();
```

xtutilp.h—private header file for Xtutil

```
/*
 * @(#) sccs/s.xtutilp.h 1.4 last delta 2/4/90 22:11:01
 *
 * Types and definitions private to libxtutil.a
 */
#ifndef GOT_xtutil_h
#include "xtutil.h"
#define GOT_xtutil_h
#endif

typedef struct _CallbackRecord {
    FUNC    func;
    caddr_t data;
} CallbackRecord;

typedef struct __XtutilPriv {
    Boolean inited;      /* has this struct been initialized? */

    Widget  toplevelWidget; /* toplevel widget in this tree */
    Window  toplevelWindow; /* window of toplevel shell widget */
    Display *ourDisplay;    /* display we are on */
    Screen  *ourScreen;     /* screen we are using */
    Window  rootWindow;     /* root window of display */

    String  applname;       /* application name */
    String  sysname;        /* system name */
    String  nodename;       /* node name */
    int gid;            /* UNIX group ID for application's user */
    int uid;            /* UNIX user ID for application's user */
} _XtutilPriv;
extern _XtutilPriv _xtutilPriv;
void    InitXtutil();
```

```
#define DELIM    0x1f /* OL FM and WSM protcol string delimiter */
#define SPACE    0x20        /* ASCII space character */
void    InitTokenizer();    /* reset the token finder */
String  NextToken();     /* get next string token up to DELIM */
```

About the Author

John David Miller led the development of Graphic Software Systems' UNIX and DOS X servers, starting back in 1986 with X Version 10 Release 4. John is now Project Leader in charge of new technology research and development for GSS's Workstation Business Unit.

Bibliography

AT&T OPEN LOOK^{tm} Graphical User Interface: Functional Specification. AT&T. 1989

AT&T OPEN LOOK^{tm} Graphical User Interface: Level 1 Trademark Guide. AT&T. 1990

AT&T OPEN LOOK^{tm} Graphical User Interface: Programmer's Guide and Programmer's Reference Manual. AT&T. 1990

AT&T OPEN LOOK^{tm} Graphical User Interface: Style Guide. AT&T. 1989

AT&T OPEN LOOK^{tm} Graphical User Interface: User's Guide. AT&T. 1990

Cox, Brad J. *Object Oriented Programming.* Addison-Wesley. 1986

Goldberg, A., and D. Robson. *Smalltalk-80: The Language and its Implementation.* Addison-Wesley. 1983

Human Interface Guidelines: The Apple Desktop Interface. Apple Computer, Inc. 1986

Kernigan, Brian W., and Dennis M. Ritchie. *The C Programming Language.* Prentice Hall. 1978

Jacobs, Thomas W.R. *The XView Toolkit: An Architectural Overview.* Xhibition. 1989

Jones, Oliver. *Introduction to the X Window System.* Prentice Hall. 1989

Nye, Adrian. *Xlib Programming Manual.* O'Reilly & Associates. 1988

_____. *Xlib Reference Manual.* O'Reilly & Associates. 1988

O'Reilly, Tim. *Xlib User's Guide.* O'Reilly & Associates. 1988

_____. "The Toolkits (And Politics) of X Windows." *Unix World.* February, 1989

Roberts, W.T., et al. *NeWS and X, Beauty and the Beast?.* Department of Computer Science, Queen Mary College. 1988

Rosenthal, David S.H. *Inter-Client Communication Conventions Manual.* Sun Microsystems. 1989

Scheifler, Robert W. *X Window System.* Digital Press. 1988

_____. "The X Window System". *Transactions on Graphics*, #63. Association for Computing Machinery. 1986

Smalltalk/V Tutorial and Programming Handbook. Digitalk. Inc. 1986

Stroustrup, Bjarne. *The C++ Programming Language.* Addison-Wesley. 1986

_____. "What is "Object-Oriented Programming?". *Proceedings of the Summer'87 ECOOP Conference.* June, 1987

Widener, Glenn. *Inter-Client Communications Conventions.* Xhibition. 1989

Winston, Patrick Henry. *LISP.* Addison-Wesley. 1984

Young, Douglas A. *X Window Systems : programming and applications with Xt.* Prentice-Hall. 1989

Index